BILL BRYSON

Bryson's Dictionary For Writers and Editors

Bill Bryson's bestselling books include *A Walk in the Woods, I'm a Stranger Here Myself, In a Sunburned Country, Bryson's Dictionary of Troublesome Words, A Short History of Nearly Everything* (which earned him the 2004 Aventis Prize), and *The Life and Times of the Thunderbolt Kid.* Bryson lives in England with his wife and children.

Bryson's Dictionary
for Writers *and* Editors

Bryson's Dictionary

for WRITERS *and* EDITORS

BILL BRYSON

Anchor Books
A Division of Random House, Inc.
New York

FIRST ANCHOR BOOKS EDITION, MAY 2009

Earlier editions of this work were published as *The Penguin
Dictionary for Writers and Editors* in Great Britain in hardcover
by Viking, London, in 1991 and in paperback by Penguin
Books, London, in 1994.

LIBRARY OF CONGRESS CATALOGING-IN-PUBLICATION DATA
Bryson, Bill.
    Bryson's dictionary for writers and editors / Bill Bryson.
        p. cm.
1. English language—Usage—Dictionaries. I. Title. II. Title:
Dictionary for writers and editors.

PE1628.B79 2008
423'.1—dc22
2007034363

Anchor ISBN 978-0-7679-2270-8

www.anchorbooks.com

Printed in the United States of America
10 9 8 7 6 5 4 3 2 1

Contents

This book is intended as a quick, concise guide to the problems of English spelling and usage most commonly encountered by writers and editors. How do you spell *supersede* and *broccoli* and *accessible*? Do I write *archaeology* or *archeology*? What's the difference between a cardinal number and an ordinal number? Is it *Capital* Reef National Park or *Capitol* Reef National Park? What did Belize used to be called? Doesn't Calcutta have a new name now? (It does—Kolkata.) What do we now call the Chinese river that I knew in my school days as the Hwang Ho? In short, what are the answers to all those points of written usage that you kind of know or ought to know but can't quite remember?

It is a personal collection, built up over thirty years as a writer and editor in two countries, and so inevitably—inescapably—it reflects my own interests, experiences, and blind spots. You may not need, as I do, to be reminded that it is Anjelica Huston but Whitney Houston, or have occasion at any point in your life to write the name of the district of Sydney known gloriously and unimprovably as Woolloomooloo. But I very much hope that what follows is broad enough and general enough to be frequently useful to nearly everyone.

To keep it simple, I have freely resorted to certain short cuts. Pronunciations have been simplified. I have scorned the International Phonetic Alphabet, with its dogged reliance on symbols such as θ, eɪ, and ð, on the grounds that hardly anyone readily comprehends them, and instead I have attempted to convert tricky pronunciations into straightforward phonetic equivalents. Often these are intended as no more than rough guides—anyone who has ever heard the throat-clearing noise that is a Dutchman pronouncing 's Gravenhage (the formal name of The Hague) will realize what a feebly approximate thing my suggested version is—and I unhesitatingly apologize for any shortcomings in this respect.

I have also been forced on occasion to be arbitrary over spelling. Dictionaries are sometimes remarkably out of step with the rest of the world on certain matters of usage and orthography—in this respect I can cite no better example than the *Oxford English Dictionary*'s interesting but lonely insistence that *Shakespeare* should be spelled *Shakspere*—but there is usually a rough consensus, which I have sought to follow, though I try always to note alternatives when they are freely accepted.

I have tried also to keep cross-references to a minimum. In my view one of the more grating irritants of research is to hunt through several pages looking for "Khayyám, Omar," only to be told "See Omar Khayyám." So I have frequently put such information not only where it should be but also where a hurried reader might mistakenly look for it. The price for this is a certain repetition, for which I additionally apologize.

Some issues of style—whether you should write *shopkeeper* or *shop-keeper*, for instance—have been deliberately excluded. Such matters often are so overwhelmingly a question of preference, house style, or fashion that my choices would be simply that: my choices. I would suggest that in such instances you should choose what seems most sensible, and strive to be consistent.

In the updating and typing of this new edition, I am hugely indebted to Meghan Bryson and Felicity Bryson Gould, respectively my daughter-in-law and daughter, for their unstinting and good-natured help, and as always I am especially indebted to my dear wife, Cynthia, for her patience and support throughout.

Bryson's Dictionary
for Writers *and* Editors

Aachen. City in Germany; in French, Aix-la-Chapelle.

a/an. Errors involving the indefinite articles *a* and *an* are almost certainly more often a consequence of haste and carelessness than of ignorance. They are especially common when numbers are involved, as here: "Cox will contribute 10 percent of the equity needed to build a $80 million cable system" or "He was assisted initially by two officers from the sheriff's department and a FBI agent." When the first letter of an abbreviation is pronounced as a vowel, as in "FBI," the preceding article should be *an*, not *a*.

Aarhus. City in Denmark; in Danish, Århus.

abacus, pl. *abacuses.*

abaft. Toward the stern, or rear, of a ship.

abattoir.

Abbas, Mahmoud. (1935–) President of Palestinian National Authority (2005–).

ABC. American Broadcasting Companies (note plural), though the full title is no longer spelled out. It is now part of the Walt Disney Company. The television network is ABC-TV.

abdomen, but **abdominal.**

Abdulaziz International Airport, King, Jeddah, Saudi Arabia.

Abdul-Jabbar, Kareem. (1947–) American basketball player; born Lew Alcindor.

aberrant, aberration.

abhorrent.

Abidjan. Former capital of Côte d'Ivoire.

ab incunabulis. (Lat.) "From the cradle."

abiogenesis. The concept that living matter can arise from nonliving matter; spontaneous generation.

-able. In adding this suffix to a verb, the general rule is to drop a silent *e* (*livable, lovable*) except after a soft *g* (*manageable*) or sibilant *c* (*peaceable*). When a verb ends with a consonant and a *y* (*justify, indemnify*) change the *y* to *i* before adding -*able* (*justifiable, indemnifiable*). Verbs ending in -*ate* drop that syllable before adding -*able* (*appreciable, demonstrable*).

-able, -ible. There are no reliable rules for knowing when a word ends in -*able* and when in -*ible;* see Appendix for a list of some of the more frequently confused spellings.

ab origine. (Lat.) "From the beginning."

abracadabra.

abridgment.

abrogate. To abolish.

Absalom. In the Old Testament, third son of David.

Absalom, Absalom! Novel by William Faulkner (1936).

Absaroka Range, Rocky Mountains.

abscess.

absinth.

abstemious.

Abu Dhabi. Capital city of and state in the United Arab Emirates.

Abuja. Capital of Nigeria.

Abu Simbel, Egypt; site of temples built by Ramses II.

abyss, abyssal, but **abysmal.**

Abyssinia. Former name of Ethiopia.

acacia.

Académie française. French literary society of forty members who act as guardians of the French language; in English contexts, *Française* is usually capitalized.

Academy of Motion Picture Arts and Sciences Institution responsible for the Oscars.

a capella. Singing without musical accompaniment.

Acapulco, Mexico. Officially, Acapulco de Juárez.

Accademia della Crusca. Italian literary academy.

accelerator.

accessible.

accessory.

acciaccatura. Grace note in music.

accidentally. Not *-tly.*

accolade.

accommodate. Very often misspelled: note *-cc-, -mm-.*

accompanist. Not *-iest.*

accouterment.

Accra. Capital of Ghana.

Acheson, Dean. (1893–1971) American diplomat and politician; secretary of state, 1949–1953.

Achilles. King of the Myrmidons, most famous of the Greek heroes of the Trojan War.

Achilles' heel. (Apos.)

acidulous, assiduous. *Acidulous* means tart or acidic. *Assiduous* means diligent.

acknowledgment.

acolyte. Not *-ite.*

Aconcagua, Cerro. Mountain in the Andes in Argentina, highest peak (at 22,835 feet; 6,960 meters) in the Western Hemisphere.

Açores. Portuguese spelling of *Azores.*

acoustics. As a science, the word is singular ("Acoustics was his line of work"). As a collection of properties, it is plural ("The acoustics in the auditorium were not good").

acquiesce, acquiescence.

acquit, acquittal, acquitted.

of land measuring 43,560 square feet, 4,840 square
ivalent to 4,047 square meters, 0.405 hectare.

acronym. is a word formed from the initial letter or letters of a group
of words, as in NATO (North Atlantic Treaty Organization).

acrostic. Writing in which the first, and sometimes the last, letter of
each line spells a word when read vertically; a type of word game
based on the same principle.

Actaeon. In Greek mythology, a hunter who is turned into a stag by
Artemis after he spies her bathing.

activity. Often a sign of prolixity, as here: "The warnings followed a
week of earthquake activity throughout the region." Just make it
"a week of earthquakes."

acute, chronic. These two are sometimes confused, which is a little
odd, as their meanings are sharply opposed. *Chronic* pertains to
lingering conditions, ones that are not easily overcome. *Acute*
refers to those that come to a sudden crisis and require immedi-
ate attention. People in the Third World may suffer from a
chronic shortage of food. In a bad year, their plight may become
acute.

AD. *Anno Domini* (Lat.) "The year of the Lord." AD should be written before the year (AD 25) but after the century (fourth century AD) and is usually set in small caps. See also ANNO DOMINI
and BC.

adage. Even the most careful users of English frequently, but unnecessarily, refer to an "old adage." An adage is by definition old.

adagio. Slowly, slow movement. Pl. *adagios*.

adapter, adaptor. The first is one who adapts (as in a book for theatrical presentation); the second is the device for making appliances
work abroad and so on.

Addams, Charles. (1912–1988) American cartoonist, long associated
with *The New Yorker*.

Addams, Jane. (1860–1935) American social activist and reformer;
Nobel Peace Prize 1931.

Addenbrooke's Hospital, Cambridge, England.

addendum, pl. *addenda.*

Addis Ababa. Capital of Ethiopia.

adduceable. Capable of being proved.

Ade, George. (1866–1944) American playwright.

Adenauer, Konrad. (1876–1967) West German chancellor (1949–1963).

adenoid, adenoidal.

ad hoc. (Lat.) Toward this, for a particular purpose.

ad infinitum. (Lat.) Without limit, to infinity.

Adirondack Mountains.

adjudicator.

ad lib. (Lat.) From *ad libitum*, "at will."

ad loc. (Lat.) From *ad locum*, "at the place." Note period after *loc.*

administer. Not *administrate.*

Admiral's Cup. Series of yachting races held every two years.

admissible, but **admittable.**

admit to is nearly always wrong. You admit a misdeed; you do not admit to it.

ad nauseam. (Lat.) Not *-um.* To the point of nausea.

ADR. American depository (not *-ary*) receipt. A financial instrument.

adrenaline is the preferred spelling, but **adrenalin** is accepted.

advance planning is common but always redundant. All planning must be done in advance.

adverse, averse. *Adverse* means hostile and antagonistic (think of *adversary*). *Averse* means reluctant or disinclined (think of *aversion*).

adviser, but **advisory.**

advocaat. A liqueur.

Aeaea. In Greek mythology, the island inhabited by Circe.

Aegean Sea. Area of the Mediterranean between Greece, Turkey, and Crete.

Aegina. Town and island off the southeastern coast of Greece.

Aeneid. Epic poem by Virgil.

Aeolian Islands. Group of islands off northeastern Sicily; also called Lipari Islands.

Aeolus. Greek god of winds.

aerate.

aerie. Eagle's nest.

Aer Lingus. Irish airline.

Aerolíneas Argentinas.

AeroMéxico.

Aeroperú. Former Peruvian national airline; ceased business in 1999.

aerosol.

aerospace.

Aérospatiale. French aviation company.

aerosphere. One of the lower levels of the atmosphere.

Aeschylus. (c. 525–c. 450 BC) Greek playwright.

Aesculapius (Lat.)**/Asclepius** (Grk.). Roman and Greek god of medicine.

aesthetic is normally the preferred spelling, though **esthetic** is acceptable.

Afars and Issas, French Territory of. Former name of Djibouti.

affaire de coeur. (Fr.) Love affair.

affaire d'honneur. (Fr.) A duel.

affect, effect. As a verb, *affect* means to influence ("Smoking may affect your health") or to adopt a pose or manner ("He affected ignorance"). *Effect* as a verb means to accomplish ("The prisoners effected an escape"). As a noun, the word needed is almost always *effect* (as in "personal effects" or "the damaging effects of war"). *Affect* as a noun has a narrow psychological meaning to do with emotional states (by way of which it is related to *affection*).

affettuoso. In music, to play with feeling.

affidavit.

affinity denotes a mutual relationship. Strictly, one should not speak of someone or something having an affinity for another, but rather with or between.

affrettando. In music, speeding up.

affright. Note *-ff-*.

aficionado, pl. *aficionados.*

AFL-CIO. American Federation of Labor and Congress of Industrial Organizations.

à fond. (Fr.) Thoroughly.

a fortiori. (Lat.) With even stronger reason, all the more so.

Afrikaans, Afrikaners. The first is a language; the second a group of people.

Afwerki, Issaias (or **Isaias**). (1946–) President of Eritrea.

Ag. Chemical symbol for silver.

AG. *Aktiengesellschaft* (Ger.) Roughly equivalent to *Inc.*

Agamemnon. In Greek mythology, king of Argos and commander of the Greek army in the Trojan War; also (in italics) the title of a play by Aeschylus, the first part of the *Oresteia* trilogy.

Agassiz (Jean) Louis (Rodolphe). (1807–1873) Swiss-born American naturalist.

à gauche. (Fr.) To the left.

agent provocateur, pl. *agents provocateurs.*

aggravate. Strictly, means to make a bad situation worse. If you walk on a broken leg, you may aggravate the injury. People can never be aggravated, only circumstances.

aggression, aggressiveness. *Aggression* always denotes hostility. *Aggressiveness* can denote hostility or merely boldness.

aggrieve.

Agincourt, Battle of. 1415.

agoraphobia. Fear of open spaces.

Agra, India, site of Taj Mahal.

agreeable.

Aguascalientes. City and state in central Mexico.

Aguilera, Christina. (1980–) American singer.

Agusta. Not *Aug-*. Italian helicopter company; formally, Gruppo Agusta.

Ahmadinejad, Mahmoud. (1956–) President of Iran (2005–).

à huis clos. (Fr.) "Behind closed doors."

Ah, Wilderness! Comedic play by Eugene O'Neill (1933).

aid and abet. A tautological gift from the legal profession. The two words together tell us nothing that either doesn't say on its own. The only distinction is that *abet* is normally reserved for contexts involving criminal intent. Thus it would be careless to speak of a benefactor abetting the construction of a church or youth club.

aide-de-camp, pl. *aides-de-camp.*

aide-mémoire, pl. same.

AIDS is not correctly described as a disease. It is a medical condition. The term is short for *acquired immune deficiency syndrome.*

aiguillette. Ornamental braid worn on the shoulder of a uniform.

Airbus Industrie. European aircraft manufacturer, now called **Airbus SAS;** it is a subsidiary of EADS NV.

Air France–KLM. Franco-Dutch airline formed from merger of two national carriers in 2004.

Air Line Pilots Association. Group that looks after the interests of American commercial pilots.

AirTran Airways.

Aix-en-Provence, France. Note hyphens.

Aix-la-Chapelle. (Hyphens.) French name for Aachen, Germany.

Aix-les-Bains, France. Note hyphens.

Ajaccio. Capital of Corsica and birthplace of Napoleon.

AK is the postal abbreviation of Alaska.

AL is the postal abbreviation of Alabama.

Ala. is the traditional abbreviation of Alabama.

à la. The adjectival forms of proper nouns in French do not take capital letters after *à la*: *à la française, à la russe, à la lyonnaise.*

alabaster.

Aladdin.

Alamein, El/Al. Egyptian village that gave its name to two battles of World War II.

Alamogordo, New Mexico, site of first atomic bomb explosion.

À la recherche du temps perdu. Novel by Marcel Proust, published in English as *Remembrance of Things Past.*

"Alas! poor Yorick! I knew him, Horatio" is the correct version of the quotation from *Hamlet.*

Alaska Airlines. Not *Alaskan.*

Albigenses, Albigensians. Religious sect during eleventh to thirteenth centuries, also known as Cathars.

Albright, Madeleine. (1937–) Czech-born American diplomat and academic.

albumen, albumin. *Albumen* is the white of an egg; *albumin* is a protein within the albumen.

Albuquerque, New Mexico.

Alcaeus. (c. 600 BC) Greek poet.

Alcatraz. Island and former prison in San Francisco Bay.

Alcibiades. (c. 450–404 BC) Athenian statesman and general.

Alcott, Louisa May. (1833–1888) American writer, daughter of **Amos Bronson Alcott** (1799–1888), author and philosopher.

Aleixandre, Vicente. (1898–1984) Spanish poet, awarded Nobel Prize for Literature 1977. Pronounced *ah-lay-hahn'-dray.*

Aleutian Islands, Alaska.

alfalfa.

Alfa-Romeo for the Italian make of automobile. Not *Alpha-.*

Al-Fatah. Palestinian political organization. Drop *Al* when it is preceded by an article ("a Fatah spokesman," "the Fatah organization").

Alfredsson, Daniel. (1972–) Swedish ice hockey player.

Alfredsson, Helen. (1965–) Swedish professional golfer.

alfresco. (One word.)

algae is plural; a single organism is an **alga.**

Algonquin Hotel, New York City.

Algonquin Indians.

algorithm.

Ali, Muhammad. (1942–) American heavyweight boxer, three-time world champion; born Cassius Marcellus Clay.

à l'italienne. (Fr., no cap.) In the Italian style.

alkali, pl. *alkalis, alkalies.*

al-Khwarizmi, Muhammad ibn Musa. (c. 780–c. 850) Arab mathematician, often called the father of algebra.

Allahabad. City in Uttar Pradesh, India.

allege, allegedly, allegation.

Allegheny Mountains and **Allegheny River,** but **Alleghany Corporation** and **Allegany** for the town, county, Indian reservation, and state park in New York. The plural of the mountains is **Alleghenies.** In short, there is huge variation in the spelling from place to place, so double-check.

Allen, William Hervey. (1889–1949) Not *Harvey*; American novelist.

Allende, Salvador. (1908–1973) President of Chile (1970–73).

All God's Chillun Got Wings. Play by Eugene O'Neill (1924).

Allhallowmass. (One word.) Alternative name for All Saints' Day.

all intents and purposes is a tautology; use just "to all intents."

All Nippon Airways. Not *-lines.*

allophone. In Canadian usage, someone who does not speak French.

allot, allotted, allotting, allottable.

all right. Not *alright.*

All Saints' Day. November 1.

All Souls College, Oxford University. Not *Souls',* etc.

all time. Many authorities object to this expression in constructions such as "She was almost certainly the greatest female sailor of all time" (*Daily Telegraph*) on the grounds that *all time* extends to the future as well as the past and we cannot possibly know what lies ahead. A no less pertinent consideration is that such assessments, as in the example just cited, are bound to be hopelessly subjective and therefore have no place in any measured argument.

allusion. "When the speaker happened to name Mr. Gladstone, the allusion was received with loud cheers" (cited by Fowler). The word is not, as many suppose, a more impressive synonym for *reference*. When you allude to something, you do not specifically mention it but leave it to the reader to deduce the subject. Thus it would be correct to write, "In an allusion to the president, he said: 'Some people make better oil men than politicians.' " The word is closer in meaning to *implication* or *suggestion*.

Allyson, June. (1917–2006) American film actress; real name Ella Geisman.

Al Manāmah/Al Manama. Capital of Bahrain.

Almaty. Largest city in Kazakhstan. The capital is Astana.

Almodóvar, Pedro. (1949–) Spanish filmmaker.

Alpes-de-Haute-Provence. Department of France.

Al Qaeda (from the Arabic *al-qā'ida*) is the most common spelling in American English for the terrorist group, but there are many variants, including commonly **Al Qaida, al-Qaeda,** and **al-Qaida.**

Al Qahirah/El Qahira. Arabic name for Cairo.

alright is never correct; make it **all right.**

ALS. Amyotrophic lateral sclerosis, a muscle-wasting disease. Also known as Lou Gehrig's disease, after the baseball player who suffered from it.

altar, alter. The first is a table used in worship; the second means to change.

altercation means a heated exchange of words. If blows are traded or shoving is involved, it is not properly an altercation.

Althing. Parliament of Iceland.

altocumulus, altostratus (each one word) for types of cloud.

alumnae, alumni. *Alumni* is the masculine plural for a collection of college graduates. In the context of an all-female institution, the correct word is *alumnae*. The singular forms are *alumna* (feminine) and *alumnus* (masculine).

alyssum. Border plant.

Alzheimer's disease, but in formal medical contexts the non-possessive form **Alzheimer disease** is increasingly used instead.

a.m./AM. *Ante meridiem* (Lat.) Before midday.

Amalienborg Palace. Residence of Danish royal family in Copenhagen.

amanuensis. One who takes dictation; pl. *amanuenses.*

amaretto. Liqueur; pl. *amarettos.*

Amarillo, Texas.

amaryllis.

ambergris. Substance used in the manufacture of perfumes.

ambidextrous. Not -*erous.*

ambience.

ambiguous, equivocal. Both mean vague and open to more than one interpretation. But whereas an *ambiguous* statement may be vague by accident or by intent, an *equivocal* one is calculatedly unclear.

Amenhotep. Name of four kings in the eighteenth dynasty of ancient Egypt.

America's Cup. Yacht races.

americium. (Not cap.) Chemical element.

AmeriCorps. Voluntary service organization.

AmerisourceBergen. (One word.) Pharmaceutical supply company.

Améthyste, Côte d', France.

Amharic. Semitic language; official tongue of Ethiopia.

amicus curiae. (Lat.) "Friend of the court." Pl. *amici curiae.*

amid, among. *Among* applies to things that can be separated and counted, *amid* to things that cannot. Rescuers might search among survivors, but amid wreckage.

amniocentesis. The withdrawing of amniotic fluid from a pregnant woman's uterus.

à moitié. (Fr.) In part, halfway.

amok is generally the preferred spelling, but **amuck** is an accepted alternative.

among, between. A few authorities insist that *among* applies to more than two things and *between* to only two. But by this logic you would have to say that St. Louis is among California, New York, and Michigan, not between them. Insofar as the two words can be distinguished, *among* should be applied to collective arrangements (trade talks among the members of the European Community) and *between* to reciprocal arrangements (a treaty between the United Kingdom, the United States, and Canada).

amoral, immoral. *Amoral* describes matters in which questions of morality do not arise or are disregarded; *immoral* applies to things that are evil.

amour-propre. (Fr.) Self-respect.

Ampère, André Marie. (1775–1836) French physicist. The unit of electricity named after him is **ampere** (no cap., no accent).

amphetamine.

amphibian, amphibious.

Amphitryon. In Greek mythology, a Mycenaen king whose wife, Alcmene, gave birth to Hercules after Zeus tricked her into sleeping with him.

ampoule/ampule/ampul. All three spellings are accepted, but **ampoule** is generally preferred.

Amtrak for the passenger railroad corporation. The company's formal designation is the National Railroad Passenger Corporation, but this is almost never used, even on first reference.

Amundsen, Roald. (1872–1928) Norwegian explorer, first person to reach the South Pole (1911).

Anacreon. (c. 563–c. 478 BC) Greek poet.

anathema, pl. *anathemas.*

Anaxagoras. (c. 500–428 BC) Greek philosopher.

Anaximander. (c. 611–c. 547 BC) Greek philosopher.

ancien régime. (Fr.) "The old order."

ancillary.

Andalusia. Region of Spain. In Spanish, Andalucía.

Andersen, Hans Christian. (1805–1875) Not *-son.* Danish writer of children's tales.

Anderson, Marian. (1897–1993) Celebrated contralto.

Andhra Pradesh. Indian state.

Andorra is a principality; the capital is Andorra la Vella.

Andrejewski, Jerzy. (1909–1983) Polish novelist.

Andretti, Mario. (1940–) American racecar driver.

Andrews Air Force Base, Maryland. (No apos.)

androgenous, androgynous. The first applies to the production of male offspring; the second means having both male and female characteristics.

Andromache. In Greek mythology, the wife of Hector.

Androscoggin. A county, river, and lake in Maine.

and which. Almost always *and which* should be preceded by a parallel *which* ("The home run, which was his tenth of the month and which was the longest hit in the park this year . . ."). The stricture applies equally to such constructions as *and that, and who, but which,* and *but who.* See also THAT, WHICH.

anesthesia, anesthesiologist.

aneurysm.

Anfinsen, Christian B(oehmer). (1916–1995) American biochemist, awarded Nobel Prize for Chemistry in 1972.

anfractuosity. Having many turns.

Angelico, Fra. (1387–1455) Florentine painter, also known as Fra Giovanni da Fiesole.

Angkor. Complex of ruins in Cambodia. **Angkor Wat** is a single temple within the compound.

Angleterre. French for England.

anglicize. (Lowercase.)

angora. Type of wool. **Angora** is the former name of Ankara, Turkey.

Angostura bitters.

angstrom/ångström. (Abbr. Å.) Unit used to measure wavelengths of light, and equal to one ten-billionth of a meter; named for **Anders Ångström** (1814–1874), Swedish physicist.

Anheuser-Busch. Brewery.

Anhui. Chinese province, formerly spelled *Anhwei.*

Aniakchak National Monument and Preserve, Alaska.

animus, but **animosity.**

aniseed. A flavorful seed.

anisette. A drink flavored with aniseed.

Ankara. Capital of Turkey.

Annabessacook, Lake, Maine.

Annapolis. Capital of Maryland.

Annapurna. A cluster of mountains in the Himalayas, of which the highest peak is Annapurna I (26,545 feet; 8,091 meters).

Ann Arbor, Michigan, home of the University of Michigan.

Anne Arundel County, Maryland.

Anne of Cleves. (1515–1557) Fourth wife of Henry VIII.

annex for both noun and verb.

Annieopsquotch Mountains, Newfoundland, Canada.

annihilate.

)41–) American actress; born Ann-Margret Olsson.
n and irregular spelling *Margret*.

at., cap. *D* only.) "The year of the Lord." See also AD.

(Lat.) Remarkable year.

anomaly, anomalous.

anonymous, anonymity.

Anouilh, Jean. (1910–1987) French playwright; pronounced *an'-wee*.

Anschluss. (Ger.) A union; particularly applied to that of Germany and Austria in 1938.

Antananarivo. Capital of Madagascar.

Antassawamock Neck, Massachusetts.

antebellum. (Lat.) "Before the war"; especially applied to the period before the American Civil War.

antecedence, antecedents. *Antecedence* means precedence; *antecedents* are ancestors or other things that have gone before.

antediluvian. Antiquated, primitive.

ante meridiem. (Lat.) "Before midday." Abbr. a.m./AM; not to be confused with **antemeridian** (one word), meaning of or taking part in the morning.

antennae, antennas. Either is correct as the plural of *antenna*, but generally *antennae* is preferred for living organisms ("a beetle's antennae") and *antennas* for manmade objects ("radio antennas made possible the discovery of quarks").

anticipate. To anticipate something is to look ahead to it and prepare for it, not to make a reasonable estimate. A tennis player who anticipates his opponent's next shot doesn't just guess where it is going to go but is there to meet it.

Anti-Defamation League.

Antigone. In Greek mythology, daughter of Oedipus; also (in italics) the title of a play by Sophocles.

Antigua and Barbuda. Caribbean state; capital St. John's.

antipasto. (It.) Appetizer, hors d'oeuvre; pl. *antipasti*.

Antipodean. Of Australia or New Zealand.

antirrhinum. Note *-rr-*. A flower, also known as a snapdragon

Antofagasta, Chile.

Antonioni, Michelangelo. (1912–2007) Italian film director.

Antony and Cleopatra. Not *Anthony.* Play by Shakespeare (c. 1606).

Antwerpen. The Flemish name for Antwerp, Belgium; the French name is Anvers.

anxious. Since *anxious* comes from *anxiety,* it should contain some connotation of being worried or fearful and not merely eager or expectant.

any. A tricky word at times, as here: "This paper isn't very good, but neither is any of the others." A simple and useful principle is to make the verb always correspond to the complement. Thus: "neither is any other" or "neither are any of the others."

anybody, anyone, anything, anyway, anywhere. *Anything* and *anywhere* are always one word. The others are normally one word except when the emphasis is on the second element (e.g., "He received three job offers, but any one would have suited him"). *Anybody* and *anyone* are singular and should be followed by singular pronouns and verbs. A common fault—so common, in fact, that some no longer consider it a fault—is seen here: "Anyone can relax so long as they don't care whether they or anyone else ever actually gets anything done." The problem, clearly, is that a plural pronoun ("they") is being attached to a singular verb ("gets"). Such constructions may in fact be fully defensible, at least some of the time, though you should at least know why you are breaking a rule when you break it.

à outrance. (Fr.) Not *à l'outrance.* To the very last, to the death.

Apalachicola. Florida river.

Aparicio, Luis. (1934–) Venezuelan-born baseball player.

Apeldoorn, the Netherlands.

Apennines for the Italian mountain range. Note *-nn-* in middle. In Italian, Appennini.

aperitif, pl. *aperitifs.*

Apfelstrudel. (Ger.) Apple strudel.

aplomb.

apocalypse, apocalyptic.

apogee. The highest or most distant point, usually in reference to orbiting bodies. Its opposite is *perigee*.

Apollinaire, Guillaume. (1880–1918) French writer and critic; born Wilhelm Apollinaris de Kostrowitzky.

Apollo. Greek god of light, son of Zeus.

"Apologie for Poetrie, An." Title of the essay by Sir Philip Sidney, also published as "The Defence of Poesie" (1595).

aposiopesis. The sudden breaking off of a thought or statement; pl. *aposiopeses.*

apostasy. The abandoning of one's faith; pl. *apostasies.*

apostatize.

a posteriori. (Lat.) From what is after; in logic, moving from effect to cause, reasoning from experience.

apothegm. A witty or pithy maxim.

apotheosis. Deification (generally used figuratively); pl. *apotheoses.*

Appalachian Mountains, eastern United States.

appaloosa. Horse. A breed of saddle horse.

apparatchik. Party functionary, especially of the Communist Party.

apparel.

apparition.

appellant, appellate.

appendices, appendixes. Either is correct.

applicator.

appoggiatura. In music, an accented nonharmonized note that precedes a harmonized note.

Appomattox, Virginia; where the Confederacy surrendered to the Union to end the Civil War (April 9, 1865).

appraise, apprise. *Appraise* means to assess or evaluate. *Apprise* means to inform. An insurance assessor appraises damage and apprises owners.

appreciate has a slightly more specific meaning than writers sometimes give it. If you appreciate something, you value it ("I appreciate your concern") or you understand it sympathetically ("I appreciate your predicament"). But when there is no sense of sympathy or value (as in "I appreciate what you are saying, but I don't agree with it") *understand* or *recognize* or the like would be better.

apprehensible.

après-midi. (Fr.) Afternoon.

après-ski. (Fr., hyphen.) The period after a day's skiing.

April Fools' Day.

a principio. (Lat.) From the beginning.

a priori. (Lat.) From what is before; in logic, an argument proceeding from cause to effect.

apropos. In French, *à propos.*

Apuleius, Lucius. (fl. second c. AD) Roman satirist.

Apulia. Region of Italy known in English as Puglia.

Aqaba, Gulf of. An arm of the Red Sea. Aqaba is also the name of a town in Jordan.

aqua vitae. (Lat.) "Water of life"; used to describe whiskeys and other alcoholic spirits.

aqueduct, but **aquifer.**

aquiline. Like an eagle.

Aquinas, St. Thomas. (1225–1274) Italian theologian, canonized 1323.

À quoi bon? (Fr.) What for? What's the point?

arabic numerals. Not cap.

Arafat, Yasir. (1929–2004) Born Mohammed Abdel Raouf Arafat; leader Palestine Liberation Organization (1969–2004), awarded Nobel Peace Prize with Shimon Peres and Yitzhak Rabin (1994).

Aramaic. Semitic language.

Aran Island and **Aran Islands** (Ireland) but **Isle of Arran** (Scotland). The sweater is spelled *Aran.*

Arc de Triomphe, Paris. Officially, Arc de Triomphe de l'Étoile.

arc-en-ciel. (Fr.) Rainbow; pl. *arcs-en-ciel.*

archaea. Type of unicellular organism.

archaeology is normally preferred, but **archeology** is accepted.

archaic, archaism.

archetype.

Archilochus of Paros. (c. 714–c. 676 BC) Greek poet.

Archimedes. (c. 287–212 BC) Greek mathematician and engineer.

archipelago, pl. *archipelagos.*

Arctic Circle, Arctic Ocean, but **arctic fox.**

Ardennes. Wooded plateau region in southern Belgium, northeastern France, and Luxembourg.

Arezzo, Italy.

arguable.

Århus. Danish for Aarhus; city in Denmark.

Aristides. (c. 530–c. 468 BC) Athenian statesman.

Aristophanes. (c. 448–c. 380 BC) Greek dramatist.

armadillo, pl. *armadillos.*

Armageddon.

armament.

armature.

aroma applies only to agreeable smells; there is no such thing as a bad aroma.

Aroostook River, Maine and New Brunswick.

Arran, Isle of, Scotland. See also ARAN ISLAND.

arrière-pensée. (Fr.) Ulterior motive, mental reservation.

arrivederci. (It.) Goodbye.

arriviste. Disagreeably ambitious person.

Arrol-Johnston. British automobile of early 1900s.

arrondissement. Principal division of French departments and some larger cities.

Arrows of the Chace, not *Chase,* by John Ruskin.

Artemis. Greek goddess of the moon, associated with hunting. The Roman equivalent is Diana.

arteriosclerosis.

Arthur Andersen. Not -*son*. Accountancy firm.

Arthur, Chester Alan. (1829–1886) U.S. president (1881–1885).

artichoke.

artifact, artefact. The first spelling is generally preferred, but either is correct.

Aruba. Caribbean island, a self-governing dependency of the Netherlands; capital Oranjestad.

Asahi Shimbun. Japanese newspaper.

as . . . as. "A government study concludes that for trips of 500 miles or less . . . automotive travel is as fast or faster than air travel, door to door" (George Will, syndicated columnist). The problem here is what is termed an incomplete alternative comparison. If we remove the "or faster than" phrase from the sentence, the problem becomes immediately evident: "A government study concludes that for trips of 500 miles or less . . . automotive travel is as fast than air travel, door to door." The writer has left the "as fast" phrase uncompleted. The sentence should say "as fast as or faster than air travel."

ascendancy, ascendant.

Asch, Sholem. (1880–1957) Polish-born American novelist.

ASCII. Short for American Standard Code for Information Interchange; computer terminology.

Asclepius. Use **Aesculapius.**

ASEAN. Association of South East Asian Nations, formed 1967; members are Brunei, Cambodia, Indonesia, Laos, Malaysia, Myanmar/Burma, the Philippines, Singapore, Thailand, and Vietnam.

aseptic.

as far as is commonly misused, as here: "As far as next season, it is too early to make forecasts" (*Baltimore Sun*). The error here has been exercising authorities since at least Fowler's heyday and shows no sign of abating, either as a problem or as something that exercises authorities. The trouble is that "as far as" serves as a conjunction and as such requires a following verb. The solution is either to remove the conjunction ("As for next season, it is too early to make forecasts") or to supply the needed verb ("As far as next season goes, it is too early to make forecasts").

Ashbery, John. (1927–) American poet and critic.

Asheville, North Carolina.

Ashgabat. Capital of Turkmenistan; also sometimes spelled *Ashkhabad.*

Ashkenazi. An East or Central European Jew; pl. *Ashkenazim.*

Ashkenazy, Vladimir. (1937–) Russian-born Icelandic pianist and conductor.

Ashmolean Museum, Oxford, England.

Ashuapmuchuan River, Quebec, Canada.

Asimov, Isaac. (1920–1992) American biochemist and prolific science-fiction writer.

asinine.

Asmara. Capital of Eritrea; formerly Asmera.

asparagus.

Assad, Bashar. (1965–) President of Syria (2000–); succeeded his father, **Hafez Assad** (1928–2000).

assagai/assegai. Either spelling is correct for the African spear.

assailant.

assassin.

Assateague Island, Maryland and Virginia.

assault, battery. They are not the same in law. *Assault* is a threat of violence; *battery* is actual violence.

assessor.

asseverate. To declare.

assiduous, acidulous. *Assiduous* means diligent; *acidulous* means tart or acidic.

Assiniboine River, Manitoba, Canada.

Assisi. Town in Umbria, Italy, birthplace of St. Francis.

assonance. Words that rhyme in consonants but not vowels (e.g., *cat* and *kit*) or in vowels but not consonants (e.g., *bun* and *sponge*).

assuage, assuaging.

assume, presume. The two words are often so close in meaning as to be indistinguishable, but in some contexts they do allow a fine distinction to be made. *Assume*, in the sense of "to suppose," normally means to put forth a realistic hypothesis, something that can be taken as probable ("I assume we will arrive by midnight"). *Presume* has more of an air of sticking one's neck out, of making an assertion that may be arguable or wrong ("I presume we have met before?"). But in most instances the two words can be used interchangeably.

as to whether. *Whether* alone is sufficient.

AstraZeneca. Pharmaceuticals company.

AstroTurf (one word) is a trademark.

Asunción. Capital of Paraguay.

asymmetry, asymmetric, asymmetrical.

Atatürk, Mustapha Kemal. (1881–1938) Turkish leader and president (1923–1938).

Atchafalaya. Louisiana river and bay.

Athena. Greek goddess of wisdom.

Athenaeum. London club and other British contexts, but **Atheneum** for the U.S. publisher.

Athinai. Greek spelling of Athens.

ATM. Automated teller machine.

à tout prix. (Fr.) At any price.

attaché.

Attawapiskat. Canadian river.

Attlee, Clement (Richard). (1883–1967) British prime minister (1945–1951). Later made Earl Attlee.

attorney general, pl. *attorneys general.*

attributable.

Attucks, Crispus. (c. 1723–1770) Black American killed in the Boston Massacre.

Atwater, (Harvey) Lee. (1951–1991) American political figure.

Atwood, Margaret. (1939–) Canadian novelist.

Au, gold, is the abbreviation of *aurum* (Lat.).

aubergine. British name for eggplant.

au besoin. (Fr.) "If need be."

aubrietia. Flowering plant named after **Claude Aubriet** (1655–1742), French painter.

Auchincloss, Louis (Stanton). (1917–) American novelist.

Auchinleck. Family name of James Boswell; pronounced *aff-leck.*

Auden, W. H. (for Wystan Hugh). (1907–1973) English-born American poet.

audible.

Audubon, John James. (1785–1851) American artist and naturalist.

au fait. (Fr.) To be in the know.

au fond. (Fr.) Basically, at the bottom.

auf Wiedersehen. (Ger.) Goodbye, until we meet again.

auger, augur. An *auger* is a tool for boring holes in wood or soil; an *augur* is a prophet or soothsayer. The two words are not related.

"Auld Lang Syne." (Scot.) Literally "old long since"; traditional end-of-year song with words by Robert Burns.

Auld Reekie. (Scot.) Old Smoky; nickname for Edinburgh.

Aumann, Robert J. (1930–) Israeli-American academic; awarded Nobel Prize for Economics (2005).

au mieux. (Fr.) For the best, at best.

au naturel. (Fr.) In the natural state.

Ausable River, Ausable Chasm, New York State.

Au Sable River, Au Sable Point, Michigan.

Auschwitz. German concentration camp in Poland during World War II. In Polish, Oświęcim.

Au secours! (Fr.) A cry for help.

Ausländer. (Ger.) Foreigner.

auspicious does not mean simply special or memorable. It means propitious, promising, of good omen.

Austen, Jane. (1775–1817) English novelist.

Australia, Commonwealth of, is divided into six states (New South Wales, Queensland, South Australia, Tasmania, Victoria, Western Australia) and two territories (Australian Capital Territory, Northern Territory). The latter two should not be referred to as states.

autarchy, autarky. The first means absolute power, an autocracy; the second denotes self-sufficiency. However, neither word is well known, and in almost every instance an English synonym would bring an improvement in comprehension, if not in elegance.

Auteuil, Daniel. (1950–) Prolific French actor.

autobahn. (Ger.) Express motorway. The English plural is *autobahns*; the German is *Autobahnen.*

auto-da-fé. Execution of heretics during the Inquisition; pl. *autos-da-fé.*

autostrada. (It.) Express motorway; pl. *autostrade.*

Auvergne. Region of France.

auxiliary. Not -*ll*-.

avant-garde.

avenge, revenge. Generally, *avenge* indicates the settling of a score or the redressing of an injustice. It is more dispassionate than *revenge,* which indicates retaliation taken largely for the sake of personal satisfaction.

Avenue of the Americas, New York City. Often still referred to as Sixth Avenue, its former name.

avocado, pl. *avocados.*

avocation. Work done for personal satisfaction rather than need, usually in addition to a normal job.

avoirdupois weights. The system of weights traditionally used throughout the English-speaking world, based on one pound equaling sixteen ounces.

Avon. Former county of England, abolished 1996; also the name of several rivers in England and the title of the former prime minister Anthony Eden (Earl of Avon).

à votre santé. (Fr.) "To your health."

a while, awhile. To write "for awhile" is wrong because the idea of *for* is implicit in *awhile.* Write either "I will stay here for a while" (two words) or "I will stay here awhile" (one word).

awoke, awaked, awakened. Two common problems are worth noting:

1. *Awoken,* though much used, is generally considered not standard. Thus this sentence from an Agatha Christie novel (cited by Partridge) is wrong: "I was awoken by that rather flashy young woman." Make it *awakened.*

2. As a past participle, *awaked* is preferable to *awoke.* Thus, "He had awaked at midnight" and not "He had awoke at midnight." But if ever in doubt about the past tense, you will never be wrong if you use *awakened.*

axel, axle. An *axel* is a jump in ice skating; an *axle* is a rod connecting two wheels.

Axelrod, George. (1922–2003) American screenwriter and film director.

ayatollah. Shiite Muslim religious leader.

Ayckbourn, Sir Alan. (1939–) Prolific British playwright.

Ayers Rock (no apos.) for the Australian eminence. However, the formal and now usual name is **Uluru.**

Aykroyd, Dan. (1952–) Canadian-born actor and screenwriter.

Azerbaijan. Former republic of the Soviet Union; capital Baku. *Azerbaijani/Azeri.*

Azikiwe, Nnamdi. (1904–1996) Nigerian nationalist leader, president (1963–66).

Bb

Baader-Meinhof Gang. German underground group named after **Andreas Baader** (1943–1977) and **Ulrike Meinhof** (1934–1976); also called the Red Army Faction.

Baath Party. Formally **Baath Arab Socialist Party.**

Babbitt. Novel by Sinclair Lewis (1922).

Babington conspiracy. A plot to assassinate Queen Elizabeth I of England, named for its principal conspirator, **Antony Babington** (1561–1586).

Babi Yar. Site near Kiev where Nazis massacred Russian Jews in 1941; also the title of a poem by Yevgeny Yevtushenko and a novel by Anatoly Kuznetsov.

babushka. A Russian grandmother; also a kind of scarf.

Bacardi. A brand of rum.

baccalaureate.

baccarat. A casino game. In French, *baccara.*

Bacchae, The. Play by Euripides.

Bacchus. Roman god of wine; the Greek equivalent was Dionysus. Words derived from *Bacchus* are usually not capitalized but do retain *-cc-* spelling: *bacchanalian, bacchic, bacchantic.*

Bach, Johann Sebastian. (1685–1750) German composer and father of four others: **Wilhelm Friedemann** (1710–1784), **Carl Philipp Emanuel** (1714–1788), **Johann Christoph Friedrich** (1732–1795), and **Johann Christian** (1735–1782).

bacillus, pl. *bacilli.*

bacteria is plural. The singular is *bacterium.* Bacteria should not be confused with viruses, which are much smaller and cause different diseases.

Baden-Württemberg. German state; capital Stuttgart.

Baedeker. Famous series of travel guidebooks first published in Germany by **Karl Baedeker** (1801–1859).

Baekeland, Leo Hendrik. (1863–1944) Belgian-born American chemist who invented Bakelite.

bagatelle. A trifle.

bahadur. A title of respect in India.

Bahai. A religion; the cognate forms are **Bahaist** and **Bahaism.**

Bahamian. Of or from the Bahamas.

Bahnhof. (Ger.) Railroad station.

Bahrain. Island state in the Persian Gulf; capital Manama.

bail, bale. *Bail* is a prisoner's bond, the pieces that rest atop the stumps in cricket, and the act of scooping water. A *bale* is a bundle, as of cotton or hay. You bail out a boat, but bale out of an aircraft. A malicious person wears a baleful expression.

Baile Atha Cliath. Gaelic for Dublin.

baited breath is wrong; breath is **bated.**

Bakelite. (Cap.) Type of plastic.

Bakunin, Mikhail (Aleksandrovich). (1814–1876) Russian revolutionary.

balalaika. Stringed instrument.

Balanchine, George. (1904–1983) Russian-born American choreographer.

baldechin/baldaquin. A canopy over a throne or altar; pronounced *bald-a-kin.* In Italian, baldacchino.

Baldrige, Malcolm. (1922–1987) Not *-ridge.* American statesman.

bale, bail. A *bale* is a bundle, as of cotton or hay. *Bail* is a prisoner's bond, the pieces that rest atop the stumps in cricket, and the act of scooping water. You bail out a boat, but bale out of an aircraft. A malicious person wears a baleful expression.

Balearic Islands. Cluster of Spanish islands in the Mediterranean; in Spanish, Islas Baleares.

Balladur, Édouard. (1929–) Prime minister of France (1993–1995).

Ballesteros, Severiano. (1957–) Spanish golfer; nickname "Sevvy."

Balliol College, Oxford University.

Baluchistan. Region in Pakistan bordered by Iran and Afghanistan.

Band-Aid (hyphen) is a trademark.

bandanna. Note -*anna*, not -*ana*.

bandicoot. Type of marsupial.

banister. Handrail on a staircase.

banjos.

Banjul. Capital of Gambia; formerly called Bathurst.

BankAmerica Corporation is now **Bank of America.**

Bankers Trust. (No apos.)

Bankhead, Tallulah. (1903–1968) American actress.

Ban Ki-moon. (1944–) South Korean diplomat; secretary-general of United Nations (2007–); on second reference, Mr. Ban.

Bannister, Sir Roger (Gilbert). (1929–) First person to run a mile in less than four minutes (3 minutes, 59.4 seconds; 1954).

banns. Notice in church of intended marriage.

banshee. Evil spirit; in Gaelic, *bean sídhe*.

Bantustan. South African black homeland.

banzai, bonsai. The first is a Japanese war cry; the second is a type of Japanese gardening centered on miniature trees.

baptistery.

Barabbas. In the New Testament, the condemned thief released instead of Jesus by Pilate.

Barbadian. Of or from Barbados. The slang term *Bajan* is also sometimes used.

barbaric, barbarous. *Barbaric*, properly used, emphasizes crudity and a lack of civilizing influence. A sharpened stick might be considered a barbaric implement of war. *Barbarous* stresses cruelty and harshness and usually contains at least a hint of moral condemnation, as in "barbarous ignorance" or "barbarous treatment."

Barbarossa. Not -*rosa.* Nickname of Frederick I (c. 1123–1190), Holy Roman Emperor; German code name for the invasion of the USSR in 1941.

barbecue is the only acceptable spelling in serious writing.

Barbizon School. Group of French landscape painters, among them Millet, Daubigny, and Rousseau.

Barclays Bank, UK (no apos.).

Barents Sea.

bar mitzvah. Religious coming-of-age ceremony for Jewish boys; the ceremony for girls is a **bat mitzvah.** The plural is *mitzvoth* or *mitzvahs.*

Barnard, Christiaan. (1922–2001) South African heart surgeon. Note -*aa-* in first name.

Barnes & Noble. (Ampersand.)

Barneys New York. (No apos.) Clothing retailer.

Barnstable. Town and county, Cape Cod, Massachusetts, but **Barnstaple,** England.

Barnum, P(hineas) T(aylor). (1810–1891) American showman.

baron, baroness, baronet. A *baron* has the lowest rank in the British nobility. A baronage can be either hereditary or nonhereditary. Holders of the latter are called life peers. A *baroness* is a woman who is the wife or widow of a baron, or a peer in her own right. In British contexts, *Lord* or *Lady* can be substituted for *Baron* or *Baroness,* e.g., Baron Baden-Powell is called Lord Baden-Powell. A *baronet* is not a peer; this is a hereditary title ranking below a peer but above a knight. See also BRITISH ARISTOCRACY.

barracuda.

Barrie, J. M. (formally Sir James Matthew Barrie) (1860–1937) Scottish writer, creator of Peter Pan.

Barroso, José Manuel. (1956–) Portuguese politician, president of the European Commission (2004–2009).

Bartholdi, Frédéric Auguste. (1834–1904) French sculptor; designed Statue of Liberty.

Bartholomew Day, August 24, but the **St. Bartholomew's Day Massacre** (1572) and **St. Bartholomew's Hospital,** London (familiarly known as **Bart's**).

Bartók, Béla. (1881–1945) Hungarian pianist and composer.

Bartolommeo, Fra. (1475–1517) Florentine painter.

Basel, Basle, Bâle. Third-largest city in Switzerland. *Basel* is the usual spelling in the United States and Germany; *Basle* is the usual spelling in Switzerland and Britain; *Bâle* is the usual spelling among French speakers.

Băsescu, Traian. (1951–) President of Romania (2004–).

Bashkortostan. Russian republic.

BASIC. Short for Beginner's All-purpose Symbolic Instruction Code; computer programming language.

basically. The trouble with this word, basically, is that it is almost always unnecessary.

Basilicata. Region of Italy.

basis. More often than not, a reliable indicator of wordiness, as here: "Det. Chief Supt. Peter Topping . . . said he would review the search on a day-to-day basis." Why not make it "would review the search daily" and save five words?

Basotho. The people of Lesotho.

bas-relief.

Basse-Normandie. Region of France; capital Caen.

Basseterre. Capital of St. Kitts and Nevis.

basset hound.

Bastille Day. July 14 (1789).

Bataan. Peninsula of the Philippines, famous for a long forced march of defeated Allied soldiers by Japanese in which many thousands died in World War II.

bated breath, not *baited. Bated* is a cousin of *abated* and so implies something that is withheld.

bathos. From the Greek *bathus,* meaning "deep," *bathos* can be used to indicate the lowest point or nadir, or triteness and insincerity. But its usual use is in describing an abrupt descent from an elevated position to the commonplace. It is not the opposite of *pathos,* which has to do with feelings of pity or sympathy.

Bathsheba. In the Old Testament, the wife of Uriah and then David, and mother of Solomon.

bathyscaph. Research submarine.

battalion.

Battelle Memorial Institute, Columbus, Ohio.

Baudelaire, Charles (Pierre). (1821–1867) French poet.

Baudouin I, (Albert Charles Léopold Axel Marie Gustave). (1930–1993) King of the Belgians (1951–1993).

Bauhaus. German school of arts and architecture, founded by Walter Gropius (1883–1969).

Baum, L(yman) Frank. (1856–1919) American writer of children's stories; created *The Wonderful Wizard of Oz.*

Bausch & Lomb. Eye-care company.

Bayern. German for Bavaria.

Bayonne. Name of cities in France and New Jersey.

Bayreuth, Bavaria.

BC always goes after the year (e.g., 42 BC); usually set in small caps. See also AD.

BCE. Before the Christian era.

be (with a participle). Almost always a wordy way of getting your point across, as here: "He will be joining the board of directors in March." Quicker to say, "He will join the board of directors in March."

Beachy Head, East Sussex, England.

Beardsley, Aubrey. (1872–1898) British artist.

béarnaise sauce.

Beaufort, South Carolina; pronounced *bew-furt.*

Beaufort scale. Measures wind velocity on a scale of 0 to 12, with 0 representing dead calm and 12 representing a hurricane.

Beaujolais. French region and wine.

Beaumarchais, Pierre Augustin Caron de. (1732–1799) French playwright whose works inspired *The Barber of Seville* and *The Marriage of Figaro.*

beau monde. (Fr.) The fashionable world; pl. *beaux mondes.*

Beauregard, Pierre (Gustave Toutant de). (1818–1893) Confederate general in the Civil War.

Beauvoir, Simone (Lucie Ernestine Marie Bertrand) de. (1908–1986) French author.

beaux arts. (Fr.) The fine arts.

béchamel sauce.

Becher's Brook. Celebrated jump on English Grand National horse racing course.

Bechuanaland. Former name of Botswana.

Becket, St. Thomas (à). (1118–1170) Archbishop of Canterbury, murdered by followers of Henry II.

Beckett, Samuel. (1906–1989) Irish poet, playwright, and novelist.

becquerel. Unit of radioactivity, named after **Antoine Henri Becquerel** (1852–1908), French physicist.

Bedloe's Island. Former name of Liberty Island, New York; site of the Statue of Liberty.

bedouin is plural; the singular is *bedi. Bedu* is an alternative plural.

Beecher, Henry Ward. (1813–1887) American preacher.

Beelzebub. Satan.

Beene, Geoffrey. (1927–2004) American fashion designer.

Beerbohm, Sir (Henry) Max(imilian). (1872–1956) British writer and critic.

Beethoven, Ludwig van. (1770–1827) German composer.

before, prior to. There is no difference between these two except length and a certain inescapable affectedness on the part of *prior to*. To paraphrase Theodore Bernstein, if you would use "posterior to" instead of "after," then by all means use "prior to" instead of "before."

Beggar's Opera, The. Not *Beggars'*; by John Gay (1728).

Begin, Menachem. (1913–1992) Polish-born Israeli prime minister (1977–83); Nobel Peace Prize shared with Anwar el-Sadat (1978).

behalf. A useful distinction exists between *on behalf of* and *in behalf of*. The first means acting as a representative, as when a lawyer enters a plea on behalf of a client, and often denotes a formal relationship. *In behalf of* indicates a closer or more sympathetic role and means acting as a friend or defender. "I spoke on your behalf" means that I represented you when you were absent. "I spoke in your behalf" means that I supported you or defended you.

Behn, Aphra. (1640–1689) English writer.

behoove (British **behove**). An archaic word, but still sometimes a useful one. Two points need to be made:

1. The word means necessary or contingent, but is sometimes wrongly used for "becomes," particularly with the adverb *ill*, as in "It ill behooves any man responsible for policy to think how best to make political propaganda" (cited by Gowers).

2. It should be used only impassively and with the subject *it*. "The circumstances behoove us to take action" is wrong. Make it instead "It behooves us in the circumstances to take action."

Beiderbecke, Bix. (1903–1931) Jazz musician; born Leon Bismarck Beiderbecke.

Beijing (Pinyin)**/Peking.**

Bekaa Valley, Lebanon.

Belarussian (or **Belarusian**) for someone or something from Belarus. The language is also Belarussian.

beleaguered. Not -*ured.*

Belém. Brazilian city, formerly Pará.

Belize. Central American republic, formerly British Honduras.

Belknap Press, The. Part of Harvard University Press.

belladonna. A highly toxic perennial herbaceous plant.

belle époque. (No caps.) The period just before World War I.

Belleisle, County Fermanagh, Northern Ireland, and New Brunswick, Canada; **Belle-Île,** Brittany, France; **Belle Isle,** Florida; **Strait of Belle Isle,** Newfoundland, Canada.

Bellerophon. In Greek mythology, a warrior who killed the Chimera and was crippled trying to fly Pegasus over Mount Olympus.

belles-lettres. Writing that has a literary or aesthetic, as opposed to purely informational, value. The word is usually treated as a plural, but may be used as a singular. For reasons unconnected to logic, the hyphen is lost and the word itself contracted in the related terms *belletrist, belletrism,* and *belletristic.*

bellicose. Warlike.

bellwether. Not -*weather. Wether* is an Old English word for a castrated sheep. A bellwether is a sheep that has a bell hung from its neck, by which means it leads the herd from one pasture to another. In general use, it signifies something that leads or shows the way. A bellwether stock is one that is customarily at the head of the pack. It does not mean a harbinger or foreteller of events.

Belsen. Concentration camp in Lower Saxony, Germany, during World War II, full name **Bergen-Belsen.**

beluga is a type of sturgeon, and not a manufacturer or producer of caviar, as is sometimes thought, so the word should not be capitalized (except of course at the start of a sentence).

Ben Ali, Zine El Abidine. (1936–) President of Tunisia (1987–).

Bendl, Karel. (1838–1897) Czech composer.

Benedick. Character in *Much Ado About Nothing* by William Shakespeare.

beneficence.

Benelux. Short for Belgium, Netherlands, and Luxembourg.

Beneš, Eduard. (1884–1948) Czechoslovakian prime minister (1921–1922) and president (1935–1938, 1939–1945 [in exile], and 1945–1948).

Benét, Stephen Vincent. (1898–1943) American writer, brother of **William Rose Benét** (1886–1950), also a writer.

Benghazi. Libyan city.

Ben-Gurion, David. (1886–1973) Israeli prime minister (1948–1953, 1955–1963); born David Grün.

benignancy/benignity.

Bening, Annette. (1958–) American actress.

benison. A blessing.

Bentsen, Lloyd. (1921–2006) American Democratic politician, secretary of the treasury (1993–1994); ran as vice presidential candidate in 1988.

ben venuto. (It.) "Welcome."

benzene, benzine. Both are liquid hydrocarbons commonly used as solvents. Benzene is primarily associated with the production of plastics, while benzine most often is encountered as a solvent used in dry-cleaning establishments. At all events, they are quite different substances and not merely alternative spellings of a single compound.

Beograd. Serbian for Belgrade.

Beowulf. Not -*wolf.* Anglo-Saxon epic.

Berchtesgaden. Not -*garden.* Bavarian tourist center where Hitler had a country retreat.

bereft. To be bereft of something is not to lack it but to be dispossessed of it, to lose it. A spinster is not bereft of a husband, but a widow is. (The word is the past participle of *bereave.*)

Bérégovoy, Pierre. (1925–1993) Prime minister of France (1992–1993).

Berenson, Bernard (or **Bernhard**). (1865–1959) Lithuanian-born American art critic.

Beretta. Italian manufacturer of handguns.

Bergdorf Goodman. New York department store.

Berkeleian. Of or from the philosophy of George Berkeley (1685–1753).

Berkeley, California, and **Berkeley Square,** London. The latter is pronounced *bark-lee.*

Berkeley, Busby. (1895–1976) Hollywood choreographer.

berkelium. Chemical element.

Berklee Performance Center, Boston, Massachusetts.

Bermudan. Not *-ian.*

Bern is the normal English spelling for the capital of Switzerland, though **Berne** is also accepted.

Bernabéu Stadium. In Madrid (formally **Santiago Bernabéu Stadium**), home of Real Madrid.

Bernanke, Ben. (1953–) American economist, chairman of the U.S. Federal Reserve Board (2006–).

Bernhardt, Sarah. (1844–1923) French actress, called "the Divine Sarah"; born Henriette-Rosine Bernard.

Bernini, (Giovanni) Lorenzo. (1598–1680) Italian sculptor and architect.

Bertelsmann. German media group.

Bertolucci, Bernardo. (1940–) Italian film director.

beryllium. Chemical element.

beseech.

besides means "also" or "in addition to," not "alternatively." Partridge cites this incorrect use: "The wound must have been made by something besides the handle of the gear-level." Make it "other than."

besiege. Not *-ei-.*

Bessarabia. Former name of Moldova.

Bessemer process. Steelmaking method named after Sir Henry Bessemer (1813–1898), British metallurgist.

bestseller, bestsellerdom (one word), but **best-selling** (hyphen).

Betelgeuse. Star in Orion constellation.

bête noire. (Fr.) Something much disliked; pl. *bêtes noires*.

Bettelheim, Bruno. (1903–1990) Austrian-born American child psychologist.

bettor for one who bets.

between, among. A few authorities continue to insist that *between* applies to two things only and *among* to more than two, so that we should speak of dividing some money between the two of us but among the four of us. That is useful advice as far as it goes, but it doesn't always go very far. It would be absurd, for instance, to say that Chicago is among New York, Los Angeles, and Houston. More logically, *between* should be applied to reciprocal arrangements (a treaty between the United States, the United Kingdom, and Canada) and *among* to collective arrangements (trade talks among the members of the European Union).

between you and I is always wrong. Make it "between you and me." The object of a preposition should always be in the accusative. More simply, we don't say "between you and I" for the same reason that we don't say "give that book to I."

Bevan, Aneurin (1897–1960), but **Ernest Bevin** (1881–1951) for the British politicians.

Bhagavadgita. Sacred Hindu text, part of the Sanskrit epic *Mahabharata*.

Bhumibol (Adulyadej). (1927–) King of Thailand (1946–).

Bhutan. Asian kingdom; capital Thimphu. Natives are *Bhutanese* (sing. and pl.).

biannual, biennial. *Biannual* means twice a year; *biennial* means every two years.

biased.

biathlon for the sport in which competitors ski across country and shoot set targets.

Bible (cap.), but **biblical** (no cap.).

Big Ben, strictly speaking, is not the famous clock on the Houses of Parliament in London, but just the great hour bell, so a passing visitor will hear Big Ben but never see it. The formal name of the clock, for what it is worth, is the clock on St. Stephen's Tower on the Palace of Westminster.

bildungsroman. (Ger.) Novel dealing with a character's early life and psychological development.

Biletnikoff, Fred. (1943–) Football player. The **Biletnikoff Award** is named for him.

billabong. Australian backwater; literally "dead stream."

billet-doux. (Fr.) Love letter; pl. *billets-doux.*

Billingsgate. For the historic London fish market; when lowercased it denotes foul or abusive speech of the type once heard there.

bimonthly, biweekly, and similar designations are almost always ambiguous. It is far better to say "every two months," "twice a month," etc., as appropriate.

biriani (or **biryani**). Indian meat and rice dish.

Bishkek. Capital of Kyrgyzstan.

Bishopsgate, London.

Bismarck, Prince Otto (Eduard Leopold) von. (1815–1898) German chancellor (1871–90).

bivouac, bivouacked, bivouacking.

BlackBerry. Communications device.

Blackfeet. Native American tribe or a member thereof; never *Blackfoot.*

Blagojevich, Rod. (1956–) Governor of Illinois (2003–).

blatant, flagrant. The words are not quite synonymous. Something that is *blatant* is glaringly obvious and contrived ("a blatant lie") or willfully obnoxious ("blatant commercialization") or both.

Something that is *flagrant* is shocking and reprehensible ("a fla-grant miscarriage of justice"). If I tell you that I regularly travel to the moon, that is a blatant lie, not a flagrant one. If you set fire to my house, that is a flagrant act, not a blatant one.

blazon means to display or proclaim in an ostentatious manner. Trails are blazed, not blazoned.

Bleecker Street, New York City.

Blériot, Louis. (1872–1936) French aviator.

blitzkrieg. (Ger.) "Lightning war"; an overwhelming attack.

Blixen, Karen, Baroness. (1885–1962) Danish writer, who used the pseudonym Isak Dinesen.

Bloemfontein, South Africa, capital of Orange Free State.

Bloomberg, Michael. (1942–) American businessman and politician, mayor of New York City (2002–).

blueprint as a metaphor for a design or plan is much overworked. At least remember that a blueprint is a completed plan, not a pre-liminary one.

Blumberg, Baruch S(amuel). (1926–) American scientist, joint winner of 1976 Nobel Prize for Physiology or Medicine.

BMW. Short for Bayerische Motoren Werke.

B'nai B'rith. Jewish organization.

Boadicea. (d. AD 62) Traditional spelling for queen of the Iceni, a British Celtic tribe, but now more often spelled **Boudicca**.

Boboli Gardens, Florence, Italy.

Boccaccio, Giovanni. (1313–1375) Italian writer.

bocce, boccie. Bowling game.

Bodensee. The German name for Lake Constance.

Bodhisattva. In Buddhism, an enlightened one.

Bodleian Library, Oxford University; pronounced *bodd-lee-un.*

Boeotia. Region of ancient Greece, centered on Thebes.

Boethius, Anicius Manlius Severinus. (c. 480–c. 524) Roman statesman and philosopher.

Boettcher Concert Hall, Denver.

boffo. A huge success.

Bofors gun. (Cap.) Named for a town in Sweden.

Bogdanovich, Peter. (1939–) American film director.

bogey, bogie, bogy. *Bogey* is the invariable spelling for contexts involving golf strokes, *bogy* generally is reserved for malevolent spirits, and *bogie* is a technical term used to describe parts of wheels or tracks on mechanical conveyances.

Bogotá. Capital of Colombia.

Bohème, La. Opera by Giacomo Puccini (1896).

Bohr, Niels. (1885–1962) Danish physicist, won Nobel Prize for Physics (1922).

Bois de Boulogne. Paris park.

bok choy. Chinese vegetable.

Boleyn, Anne. (c. 1507–1536) Second wife of Henry VIII.

bolívar. Monetary unit of Venezuela, named for **Simón Bolívar** (1783–1830), Venezuelan-born revolutionary.

Bolivia. South American republic; the seat of government is La Paz, but the official capital is Sucre.

Böll, Heinrich. (1917–1985) German writer, awarded the Nobel Prize for Literature in 1972.

bollito misto, pl. *bolliti misti.* An Italian stew.

bollix. To botch or bungle.

Bombay. Now known as Mumbai.

bon appétit. (Fr.) Eat well, enjoy your food.

Bonhams. (No apos.) London auction house.

bonhomie. (Fr.) Good nature.

Bonnard, Pierre. (1867–1947) French painter.

bonne nuit. (Fr.) Good night, but **bonsoir** for good evening.

bonsai, banzai. *Bonsai* is the Japanese art of growing dwarf shrubs; *banzai* is a Japanese salute, literally "May you live 10,000 years."

bonsoir. (Fr.) Good evening, but **bonne nuit** for good night.

bon vivant, bon viveur. The first is a person who enjoys good food; the second a person who lives well.

Book-of-the-Month Club.

Boonyaratglin, Gen. Sonthi. (1946–) Leader of military coup in Thailand in 2006; on second reference he is Gen. Sonthi.

Boorstin, Daniel. (1914–2004) American historian.

Bophuthatswana. Former South African black homeland; capital Mmabatho. Reintegrated into South Africa in 1994.

bordellos.

Borders Books and Music. (No apos.) ⸱

Borghese. Noble Italian family.

Borgia, Rodrigo. (1431–1503) Pope Alexander VI, father of **Cesare Borgia** (1476–1507) and **Lucrezia Borgia** (1480–1519).

Borglum, Gutzon. (1871–1941) American sculptor, designer of the presidential memorial at Mount Rushmore; full name John Gutzon de la Mothe Borglum.

Bormann, Martin. (1900–1945) Nazi politician.

born, borne. Both are past participles of the verb *bear*, but by convention they are used in slightly different ways. *Born* is limited to the idea of birth ("He was born in December"). *Borne* is used for the sense of supporting or tolerating ("She has borne the burden with dignity"), but is also used to refer to giving birth in active constructions ("She has borne three children") and in passive constructions followed by "by" ("The three children borne by her . . .").

Borodin, Alexander (Porfiryevich). (1833–1887) Russian composer.

borscht.

Börse, Borsa, Bourse. Respectively German, Italian, and French for stock exchange.

Bosch, Hieronymus. (c. 1450–1516) Dutch painter, born Hieronymus van Aken.

bo's'n, bosun, bo'sun are all abbreviations of **boatswain**, a naval officer; not to be confused with **boson,** a type of subatomic particle.

Bosnia and Herzegovina/Bosnia-Herzegovina. Serbian republic, formerly part of Yugoslavia; capital Sarajevo.

Bosporous, not *Bosph-,* for the strait separating Europe and Asia.

BOSS. Bureau for (not *of*) State Security, former South African intelligence department.

both. Three small problems to note:

1. *Both* should not be used to describe more than two things. Partridge cites a passage in which a woman is said to have "a shrewd common sense . . . both in speech, deed and dress." Delete *both.*

2. Sometimes it appears superfluously: ". . . and they both went to the same school, Charterhouse" (*Observer*). Either delete *both* or make it ". . . they both went to Charterhouse."

3. Sometimes it is misused for *each.* To say that there is a supermarket on both sides of the street suggests that it is somehow straddling the roadway. Say either that there is a supermarket on each side of the street or that there are supermarkets on both sides. (See also EACH.)

both . . . and. "He was both deaf to argument and entreaty" (cited by Gowers). The rule involved here is that of correlative conjunctions, which states that in a sentence of this type *both* and *and* should link grammatically similar entities. If *both* is followed immediately by a verb, *and* should also be followed immediately by a verb. If *both* immediately precedes a noun, then so should *and.* In the example above, however, *both* is followed by an adjective (*deaf*) and *and* by a noun (*entreaty*).

The sentence needs to be recast, either as "He was deaf to both argument [noun] and entreaty [noun]" or as "He was deaf both to argument [preposition and noun] and to entreaty [preposition and noun]."

The rule holds true equally for other such pairs: "not only . . . but also," "either . . . or," and "neither . . . nor."

Botswana. Southern African republic, formerly Bechuanaland; capital Gaborone. The people are **Batswana** (sing. and pl.).

Botticelli, Sandro. (c. 1445–1510) Italian painter, born Alessandro di Mariano di Vannik Filipepi.

bottleneck, as Gowers notes, is a useful, if sometimes overworked, metaphor to indicate a point of constriction. But it should not be forgotten that it is a metaphor and therefore capable of cracking when put under too much pressure. To speak, for instance, of "a worldwide bottleneck" or "a growing bottleneck" sounds a note of absurdity. Bottlenecks, even figurative ones, don't grow, and they don't encompass the earth.

Boucicault, Dion. (1822–1890) Irish playwright; pronounced *boo'-see-ko.*

Boudicca (d. AD 62) is now the more common spelling for the Celtic queen traditionally known as **Boadicea.** Queen of the Iceni, she led an unsuccessful revolt against the Romans.

bougainvillea.

bouillabaisse. Not *-illi-.*

bouillon. Not *-ion.* Broth.

bourgeois, bourgeoisie.

Bourgogne. The French name for Burgundy.

boustrophedon. Writing in which alternate lines go from right to left and left to right.

boutonnière. Flower for buttonhole.

Boutros-Ghali, Boutros. (1922–) Egyptian politician and civil servant; secretary-general of the United Nations (1992–1996).

Bouygues Group. French construction company.

bouzouki. Greek stringed musical instrument.

Bowes Lyon. (No hyphen.) Family name of the late British Queen Mother.

boyfriend, girlfriend. (Each one word.)

boysenberry.

Brady, Mathew. (1823–1896) American Civil War photographer. Note irregular spelling of first name.

braggadocio. Hollow boasting, after the character Braggadochio in Spenser's *Fairie Queene.*

Brahman/Brahmin. The first is a member of a Hindu caste; the second is used to describe long-established socially exclusive people ("Boston Brahmins"). The breed of cattle is spelled *Brahman.*

Brahmaputra. Asian river.

Brahms, Johannes. (1833–1897) German composer.

Braille, Louis. (1809–1852) French inventor of the embossed reading system for the blind.

Bramante, Donato di Pasuccio d'Antonio. (1444–1514) Italian architect and artist.

Brancusi, Constantin. (1876–1957) Romanian sculptor.

Brandeis, Louis D(embitz). (1856–1941) American jurist; Brandeis University is named for him.

Brandywine. Creek in Pennsylvania and Delaware, site of a battle in the Revolutionary War.

Braque, Georges. (1882–1963) French Cubist painter.

Brasenose College, Oxford University.

Brasília. Capital of Brazil.

Braun, Wernher von. (1912–1977) German-born American space scientist.

bravado should not be confused with *bravery.* It is a swaggering or boastful display of boldness, often adopted to disguise an underlying timidity. It is, in short, a false bravery and there is nothing courageous about it.

BRD. Abbreviation of Bundesrepublik Deutschland.

breach, breech. Frequently confused. *Breach* describes an infraction or a gap. It should always suggest *break*, a word to which it is related. *Breech* applies to the rear or lower portion of things. The main expressions are *breach of faith* (or *promise*), *breech delivery*, *breeches buoy*, *breechcloth*, and *breech-loading gun*.

Breakspear, Nicolas. (c. 1100–1159) Pope Adrian IV.

Brest-Litovsk, Treaty of. (1918) Treaty that ended Russian involvement in World War I.

Bretagne. French for Brittany.

Bretton Woods. Mountain resort in New Hampshire, site of 1944 conference that led to the establishment of the International Monetary Fund and World Bank.

Breuer, Marcel. (1902–1981) Hungarian-born American architect and designer.

Breugel/Breughel. Use **Brueghel.**

Brezhnev, Leonid (Ilyich). (1906–1982) Leader of the Soviet Union (1977–1982).

bric-a-brac.

Bridge of San Luis Rey, The. Novel by Thornton Wilder (1927).

brie. (Not cap.) Cheese.

Brillat-Savarin, Anthelme. (1755–1826) French gastronome.

Bristol-Myers Squibb. U.S. pharmaceuticals company.

Britannia, Britannic, but **Brittany** for the region (formerly a province) of France. The song is "Rule, Britannia," with a comma.

British aristocracy, or peerage, comprises, in descending order, the ranks duke, marquess, earl/countess, viscount, and baron/baroness. Male peers below the rank of duke may be referred to as Lord (i.e., the Earl of Avon may be called Lord Avon), and all peeresses may be referred to as Lady. However, not every lord is a peer. The eldest son of a duke, marquess, or earl, for instance, may use one of his father's minor titles as a courtesy title and call himself the Marquess of X or Earl of Y, but he is not a peer and is not allowed to sit in the House of Lords. Younger sons of dukes and marquesses may put *Lord* in front of their names: Lord John X. Their wives are then called Lady John X. Daughters of dukes, marquesses, and earls will similarly put *Lady* before their names: Lady Mary Y. Wives of other kinds of peers, and of knights and baronets, are referred to as Lady X or Lady Y; that is, their first names are not used. Sir John Blogg's wife is simply Lady Blogg, not Lady Mary Blogg. Life peers are people of distinction who are elevated to the peerage but whose titles die with them.

British Guiana. Former name of the South American country now known as **Guyana.**

British Honduras. Former name of Belize.

British Indian Ocean Territory. Group of 2,300 scattered islands in the Indian Ocean run as a British colony; principal island Diego Garcia.

Britten, (Edward) Benjamin. (1913–1976) English composer; later Baron Britten of Aldeburgh.

Brobdingnag. Not *-dig-*. Place inhabited by giants in *Gulliver's Travels.*

broccoli.

Bronfman, Edgar M(iles). (1929–) Canadian businessman.

Brontë, Anne (1820–1849), **(Patrick) Branwell** (1817–1848), **Charlotte** (1816–1855), and **Emily (Jane)** (1818–1848): English literary family. Among their best-known works are Emily's *Wuthering Heights*, Charlotte's *Jane Eyre*, and Anne's *The Tenant of Wildfell Hall.*

brontosaurus. Not *bronta-*. Type of dinosaur.

Brooke, Rupert (Chawner). (1887–1915) English poet.

Brookings Institution (not *Institute*), Washington, D.C.; named after **Robert Somers Brookings** (1850–1932), American philanthropist.

Brooks, Van Wyck. (1886–1963) American critic and historian.

brouhaha. An uproar.

Brown v. Board of Education. 1954 landmark civil rights case in which the Supreme Court ruled that segregated schools were illegal. See also PLESSY V. FERGUSON.

brucellosis. Disease of cattle.

Brueghel, Pieter, the Elder. (c. 1520–1569) Not -*eu*-. Flemish painter and father of two others: **Pieter Brueghel the Younger** (1564–1638) and **Jan Brueghel** (1568–1625).

Bruges (Fr.)/**Brugge** (Flemish). Historic city in northern Belgium.

Brummell, (George Bryan) Beau. (1778–1840) Celebrated English dandy.

Brundtland, Gro Harlem. (1939–) Norwegian prime minister (1981, 1986–1989, 1990–1996).

Bruneau-Jarbidge. Site of historic supervolcano in Idaho.

Brunei. Independent oil-rich state on Borneo; capital Bandar Seri Begawan. A native is a Bruneian.

Brunel, Isambard Kingdom. (1806–1859) British engineer; son of **Sir Marc Isambard Brunel** (1769–1849), also an engineer.

Brunelleschi, Filippo. (c. 1377–1446) Renaissance architect and sculptor.

Brunhild. In Scandinavian sagas, she is a Valkyrie, or priestess, in a deep sleep. In Wagner's *Ring* cycle, the name is spelled *Brünnhilde*.

Brussels. Capital of Belgium. In French, Bruxelles; in Flemish, Brussel.

brussels sprouts. (No cap., no apos.)

Bryan, William Jennings. (1860–1925) American lawyer, orator, and politician.

Bryant, William Cullen. (1794–1878) American journalist, critic, and poet.

Brzezinski, Zbigniew K. (1928–) Polish-born American academic and statesman.

BSE. Bovine spongiform encephalopathy, more commonly known as mad cow disease.

BST. Bovine somatotropin, a genetically engineered hormone used to increase milk production in cows.

BTU. British thermal unit, the amount of heat required to raise the temperature of one pound of water by one degree Fahrenheit.

Buccleuch. Ancient British dukedom; pronounced *buck-loo'*.

Bucharest. Capital of Romania; in Romanian, Bucureşti.

Buddenbrooks. Novel by Thomas Mann (1901).

Buddha, Buddhist, Buddhism.

Buddleia. Genus of shrub.

buenos días (for "good day" or "hello" in Spanish), but *buenas* (not -*os*) *noches* ("good night") and *buenas tardes* ("good afternoon").

buffalo. The plural can be either *buffalo* or *buffaloes*.

Bugatti. Sports car.

Bujumbura. Capital of Burundi.

Bulfinch, Charles. (1763–1844) American architect.

Bulfinch's Mythology. Subtitle of *The Age of Fable* by Thomas Bulfinch (1796–1867).

bull's-eye, in the sense of a target.

Bulwer-Lytton, Edward. (1803–1873) Also Baron Lytton, English writer and politician, celebrated for penning the classically bad opening line "It was a dark and stormy night" in his novel *Paul Clifford* (1830). The annual Bulwer-Lytton Fiction Contest, for a mock bad opening line, is named in his honor.

bumf. Assorted papers.

Bumppo, Natty. Note -*pp*-. Hero of James Fenimore Cooper stories.

Bunche, Ralph (Johnson). (1904–1971) American statesman; one of the founders of the United Nations. Awarded Nobel Peace Prize (1950).

Bundesbank. Central bank of Germany.

Bundesrat, Bundestag. The *Bundesrat* (Federal Council) is the upper house of the German parliament; the *Bundestag* (Federal Assembly) is the lower house.

Bundesrepublik Deutschland. (Abbr. BRD.) Federal Republic of Germany.

Bundeswehr. German armed forces.

Bunsen burner. (One cap.)

Buoniconti, Nick. (1940–) American football player.

buoy is pronounced *boy*, not *boo-ee*. Think of **buoyant**.

burgeon does not mean merely to expand or thrive. It means to bud or sprout, to come into being. For something to burgeon, it must be new. Thus, it would be correct to talk about the burgeoning talent of a precocious youth, but to write of "the ever-burgeoning population of Cairo" is wrong. Cairo's population has been growing for centuries, and nothing, in any case, is ever-burgeoning.

bürgermeister. (Ger.) Mayor.

Burgess, (Frank) Gelett. (1866–1951) American humorist.

Burgundy. Region of eastern France. In French, Bourgogne. The wine is **burgundy** (lowercase).

Burke and Hare. Body snatchers and murderers in Edinburgh in the early nineteenth century; they were both named William.

Burkina-Faso. Landlocked west African state, formerly Upper Volta; capital Ouagadougou. Natives are Burkinabe (sing. and pl.).

Burma, Myanmar. The first is the former official name of the Southest Asian nation and the one now preferred by most publications and other informed users outside Burma. *Myanmar* was for a time used by many publications, but now its use is mostly confined to the country's government and institutions under its influence. Some authorities write *Burma/Myanmar*. The United Nations uses just *Myanmar*.

Burne-Jones, Sir Edward Coley. (1833–1898) British painter and designer.

burnoose (or **burnous**). A hooded Arab cloak.

Burnt-Out Case, A. Novel by Graham Greene (1960).

burnt sienna. Not *siena*.

burqa. Type of enveloping dress worn by Muslim women when in public to preserve their modesty. Also spelled **burkha, burka, burqua.**

Burtts Corner, New Brunswick, Canada.

Burundi. African republic; capital Bujumbura.

Buryatiya. Russian republic.

Bury St. Edmunds, Suffolk, England. (No apos.) *Bury* is pronounced *berry*.

bus, buses, bused, busing are words relating to a form of transportation and should not be confused with *buss, busses,* etc., meaning kiss(es).

but used negatively after a pronoun presents a problem that has confounded careful users for generations. Do you say, "Everyone but him had arrived" or "Everyone but he had arrived"? The authorities themselves are divided.

Some regard *but* as a preposition and put the pronoun in the accusative—i.e., *me, her, him,* or *them.* So just as we say, "Give it to her" or "between you and me," we should say, "Everyone but him had arrived."

Others argue that *but* is a conjunction and that the pronoun should be nominative (*I, she, he,* or *they*), as if the sentence was saying, "Everyone had arrived, but he had not."

The answer perhaps is to regard *but* sometimes as a conjunction and sometimes as a preposition. Two rough rules should help.

1. If the pronoun appears at the end of the sentence, you can always use the accusative and be on firm ground. Thus, "Nobody knew but her"; "Everyone had eaten but him."

2. When the pronoun appears earlier in the sentence, it is almost always better to put it in the nominative, as in "No one but he had seen it." The one exception is when the pronoun is influ-

enced by a preceding preposition, but such constructions are relatively rare and often clumsy. Two examples might be "Between no one but them was there any bitterness" and "To everyone but him life was a mystery." See also THAN (3).

Buthelezi, Mangosuthu. (1928–) South African politician, founder of Inkatha Freedom Party.

BWIA. British West India Airways; not *Indian* or *Indies*.

byte. In computing, a unit of eight bits.

Cc

ca. (Lat.) is the abbreviation for *circa*, meaning about or approximately; often **c.** In either case, it is customary to put a period after it.

cacao. The tree from whose seed cocoa and chocolate are made.

caddie, caddy. A *caddie* is a golfer's assistant; a *caddy* is a container or small casket. The affectionate term for a Cadillac is *Caddy.*

Cadmean victory. One that leaves the victor ruined. See also PYRRHIC VICTORY.

caduceus. Staff with two winged serpents wrapped around it.

Caedmon. (fl. seventh c.) English poet.

Caerphilly cheese. (In Welsh, Caerffili.)

caesarean, not *-ian*, remains the preferred spelling for the form of childbirth properly known as a **Caesarean section,** as well as for references to Roman emperors named Caesar.

caesar salad. (Not cap.)

Cage, Nicolas. (1964–) American actor; not *Nicholas,* though his birth name was Nicholas Coppola.

cagey (pref.), **cagy** (alt.).

Caius, the Cambridge college, is formally **Gonville and Caius College.** Caius is pronounced *keys.*

Cajun. (Cap.) Native of traditionally French-speaking region of Louisiana; derived from *Acadian.*

calamine lotion.

Calaveras County, California, is the scene of the Mark Twain story "The Celebrated Jumping Frog of Calaveras County."

Calcutta, the Indian city, is now officially **Kolkata;** until the new name is fully established, the use of both on first reference is advisable.

Calderón, Felipe. (1962–) President of Mexico (2006–).

Calderón de la Barca (y Henao), Pedro. (1600–1681) Spanish playwright.

calico, pl. *calicoes.*

caliper.

Callicrates. (fl. fifth c. BC) Greek architect, co-designer (with Ictinus) of the Parthenon.

calligraphy is an art. The science of studying written text is graphology.

Callimachus. (fl. third c. BC) Greek scholar.

calliope. Fairground steam-organ, named after Calliope, the Greek muse of epic poetry.

callous, callus. The first means insensitive, the second is a thickening of the skin.

Calmann-Lévy. French publisher.

Caltech (one word) is the common name for the California Institute of Technology in Pasadena.

Calypso. Nymph who delayed Odysseus for seven years on his way home from Troy.

camaraderie.

Cambodia has been variously known in recent decades as the Khmer Republic, Democratic Kampuchea, and the People's Republic of Kampuchea, but in 1989 it resumed its historical name of Cambodia.

Cambridgeshire. English county.

Camden Yards. Baseball stadium, home of Baltimore Orioles; formally it is **Oriole Park at Camden Yards.**

camellia for the flower. Not *camelia.*

Camembert. (Cap.) Soft French cheese and the village in Normandy for which it is named.

Cameroon/Cameroun. The first is the English spelling; the second is the French (and local) spelling for the West African republic formerly called the Cameroons. Its capital is Yaoundé.

Camisards. French Calvinists disaffected by the revocation of the Edict of Nantes (1703).

camisole.

Camorra. Mafia-type secret society of Naples.

Campagna di Roma. Countryside around Rome.

campanile. Bell tower.

can, may. *Can* applies to what is possible and *may* to what is permissible. You can drive your car the wrong way down a one-way street, but you may not. Despite the simplicity of the rule, errors are common, even among experts. Here is William Safire writing in the *New York Times* on the pronunciation of *junta*: "The worst mistake is to mix languages. You cannot say 'joonta' and you cannot say 'hunta.' " But you can, and quite easily. What Mr. Safire meant was that you may not or should not or ought not.

Canada is a dominion, comprising ten provinces (Alberta, British Columbia, Manitoba, New Brunswick, Newfoundland and Labrador, Nova Scotia, Ontario, Prince Edward Island, Quebec, and Saskatchewan) and three territories (Yukon, Northwest, and Nunavut); capital Ottawa.

Canaletto. (1697–1768) Venetian artist, real name Giovanni Antonio Canal.

Canandaigua Lake, New York.

canard. A ridiculous story or rumor. "Gross canard" is a cliché. The French satirical magazine is *Le Canard Enchaîné*.

Canary Islands. Island group off northwest Africa; they are not a colony but are part of Spain; in Spanish, *Islas Canarias*.

Cancún. Mexican resort.

candelabrum (or **candelabra**), pl. *candelabra* (or *candelabras*). Note not *candle-*.

Candlemas. The Feast of the Purification of the Virgin Mary; February 2.

Canetti, Elias. (1905–1994) Bulgarian-born British writer; awarded Nobel Prize for Literature in 1981.

canine.

canister.

cannabis.

Cannae. Site of battle in southern Italy where Hannibal routed the Romans.

canneloni.

Cannizzaro, Stanisloa. (1826–1910) Italian chemist.

cannon, canon. A *cannon* is a gun. *Canon* is an ecclesiastical title; a canon is a body of religious writings or the works of a particular author.

cannonball. (One word.)

cannot help but is an increasingly common construction, and perhaps now may be said to carry the weight of idiom, but it is also worth noting that it is both unnecessarily wordy and a little irregular. "You cannot help but notice what a bad name deregulation has with voters" would be better (or at least more conventionally) phrased as either "You cannot help notice . . ." or "You cannot but notice . . ."

canoodle.

canopy.

Canova, Antonio. (1757–1822) Italian sculptor.

cant, jargon. Both apply to words or expressions used by particular groups. *Cant* has derogatory overtones and applies to the private vocabulary and colloquialisms of professions, social groups, and sects. *Jargon* is a slightly more impartial word and usually suggests terms used in a particular profession.

cantaloupe.

Canton, China, is now normally referred to by its Pinyin name,

Guangzhou. It is the capital of Guangdong Province, formerly Kwantung. **Cantonese** is still used to describe the food of the region, however.

Canute. (c. 995–1035) King of England, Norway, and Denmark; sometimes spelled *Cnut.*

canvas, canvass. The first is the fabric; the second is a verb meaning to solicit, especially for votes.

Cape Canaveral, Florida; called Cape Kennedy from 1963 to 1973.

Čapek, Karel. (1890–1938) Czech author.

Cape Town (two words), South Africa.

Cape Verde. Atlantic island nation off African coast; capital Cidade de Praia.

capital, capitol. *Capitol* always applies to a building, usually the place where legislatures gather in the United States. It is always capitalized when referring to the domed building in Washington, D.C., housing the U.S. Congress. The rise on which the U.S. Capitol stands is Capitol Hill. In all other senses, *capital* is the invariable spelling.

Capitol Reef National Park, Utah; not *-al.*

Capodichino International Airport, Naples, Italy.

cappuccino, pl. *cappuccinos.*

carabinieri, not *cari-,* for the Italian security force roughly equivalent to the French gendarmerie. Like gendarmes, carabinieri are soldiers employed in police duties. They are separate from, and not to be confused with, the state police (*polizia statale* in Italian), who also deal with criminal matters. *Carabinieri* is a plural; a single member of the force is a carabiniere. See also GENDARMES.

Caracalla, Marcus Aurelius Antoninus. (186–217) Roman emperor.

Caracci, Lodovico (1555–1619), **Agostino** (1557–1602), and **Annibale** (1560–1609), family of Italian painters.

carafe. A container, especially for wine or water.

Caraqueño. A person from Caracas, Venezuela.

carat, caret, karat. A *carat* is the unit of measurement used by jewelers; a *caret* is an insertion mark (∧) associated with proofreading; a *karat* is a measure of the purity of gold.

Caravaggio, Michelangelo Merisi/Amerighi da. (c. 1569–1609) Italian painter.

caraway seeds.

carbon dioxide, carbon monoxide. *Carbon dioxide* is the gas people exhale; *carbon monoxide* is the highly poisonous gas associated with car exhausts.

carburetor.

carcass.

Carcassonne. Walled city in southern France.

cardamom. A spice.

cardinal numbers, ordinal numbers. *Cardinal numbers* are those that denote size but not rank: one, two, three, etc. *Ordinal numbers* are those that denote position: first, second, third, etc.

CARE. International charity, short for Cooperative for American Relief Everywhere. Originally the *R* stood for Remittances and the *E* for Europe.

careen, career. Occasionally confused when describing runaway vehicles and the like. *Careen* should convey the idea of swaying or tilting dangerously. If all you mean is uncontrolled movement, use *career*.

caret, not *carat*, for the insertion mark (∧) associated with proofreading. See also CARAT, CARET, KARAT.

cargoes.

Caribbean.

Cariboo Mountains, Canada; part of the Rockies.

caricature.

CARICOM. Short for **Caribbean Community,** regional trade organization.

carillon.

Carioca. (Cap.) Colloquial name for a person or persons from Rio de Janeiro, Brazil.

Carisbrooke Castle, Isle of Wight, England.

Carl XVI Gustaf. (1946–) King of Sweden (1973–).

Carlyle Group. Investment company.

Carlyle Hotel, New York City.

Carlyle, Thomas. (1795–1881) Scottish historian.

Carmichael, Hoagy. (1899–1981) American songwriter; full name **Hoagland Howard Carmichael.**

Carnap, Rudolf. (1891–1970) German-born American philosopher.

Carnarvon, Lord. (Formally George Edward Stanhope Molyneux Herbert, Earl of Carnarvon) (1866–1923) English archaeologist, co-discoverer with Howard Carter of the famous tomb of Tutankhamun in Egypt.

Carnegie Institute, Pittsburgh, but **Carnegie Institution,** Washington, D.C.

Carnoustie, Scotland, site of famous golf course.

carom.

Carothers, Wallace (Hume). (1896–1937) American scientist and inventor of nylon.

carotid arteries.

carpaccio. Thinly sliced beef, named for **Vittore Carpaccio** (c. 1460–c. 1526), Italian painter.

carpal tunnel syndrome.

carpe diem. (Lat.) "Seize the day," make the most of the present.

Carpentaria, Gulf of, Australia.

Carrantuohill. Highest mountain in Ireland (31,414 feet), in Macgillicuddy's Reeks, County Kerry.

Carrara. Town in Tuscany, Italy, and the fine white marble quarried nearby.

Carrasquel, Chico. (1928–2005) Venezuelan baseball star, played mostly for Chicago White Sox.

Carrefour. French supermarket group.

Carroll, Diahann. (1935–) American singer and actress.

Carroll, Lewis. Pen name of Charles Lutwidge Dodgson (1832–1898).

cartel describes not just any alliance of businesses but one designed to maximize prices; unless a negative connotation is desired, avoid the word.

Carter Barron Amphitheatre, Washington, D.C. Note that *Amphitheatre* is spelled *-re*.

Carthusian.

Cartier-Bresson, Henri. (1908–2004) French photographer.

cartilage.

Carton, Sydney. Principal character in Dickens's *A Tale of Two Cities.*

Caruso, Enrico. (1874–1921) Italian tenor.

Cary, Joyce. (1888–1957) British author; full name Arthur Joyce Lunel Cary.

caryatid. In architecture, a female form used as a supporting pillar.

Casablanca, Morocco.

Casals, Pablo. (1876–1973) Spanish cellist.

Casanova (de Seingalt), Giovanni Jacopo/Giacomo. (1725–1798) Italian adventurer.

cashmere.

Cassamassima, The Princess. Novel by Henry James (1886).

Cassandra. In Greek mythology, she was given the power of prophecy by Apollo but doomed never to be believed. The name is now used as a synonym for any prophet of doom.

Cassatt, Mary. (1845–1926) American impressionist painter.

cassava. Root crop widely grown in Africa and parts of Asia and South America; also known as manioc, yuca, or tapioca.

Cassavetes, John. (1930–1989) American actor and director.

cassette.

Cassiopeia. A constellation in the northern hemisphere named for the mother of Andromeda in Greek mythology.

cassowary. Flightless bird.

castenets. Spanish rhythm instruments.

caster, castor. The first is the spelling for a wheel on a chair; the second is the spelling of the oil or bean.

Castile. Area of northern Spain; in Spanish, Castilla. The name appears in two Spanish regions: Castilla–La Mancha and Castilla-León.

Castlereagh, Robert Stewart, Viscount. (1769–1822) British statesman.

castrato. Castrated soprano; pl. *castrati.*

casus belli. (Lat.) Act that gives rise to war.

catalyst is not just any agent of change, but one that hastens change without becoming changed itself.

catamaran.

catarrh.

cater-corner. Not *catty-corner.*

Catharine's College, St., Cambridge University, England, but **St. Catherine's College,** Oxford.

CAT scan. Short for computerized axial tomography.

Catullus, Gaius Valerius. (c. 84–c. 55 BC) Roman poet.

Caudillo. (Sp.) "Leader"; title assumed by General Francisco Franco of Spain.

cauliflower.

cause célèbre.

caveat emptor. (Lat.) "Let the buyer beware."

caviar.

Cawley, Evonne Goolagong. (1951–) Australian tennis star.

Cayenne. Capital of French Guiana.

CBC. Canadian Broadcasting Corporation.

CBS. Columbia Broadcasting System.

CCCP. Abbreviation in the Cyrillic alphabet of Soyuz Sovyetskikh Sotsialisticheskikh Respublik (Union of Soviet Socialist Republics), former USSR.

Ceaușescu, Nicolae. (1918–1989) President of Romania (1967–89); pronounced *chow'-chess-coo.*

cedilla. Mark [,] placed under a *c* to indicate that it is pronounced in French as an *s*, in Turkish as *ch*, and in Portuguese as *sh*.

ceilidh. (Gaelic) A gathering for music and dancing; pronounced *kay'-lee.*

Cela, Camilo José. (1916–2002) Spanish novelist, awarded Nobel Prize for Literature (1989).

celebrant, celebrator. The first is the term for persons taking part in religious ceremonies. Those who gather for purposes of revelry are celebrators.

celibacy does not, as is generally supposed, indicate abstinence from sexual relations. It means only to be unmarried, particularly if as a result of a religious vow. A married person cannot be celibate, but he may be chaste.

Cellini, Benvenuto. (1500–1571) Italian sculptor, goldsmith, and author.

Celsius, centigrade. (Abbr. C.) Interchangeable terms referring to the scale of temperature invented by **Anders Celsius** (1701–1744), a Swedish astronomer. To convert Celsius to Fahrenheit, multiply the Celsius temperature by 1.8 and add 32, or use the table in the Appendix.

cement, concrete. The two are not interchangeable. *Cement* is a constituent of *concrete,* which also contains sand, gravel, and crushed rock.

cemetery. Not *-ary.*

Cenozoic era. The present geological era, beginning about 65 million years ago. In earlier periods it was sometimes also spelled **Caenozoic** or **Cainozoic**.

centavo. A monetary unit in many countries of South and Central America equivalent to one one-hundredth of the country's main unit of currency; pl. *centavos.*

center around. *Center* indicates a point, and a point cannot encircle anything. Make it "center on" or "revolve around."

Centers for Disease Control and Prevention, Atlanta. Federal institution that deals with matters of public health. Note the plural *Centers.* It is part of the U.S. Department of Health and Human Services.

centrifugal/centripetal force. *Centrifugal force* pulls away from; *centripetal force* draws toward.

Cephalonia. Greek island in the Ionian chain; in Greek, Kephallinia.

Cerberus. In Greek mythology, a three-headed dog that stood guard over the gates to the underworld.

Ceres. Roman goddess of grain, identified with the Greek goddess Demeter.

CERN. Originally Conseil Européen pour la Recherche Nucléaire, now the Organisation Européenne pour la Recherche Nucléaire, the European Organization for Nuclear Research, based in Geneva, Switzerland.

Cervantes, (Saavedra) Miguel de. (1547–1616) Spanish author.

c'est la guerre. (Fr.) "That's the way of war."

Cévennes. Mountains in southern France.

Ceylon. Former name of Sri Lanka.

Cézanne, Paul. (1839–1906) French impressionist painter.

cf. Confer. (Lat.) "Compare"; used in cross-references.

Chablais. Region of Haute-Savoie, France.

Chablis. French village and white burgundy wine (also cap.).

chacun à son goût. (Fr.) "Each to his own taste."

chacun pour soi. (Fr.) "Everyone for himself."

chador. Large piece of cloth worn by some Muslim women, which is wrapped around the body to leave only the face exposed; pl. *chadors.*

chaebol. Korean business conglomerate; pl. same.

chafe, chaff. To *chafe* means to make sore or worn by rubbing (or, figuratively, to annoy or irritate). To *chaff* means to tease good-naturedly.

chaffinch. Type of bird.

Chagall, Marc. (1889–1985) Russian-born French artist.

chagrined.

chaise-longue, pl. *chaises-longues.*

Chakvetadze, Anna. (1987–) Russian tennis player.

Chaliapin, Feodor (Ivanovich). (1873–1938) Russian opera singer.

challah (or **chalah** or **hallah**). Type of Jewish bread.

Chalon-sur-Saône, Châlons-en-Champagne, Chalonnes-sur-Loire, France.

Chamberlain, Sir (Joseph) Austen. (1863–1937) British politician, awarded Nobel Peace Prize (1925); son of **Joseph Chamberlain** (1836–1914), also a politician; half brother of **(Arthur) Neville Chamberlain** (1869–1940), British prime minister (1937–1940).

Chamberlain, Wilt. (1936–1999) American basketball player.

Chambers's Encyclopaedia.

chameleon.

chamois. The plural is also *chamois,* for both the antelope and the cloth for wiping cars.

Champagne. Region of France, formally Champagne-Ardenne; the wine is **champagne** (no cap.).

champaign. An open plain.

Champaign, Illinois.

Champaigne, Philippe de. (1602–1674) French painter.

Champigny-sur-Marne. Suburb of Paris.

Champlain, Samuel de. (1567–1635) Founder of Quebec.

Champollion, Jean François. (1790–1832) French Egyptologist who helped decipher the hieroglyphics on the Rosetta Stone.

Champs-Élysées, Paris.

Chancellor of the Duchy of Lancaster. Post in the British Cabinet that has no formal duties, enabling the holder to take up special assignments for the prime minister.

Chancellorsville, battle of. Note *-orsv-*. Battle in the Civil War.

Chandigarh. Indian city laid out by Le Corbusier.

Chang Jiang (Pinyin)/**Yangtze River.** If you use the Pinyin spelling (as many users now do) you should make at least passing reference to the Yangtze, as that name is much more widely known in the English-speaking world.

Chanukah. Use **Hanukkah.**

chaparral. Scrubby thicket of the American West.

chapati/chapatti. Type of unleavened bread from India.

chaperon.

Chappaquiddick. Island off Martha's Vineyard, Massachusetts, made internationally famous in 1969 when Senator Edward Kennedy drove a car off a bridge following a party and his passenger, Mary Jo Kopechne, died.

chargé d'affaires, pl. *chargés d'affaires.*

Charlemagne. Charles I (742–814), first Holy Roman Emperor (800–814).

Charlotte Amalie. Capital of U.S. Virgin Islands.

Charlotte Douglas International Airport, North Carolina.

Charlottenburg. Suburb of Berlin.

Charollais cattle.

chary. Doubtful, cautious; but **chariness.**

Charybdis. In Greek mythology, a whirlpool off the coast of Sicily. It is often paired metaphorically with Scylla, a six-headed monster who lived nearby. In this sense Charybdis and Scylla signify any highly unattractive—and unavoidable—dilemma.

chastise. Not *-ize.*

Chateaubriand, Francois-René, Vicomte de. (1768–1848) French statesman and writer. The steak dish named for him is usually not capitalized.

Châteaubriant, France.

Château-Lafite, Château-Margaux. French red wines.

Chatham House Rule, Not *Rules.* A rule of confidentiality formulated in 1927 at the Royal Institute of International Affairs, or Chatham House, London. Under it information gathered at a meeting may be used, but the source may not be disclosed.

Chattahoochee River, Georgia and Alabama.

Chattanooga, Tennessee.

Chatto & Windus Ltd. British publisher.

chauffeur.

Chávez, Hugo. (1954–) President of Venezuela (1999–); full name Hugo Rafael Chávez Frías.

Chayefsky, Paddy. (1923–1981) American playwright and screenwriter.

cheap, cheep. The first means inexpensive; the second refers to the sound birds make.

cheddar cheese, but Cheddar (cap.) for the place in England whence it originated.

Cheeryble brothers. Characters in Charles Dickens's *Nicholas Nickleby.*

Chelyabinsk, Siberia, Russia.

Chemnitz, Germany; formerly Karl-Marx-Stadt.

Chennai is the new official name for Madras, India, but until it is fully established both names should probably be used on first reference.

Chennault, Claire. (1890–1958) American general, organized Flying Tigers air corps in World War II.

Chequers. Official country home of the British prime minister, near Princes Risborough, Buckinghamshire.

Chernenko, Konstantin. (1911–1985) President of the Soviet Union (1984–1985).

Chernobyl. Ukrainian site of world's worst known nuclear accident (1986).

Cherokee. North American Indian people.

Chery. Chinese car manufacturer; not *Cherry.*

Chesapeake Bay, Maryland and Virginia.

Chesebrough-Pond's. U.S. cosmetics and household products company.

Cheviot Hills, England and Scotland.

ChevronTexaco. (One word.) Oil company.

Chevy. Diminutive form of *Chevrolet.*

Chevy Chase, Maryland.

Cheyenne. North American Indian people, river, and capital of Wyoming.

Chhatrapati Shivaji International Airport, Mumbai, India; note *Chh-.*

Chiang Kai-shek. (1887–1975) Leader of Nationalist Republic of China (1928–1949) and first president of Taiwan (1950–1975).

chiaroscuro. Interplay of light and shade.

Chicano, pl. *Chicanos.*

Chichén Itzá. Mexican ruins.

Chickamauga, Georgia; not *-magua.* Site of Civil War battle (1863).

chickenpox. (One word.)

chicory. Herb.

Chihuahua. City and state in Mexico and breed of dog.

chilblain. Not *chill-.*

Childe Harold's Pilgrimage. Not *Child.* Poem by Lord Byron.

children's is the only possible spelling of the possessive form of *children.*

chili, pl. *chilies.*

chimera. A wild or fanciful creation, taken from *Chimera* (sometimes *Chimaera*), a mythological beast with the head of a lion, body of a goat, and tail of a serpent.

China, Republic of. Official name of Taiwan, used almost nowhere except in Taiwan itself. The mainland country is the **People's Republic of China.**

chinchilla.

Chincoteague for bay, island, and town in Virginia or Maryland.

Chinese names. The system now used almost everywhere for transliterating Chinese names into English is Pinyin (which means transcription). This has occasioned many striking changes in the rendering of Chinese names: *Mao Tse-tung* is now *Mao Zedong; Peking* is now *Beijing.* In some cases, particularly where long-established names are concerned, older forms continue to be used—*Confucius, Hong Kong, Shanghai*—but even many of these are slowly changing. If uncertain, or where confusion is likely, it is a courtesy to give both names: "Chang Jiang River, formerly known as the Yangtze."

Chingachgook. Character in James Fenimore Cooper's novel *The Deerslayer* (1841).

chinook. Warm, dry wind that blows off the Rocky Mountains.

chipmunk. Not *-monk.*

Chippendale, Thomas. (c. 1718–1779) English furniture designer and manufacturer.

Chișinău. Capital of Moldova.

chitterlings is the formal name of the dish made from pig's intestines, but it is often more informally spelled **chitlins.**

chivvy. To hurry or harass.

chlorophyll.

chockfull (or **chock-full**). But the brand of coffee and restaurants is **Chock full o'Nuts.**

chocolate.

Choctaw. Native American group.

cholesterol.

Chomsky, Noam. (1928–) American linguist.

Chongqing. City in Sichuan Province, China; formerly referred to as **Chungking.**

Chopin, Frédéric François. (1810–1849) Polish composer.

chord, cord. A *chord* is a group of musical notes or a type of arc in geometry; a *cord* is a length of rope or similar material of twisted strands, or a stack of wood. You speak with your vocal cords.

Chou En-lai. (1898–1976) Prime minister of China (1949–1976). The name is now usually spelled **Zhou Enlai.**

Christ Church, Christchurch. *Christ Church* is the spelling and full name of the Oxford college (i.e., not *Christ Church College*). The communities in New Zealand and England are *Christchurch.*

Christiania. Former name of Oslo.

Christie's. London auction house; formally Christie, Manson & Woods, but the parent company styles itself **Christies International** (no apos.).

Christ's College, Cambridge University.

Christy Minstrels.

chromosome.

chronic, acute. *Chronic* means constant or long-standing; *acute* (when applied to an illness or a situation) means approaching a crisis.

chrysalis. The formal plural, and the one to use in scientific contexts, is *chrysalides,* but *chrysalises* is acceptable for more general writing.

chrysanthemum.

chukker. Period of play in polo.

Church of Christ, Scientist (with comma) is the formal name of the Christian Science church.

Church of Jesus Christ of Latter-day Saints. Formal title of the Mormon Church.

Churchs Ferry (no. apos.), North Dakota.

chutzpah. (Yid.) Shameless impudence, brashness.

Chuvashiya. Russian republic.

ciao. (It.) Salutation meaning either hello or goodbye.

Ciba-Geigy. Swiss pharmaceuticals company.

Cicero, Marcus Tullius. (106–43 BC) Roman orator and statesman.

Ciechanover, Aaron. (1947–) Israeli scientist, awarded Nobel Prize for Chemistry (2004).

Cimoszewicz, Wlodzimierz. (1950–) Prime minister of Poland (1996–1997).

Cincinnati, Ohio.

Cincinnatus, Lucius Quintus. (c. 519–c. 439 BC) Roman general.

Cinderella.

CinemaScope. Wide-screen film system.

cinéma vérité.

cineraria. Type of flower; pl. *cinerarias.*

cinnamon.

cinquecento. (It.) Literally "the five hundreds"; Italian name for the sixteenth century.

Cinque Ports, England; pronounced *sink.*

cipher. Not *cypher.*

circadian. Taking place in twenty-four-hour cycles.

Circe. In Greek mythology, an enchantress on the island of Aeaea who detained Odysseus and his men, turning the latter into swine and bearing a son by the former.

circumstances, in the and **under the.** A useful distinction can be drawn between the two. *In the circumstances* should indicate merely that a situation exists: "In the circumstances, I began to feel worried." *Under the circumstances* should denote a situation in which action is necessitated or inhibited: "Under the circumstances, I had no choice but to leave."

cirrhosis.

Citigroup Inc., the financial services corporation, has a habit of dazzling inconsistency with regard to capitalization and spacing when naming subsidiaries. Among its offshoots are **Citibank, Citi Cards, CitiFinancial, CitiMortgage,** and **Citi Private Bank.** Take care.

Citizens Bank Park. Philadelphia baseball stadium, home of the Phillies.

Citlatépetl. Dormant Mexican volcano.

C. Itoh. Japanese trading company.

Citroën. French automobile.

city names. Where cities have the same name as surrounding territory, it is normal to capitalize *City* even when it is not formally part of the place name. Thus, *New York City, Mexico City, Luxembourg City, Quebec City.*

Ciudad Trujillo. Former name of Santo Domingo, capital of the Dominican Republic.

Civitavecchia. Italian coastal city, north of Rome in Latium.

Clare, County, Ireland.

Claridge's Hotel, London, but **Hôtel Claridge,** Paris.

clarinetist.

Clarke, Arthur C(harles). (1917–) English science-fiction writer.

Clemenceau, Georges (Eugène Benjamin). (1841–1929) Prime minister of France (1906–1909, 1917–1920).

Clemens, Samuel Langhorne. (1835–1910) American author better known by his pen name, Mark Twain.

clerestory. A windowed wall, usually in a church.

clerihew. Four-line nonsense poem devised by **Edmund Clerihew Bentley** (1875–1956).

climactic, climatic, climacteric. *Climactic* means appearing at a climax ("the climactic scene in a movie"); *climatic* means having to do with climate and weather ("the climatic conditions of the Brazilian rainforest"); *climacteric* is a noun signifying a time of important change and is most commonly applied to menopause.

cloisonné. A type of enamel work.

close proximity is inescapably tautological. Make it "near" or "close to." See also SCRUTINY, SCRUTINIZE.

Clouseau, Inspector. Fictional character mostly portrayed by Peter Sellers in *Pink Panther* films.

Clwyd. County of northern Wales; pronounced *kloo'-wid.*

Clytemnestra. In Greek mythology, the wife of Agamemnon.

cnidarians. Members of the phylum of marine invertebrates that includes jellyfish, corals, and sea anemones. Also called *coelenterates.*

Cnossos/Cnossus. Alternative spellings for ancient capital of Crete; usually spelled **Knossos** in American usage.

Coahuila. State in northeastern Mexico.

Cobb, Irvin S(hrewsbury). (1876–1944) American journalist and humorist.

Cobh, County Cork, Ireland; pronounced *cove.*

COBOL. Common Business Oriented Language, an early computer programming language.

Coca-Cola. (Hyphen.) The diminutive term *Coke* should always be capitalized.

coccyx. Tailbone; pl. *coccyxes.*

cock-a-leekie soup.

cockney. (No cap.) A native of London's East End; pl. *cockneys.*

coconut. But the Marx Brothers Broadway show and movie is *The Cocoanuts.*

cocoon.

coelacanth for the ocean fish famed in scientific circles for its archaic qualities. Pronounced *see-luh-kanth.*

coequal is a pointless word; *co-* adds nothing to *equal* that *equal* doesn't already say alone.

Coetzee, J. M. (for John Maxwell) (1940–) South African–born Australian author, awarded Nobel Prize for Literature in 2003.

Coeur d'Alene, Idaho.

Coeur de Lion, Richard. (1157–1199) Richard the Lionheart, Richard I of England.

cogito, ergo sum. (Lat.) "I think, therefore I am." Descartes's aphorism.

cognoscente. A person who is well informed or of elevated taste; pl. *cognoscenti.*

Cohan, George M. (for Michael) (1878–1942) American songwriter and performer, playwright, and producer.

Cohen-Tannoudji, Claude. (1933–) French physicist, born in Algeria; awarded Nobel Prize for Physics (1997).

Cointreau. Liqueur.

Coleman, Ornette. (1930–) American jazz saxophonist.

coleus.

Colgate-Palmolive. (Hyphen.) Personal products company.

colic, but **colicky.**

coliseum, Colosseum. The first applies to any large amphitheater; the second is a particular amphitheater in Rome.

collapsible. Not *-able.*

collectible is the normal U.S. spelling, but *collectable* is an accepted alternative.

collectives. Deciding whether to treat nouns of multitude—words like *majority, flock, variety, group, crowd,* and so on—as singulars or plurals is entirely a matter of the sense you intend to convey. Although some authorities have tried to fix rules, such undertakings are almost always futile. On the whole, Americans lean to the singular and Britons to the plural, often in ways that would strike the other as absurd (compare the American "The couple was married in March" with the British "England are to play Hungary in their next match"). A common fault is to flounder about between singular and plural. Even Samuel Johnson stumbled when he wrote that he knew of no nation "that *has* preserved *their* words and phrases from mutability." Clearly the italicized words should be either singular both times or plural both times. See also NUMBER and TOTAL.

collisions can occur only when two or more moving objects come together. If a car runs into a stationary object, it is not a collision.

Colman, Ronald. (1891–1958) English actor.

Colombey-les-Deux-Églises. Town east of Paris where Charles de Gaulle is buried.

Colombia. South American country; capital Bogotá.

Colombo. Capital of Sri Lanka.

Colón, Cristóbal. Spanish spelling of Christopher Columbus. In his native Italy, his name was Cristoforo Colombo.

colonnade.

colossal.

Colosseum, Rome.

Colossus of Rhodes.

colostomy.

Colquhoun. Scottish name; pronounced *ko-hoon'*.

Columba, St. (521–597) Irish saint associated with the Scottish island of Iona.

Columbus Day. Second Monday in October.

combatant, combated, combating.

combustible. Capable of being burned.

Comédie-Française. National theater of France; formally, the Théâtre Français.

Comedy of Errors, The, not *A*, for the play by William Shakespeare.

Comerica Park. Detroit baseball stadium, home of the Tigers.

comestible. Foodstuff.

comic, comical. Something that is *comic* is intended to be funny ("a comic performance"). Something that is *comical* is funny whether or not that was the intention ("a comical misunderstanding").

Comiskey Park. Former Chicago baseball stadium, home of the White Sox; the team's stadium is now called U.S. Cellular Field.

commedia dell'arte. Type of farcical Italian comedy.

commence. An unnecessary genteelism. What's wrong with "begin"?

commingle. To mix together. Note *-mm-*.

commiserate.

committal.

Commodus, Lucius Aelius Aurelius. (AD 161–192) Roman emperor (AD 180–192).

Comoros. Island state off Madagascar; capital Moroni.

compact disc. Not *disk*.

comparatively. "Comparatively little progress was made in the talks yesterday" (*Guardian*). Compared with what? *Comparatively* should be reserved for occasions when a comparison is being expressed or at least clearly implied. If all you mean is *fairly* or *only a little*, choose another word. See also RELATIVELY.

compare to, compare with. These two can be usefully distinguished. *Compare to* should be used to liken things, *compare with* to consider their similarities or differences. "He compared London to New York" means that he felt London to be similar to New York. "He compared London with New York" means that he assessed the two cities' relative merits. *Compare to* most often appears in figurative senses, as in "Shall I compare thee to a summer's day?"

compatible.

compatriot for a fellow countryman. Not to be confused, in meaning or spelling, with *expatriate*.

compel, impel. Both words imply the application of a force leading to some form of action, but they are not quite synonymous. *Compel* is the stronger of the two and, like its cousin *compulsion*, suggests action undertaken as a result of coercion or irresistible pressure: "The man's bullying tactics compelled us to flee." *Impel* is closer in meaning to *encourage* and means to urge forward: "The audience's ovation impelled me to speak at greater length than I had intended." If you are compelled to do something, you have no choice. If you are impelled, an element of willingness is possible.

compendium. No doubt because of the similarity in sound to *comprehensive*, the word is often taken to mean vast and all-embracing. In fact, a *compendium* is a succinct summary or abridgment. Size has nothing to do with it. It may be as large as *The Oxford English Dictionary* or as small as a memorandum. What is important is that it should provide a complete summary in a brief way. The plural can be either *compendia* or *compendiums*. The *OED* prefers the former, most other dictionaries the latter.

complacent, complaisant. The first means self-satisfied, contented to the point of smugness. The second means affable and cheerfully obliging. If you are *complacent*, you are pleased with yourself. If you are *complaisant*, you wish to please others. Both words come from the Latin *complacere* ("to please"), but *complaisant* reached us by way of France, which accounts for the difference in spelling.

Compleat Angler, The. Book by Izaak Walton (1653).

complement, compliment/complementary, complimentary. The words come from the same Latin root, *complere*, meaning to fill up, but have long had separate meanings. *Compliment* means to praise. *Complement* has stayed closer to the original meaning: it means to fill out or make whole. So a gracious guest compliments a host; an espresso after dinner complements a meal. In the adjectival forms *complementary* and *complimentary* the words retain these senses, but *complimentary* has the additional meaning of something given without charge: a complimentary ticket, for instance.

complete. Partridge includes *complete* in his list of false comparatives—that is, words that do not admit of a comparison, such as *ultimate* and *eternal* (one thing cannot be "more ultimate" or "more eternal" than another). Technically, he is right, and you should take care not to modify *complete* needlessly. But there are occasions when it would be pedantic to carry the stricture too far. As the Morrises note, there can be no real objection to "This is the most complete study to date of that period." Use it, but use it judiciously.

complete and unabridged. Though blazoned across the packaging of countless audio books, the phrase is palpably redundant. If a work is unabridged, it must be complete, and vice versa. Choose one or the other.

compos mentis. (Lat.) "Of sound mind."

comprehensible.

compressor.

comprise. "Beneath Sequoia is the Bechtel Group, a holding company comprised of three main operating arms . . ." (*New York Times*). Not quite. It is composed of three main operating arms, not comprised of them. *Comprised of* is a common expression, but it is always wrong. *Comprise* means to contain. The whole comprises the parts and not vice versa. A house may comprise seven rooms, but seven rooms do not comprise a house—and still less is a house comprised of seven rooms. The example above should be either "a holding company comprising three main operating arms" or "composed of three main operating arms."

conceived. "Last week, 25 years after it was first conceived . . ." (*Time*). Delete "first." Something can be conceived only once. Similarly with "initially conceived" and "originally conceived."

Concertgebouw Orchestra, Amsterdam.

condone. The word does not mean to approve or endorse, senses that are often attached to it. It means to pardon, forgive, overlook. You can condone an action without supporting it.

Coney Island, New York.

confectionery. Not *-ary.*

confidant (masc.)/**confidante** (fem.) for a person entrusted with private information.

Congo, confusingly, now applies to two neighboring nations in

Africa. The larger of the two, which was called Zaire until 1997, now styles itself the Democratic Republic of the Congo; its capital is Kinshasa. Bordering it to the west is the much smaller Republic of the Congo; capital Brazzaville.

Congonhas–São Paulo International Airport, São Paulo, Brazil.

Congressional Medal of Honor, for the highest U.S. military honor, is not strictly correct. It is awarded by Congress, but its correct title is simply the Medal of Honor.

Congreve, William. (1670–1729) English playwright.

Connacht. Province of Ireland comprising five counties: Galway, Leitrim, Mayo, Roscommon, and Sligo.

Connelly, Marc. (1890–1980) American playwright. Full name: Marcus Cook Connelly.

Connemara. Galway, Ireland.

connoisseur.

ConocoPhillips. Oil company.

Conseco Fieldhouse, Indianapolis; home of the Indiana Pacers basketball team.

consensus. "General consensus" is a tautology. Any consensus must be general. Equally to be avoided is "consensus of opinion." Above all, note that *consensus* is spelled with a middle *s*, like *consent*. It has nothing to do with *census*.

consols. Consolidated annuities, a stock market term.

Constance/Bodensee. (Ger.) Lake bounded by Switzerland, Germany, and Austria; the principal lakeside city is Constance in English and French, but Konstanz in German.

Constantinople. Former name of Istanbul.

consummate. As a term of praise, the word is much too freely used. A *consummate* actor is not merely a very good one but someone who is so good as to be unrivaled or nearly so. It should be reserved to describe only the very best.

contagious, infectious. Diseases spread by contact are *contagious*.

Those spread by air and water are *infectious*. Used figuratively ("contagious laughter," "infectious enthusiasm"), either is fine.

contemptible, contemptuous. *Contemptible* means deserving contempt. *Contemptuous* means bestowing it. A contemptible offer may receive a contemptuous response.

conterminous, coterminous. Sharing a common boundary.

continual, continuous. Although the distinction is not widely observed, or indeed always necessary, there is a useful difference between the two words. *Continual* refers to things that happen repeatedly but not constantly. *Continuous* indicates an uninterrupted sequence. However, few readers will be aware of this distinction, and the writer who requires absolute clarity will generally be better advised to use *incessant* or *uninterrupted* for *continuous* and *intermittent* for *continual*.

contrary, converse, opposite, reverse. *Contrary* describes something that contradicts a proposition. *Converse* applies when the elements of a proposition are reversed. *Opposite* is something that is diametrically opposed to a proposition. *Reverse* can describe any of these. For the statement "I love you," the opposite is "I hate you"; the converse is "You love me"; the contrary would be anything that contradicted it: "I do not love you," "I have no feelings at all for you," "I like you moderately." The reverse could embrace all of these meanings.

conurbation does not describe any urban area, but rather a place where two or more sizable communities have sprawled together, such as Pasadena–Los Angeles–Long Beach in California or Amsterdam-Rotterdam-Haarlem-Utrecht in the Netherlands.

convener. Not *-or*. One who convenes.

convince, persuade. The words are not quite the same. You *convince* someone that he should believe, but *persuade* him to act. It is possible to persuade a person to do something without convincing him of the correctness or necessity of doing it. A separate distinction is that *persuade* may be followed by an infinitive, but *convince* may not. Thus the following is wrong: "The Soviet Union evidently is not able to convince Cairo to accept a rapid cease-fire." Make it either "persuade Cairo to accept" or "convince Cairo that it should accept."

coolly.

Cooper, James Fenimore. (1789–1851) American writer.

Cooper-Hewitt National Design Museum, New York.

Copland, Aaron. (1900–1990) American composer.

Copley, John Singleton. (1737–1815) American painter.

Coppola, Francis Ford. (1939–) American film director.

Corbière, (Édouard Joachim) Tristan. (1845–1875) French poet.

Corbusier, Le. Pseudonym of Charles Édouard Jeanneret (1887–1965), Swiss architect and city planner.

Corcoran Gallery of Art, Washington, D.C.

cord, chord. A *cord* is a length of rope or similar material of twisted strands; a *chord* is a group of musical notes. You speak with your vocal cords.

corduroy.

CORE. Congress of (not *for*) Race Equality, U.S. civil rights organization.

Coriolis effect. The tendency of winds of deflect to the right in the Northern Hemisphere and to the left in the Southern Hemisphere as a consequence of Earth's spin.

Corneille, Pierre. (1606–1684) French playwright.

Cornouaille, Côte de, France.

Coronado, Francisco Vásquez de. (c. 1500–1554) Spanish explorer of the New World.

Corot, Camille. (1796–1875) French painter.

Corporation for Public Broadcasting.

Correggio, Antonio Allegri da. (1494–1534) Italian painter.

corrigible. Capable of being corrected or improved.

corruptible.

cortege. (No accents.)

Cortes. Legislative assembly of Spain, but see next entry.

Cortés/Cortéz, Hernando/Hernan. (1485–1547) Spanish conqueror of Aztecs.

coruscate. Not -rr-. Glittering, dazzling, as in "coruscating wit."

Così fan tutte. Opera by Mozart (1790).

cos lettuce.

Costa-Gavras, (Henri) Constantin. (1933–) Film director.

Côte d'Azur. The French Riviera.

coterminous, conterminous. Sharing a common boundary.

cotoneaster. Type of shrub.

Cotten, Joseph. (1905–1994) Film actor.

Cottian Alps. Section of Alps between France and Italy.

couldn't of. " 'Couldn't of got it without you, Pops,' Parker said . . ." (*New Yorker*). As a shortened form of "couldn't have," *couldn't of* does unquestionably avoid the clumsy double contraction *couldn't've*, a form not often seen in print since J. D. Salinger stopped writing. However, I would submit that that does not make it satisfactory. Using the preposition *of* as a surrogate for *'ve* seems to me simply to be swapping an ungainly form for an illiterate one. If *couldn't've* is too painful to use, I would suggest simply writing *couldn't have* and allowing the reader's imagination to supply the appropriate inflection.

coulee. Ravine.

council, counsel. The first is a deliberative body (city council); the second applies to contexts involving the giving of advice or guidance (marriage counselor).

Countess Cathleen, The. Not *Kath-*. A play by William Butler Yeats (1899).

country, nation. It is perhaps a little fussy to insist too strenuously on the distinction, but strictly *country* refers to the geographical characteristics of a place and *nation* to the political and social ones. Thus the United States is one of the richest nations but largest countries.

coup de grâce. A decisive blow.

coup d'état, pl. *coups d'état.*

coup de théâtre. Dramatic turn of events.

couple. The idea, fiercely adhered to in some quarters, that *couple* must always be singular is both pointless and unsupported by wider authority. When a couple are thought of as separate individuals ("The couple were apprehended in different counties"; "The couple have been living apart since 1999"), the plural is always to be preferred.

couple of. The second word is required in sentences like "Can I borrow a couple of dollars?" To drop the "of" is a common but nonetheless grating illiteracy in any but the most casual writing.

courgette. French and British name for the vegetable known to Americans as zucchini.

Courmayeur, Italy; Alpine resort.

court-martial. (Hyphen.) The plural is *courts-martial* (though some authorities now accept *court-martials*).

Court of Session. The supreme court of Scotland.

Court of St. James's is the place to which ambassadors are posted in Great Britain. Note the apostrophe and second *s*.

Cousy, Bob. (1928–) American basketball player.

Covarrubias, Miguel. (1902–1957) Mexican artist.

Cowper, William. (1731–1800) English poet; pronounced *cooper*.

Cozzens, James Gould. (1903–1978) American author.

crackerjack, Cracker Jack. The first is an old slang term for something good; the second is the popular candied popcorn.

crass means stupid and grossly ignorant to the point of insensitivity and not merely coarse or tasteless. A thing must be pretty bad to be crass.

Cratchit, Bob. Character in Dickens's *A Christmas Carol.*

Crécy, Battle of (1346).

Creekmur, Lou. (1927–) American football player.

crème brûlée. Literally "burnt cream"; custard dessert.

creole, pidgin. A *pidgin* is a simplified and rudimentary language that springs up when two or more cultures come in contact. If that contact is prolonged and generations are born for whom the pidgin is their first tongue, the language will usually evolve into a more formalized *creole* (from the French for "indigenous"). Most languages that are commonly referred to as pidgins are in fact creoles.

crêpes suzette. (Not cap.) When *crepes* is used on its own in most circumstances the circumflex may be dropped.

crescendo is not a climax or conclusion. It is the movement toward a conclusion. Properly, it should be used only to describe a gradual increase in volume or intensity.

Cressida, Troilus and. Play by Shakespeare (c. 1601). The poem by Geoffrey Chaucer is "Troylus and Criseyde." In Boccaccio's *Il Filostrato* the spelling is *Criseida.*

crevasse, crevice. A *crevasse* is a deep fissure, particularly in thin ice; a *crevice* is a narrow and generally shallow fissure.

Crèvecoeur, J. Hector St. John. (1735–1813) Born Michel Guillaume Jean de Crèvecoeur; French-born American essayist.

cri de coeur. (Fr.) An impassioned plea.

crime passionnel. (Fr.) A crime motivated by sexual jealousy.

crisis, pl. *crises.*

criterion, pl. *criteria.*

Croat, Croatian. The first describes the people of Croatia; the second is a more general adjective ("a Croatian city").

Croce, Benedetto. (1866–1952) Italian writer, philosopher, and politician.

crocheted, crocheting.

Crockett, Davy. (1786–1836) American frontiersman and politician.

Croesus. Last king of Lydia (reigned 560–546 BC); byword for wealth.

Cro-Magnon. Early form of *Homo sapiens*, named after a hill in France.

Crome Yellow for the 1921 novel by Aldous Huxley. Not *Chrome*.

Cronos. In Greek mythology, a Titan dethroned by his son Zeus; equivalent to the Roman god Saturn. Sometimes spelled *Kronos* (esp. in UK).

crony.

Crowley, Aleister. (1875–1947) English writer and diabolist.

Crufts Dog show. (UK)

Cruikshank, George. (1792–1878) English cartoonist and illustrator.

cruzeiro. Principal unit of currency of Brazil; from 1986 to 1990 it was the *cruzado*.

Cry, the Beloved Country. Note comma. Novel by Alan Paton (1948).

CSA Czech Airlines. National airline of Czech Republic.

Csonka, Larry. (1946–) American football player.

C-Span, C-Span 2. Cable television networks; the initials are short for Cable-Satellite Public Affairs Network.

Cucamonga, California, became **Rancho Cucamonga** in 1977 when it amalgamated with the neighboring communities of Alta Loma and Etiwanda.

Cuchulain. Warrior hero of Irish mythology; pronounced *koo-hoo'-lin*.

cuckoo.

cueing.

cul-de-sac. (Hyphens.) Pl. *cul-de-sacs*.

Culloden, Battle of.

Culpeper, Virginia.

Culzean Castle, Scotland; pronounced *kuh-lane'*.

cumbrous. Not *-erous*.

cuneiform. Wedge-shaped writing.

cupful, pl. *cupfuls.*

cupola.

Curaçao. Island in the Netherlands Antilles. The liqueur produced there is spelled the same but lowercased.

curettage. A surgical scraping procedure using a curette.

curette. A surgical instrument.

Curie, Marie. (1867–1934) Polish-born French physicist. Joint winner with her husband, Pierre Curie, and Henri Becquerel, of the Nobel Prize for Physics in 1903, she was also awarded the Nobel Prize for Chemistry in 1911. Born Marie Sklodowska.

curlicue.

Curragh Incident. A near-mutiny in 1914 by British officers stationed at the Curragh, near Dublin, who refused to fire on civilians. A curragh is also a type of small boat.

current, currently. When there is a need to contrast the present with the past, *current* has its place, but all too often it is merely an idle occupier of space, as in these two examples from a single article in *Time* magazine: "The Government currently owns 740 million acres, or 32.7% of the land in the U.S. . . . Property in the area is currently fetching $125 to $225 per acre." The notion of currency is implicit in both statements, as it is in most other sentences in which *current* and *currently* appear. *Currently* should be deleted from both. (The second sentence could be further improved by changing "is fetching" to "fetches.")

curriculum vitae. Another name for a résumé.

Curtiss aircraft. Named after **Glenn Curtiss** (1878–1930), American inventor and aviator.

Curtiz, Michael. (1888–1962) Hungarian-born American film director; born Mihály Kertész.

curtsy. Not *-ey.*

curvaceous. Not *-ious.*

cut back is generally tautological, as here: "Losses in the metal stamping division have forced the group to cut back production." More succinct to say "have forced the group to cut production."

cyanosis. Turning blue from lack of oxygen.

cyclamen.

cymbal. Percussion instrument.

Cynewulf. (fl. eighth c.) Anglo-Saxon poet.

Cyrillic alphabet. Alphabet widely used for Slavonic languages. It is named after St. Cyril, who is popularly credited with its invention. Some of the characters vary slightly between Russian, Bulgarian, and other languages.

cystic fibrosis. Genetic disease.

cystitis.

Dd

Dachau. Town near Munich, site of infamous concentration camp in World War II.

Dadullah, Mullah. (1966–2007) Afghan Taliban commander; sometimes called Dadullah Akhund.

Daedalus. In Greek mythology, father of Icarus and builder of the Labyrinth; but the character in the works of James Joyce is **Stephen Dedalus** and the pseudonym used by the Italian author Umberto Eco is also **Dedalus**.

daguerreotype. Early photographic process, named after **Louis Daguerre** (1789–1851), French painter and photographer.

Dahomey. Former name of Benin.

Dai-Ichi Kangyo. Japanese bank.

Dáil Éireann. Lower house of Irish parliament; pronounced *doyle air-ran*.

DaimlerChrysler AG. German car manufacturer, separated in 2007 into **Daimler AG** and **Chrysler Holding**.

daiquiri.

Dalai Lama. The high priest of Tibet.

d'Alembert, Jean Le Rond. (1717–1783) French mathematician.

Damariscotta. Town and lake in Maine.

Danaë. Mother of Perseus in Greek mythology.

danke schön. (Ger.) "Thank you very much."

d'Annunzio, Gabriele. (1863–1938) Italian writer and adventurer.

danse macabre. Not *dance*. From the French for "a dance of death." The plural is *danses macabres*.

Dante Alighieri. (1265–1321) Italian poet; the adjective is *Dantesque.*

Danzig. Former name of Gdańsk, the Polish city.

D'Arcy Masius Benton & Bowles. Former advertising agency.

Dardanelles. The narrow channel linking the Aegean Sea and the Sea of Marmara, known in antiquity as the Hellespont.

Dar es Salaam. Former capital of Tanzania. See also DODOMA.

Darjeeling for the tea, but **Darjiling** for the Indian city for which it is named.

data is a plural. Although this fact is widely disregarded, you should at least be aware that "The data was fed into a computer" is incorrect. It is also worth observing that the sense of *data* is generally best confined to the idea of raw, uncollated bits of information, the sort of stuff churned out by computers, and not used as a simple synonym for *facts* or *reports* or *information.*

da Vinci, Leonardo, for the Florentine artist (1452–1519). On second reference he is properly referred to as "Leonardo," not as "da Vinci."

Davy, Sir Humphry. (1778–1829) Not *Humphrey.* English chemist.

Dayan, Moshe. (1915–1981) Israeli general and politician.

dB is the abbreviation for *decibel.*

DDR. Short for Deutsche Demokratische Republik; former East Germany.

DDT. Dichlorodiphenyltrichloroethane, an insecticide.

debacle. A rout or ruin; in French, *débâcle.*

De Bakey, Michael. (1908–) American heart surgeon.

de Beauvoir, Simone. (1908–1986) French author.

De Benedetti, Carlo. (1934–) Italian industrialist.

debonair. In French, it is *débonnaire.*

Debrett's Peerage and Baronetage. Guide to British aristocracy.

Debs, Eugene V(ictor). (1855–1926) American socialist and labor leader.

DeBusschere, Dave. (1940–2003) American basketball and baseball player.

Debussy, (Achille-) Claude. (1862–1918) French composer.

débutante.

decathlon. The ten events are long jump, high jump, pole vault, discus, shot put, javelin, 110-meter hurdles, and 100-, 400-, and 1,500-meter races.

deceit, deceive.

deci-. Prefix meaning one-tenth.

decimate. Literally the word means to reduce by a tenth (from the ancient practice of punishing the mutinous or cowardly by killing every tenth man). By extension it may be used to describe the inflicting of heavy damage, but it should never be used to denote annihilation, as in this memorably excruciating sentence cited by Fowler: "Dick, hotly pursued by the scalp-hunter, turned in his saddle, fired and literally decimated his opponent." Equally to be avoided are contexts in which the word's use is clearly inconsistent with its literal meaning, as in "Frost decimated an estimated 80 percent of the crops."

décolletage. A plunging neckline on clothing.

Dedalus, Stephen. Character in James Joyce works. See also DAEDALUS.

de facto. (Lat.) Existing in fact but not in law; see also DE JURE.

defective, deficient. When something is not working properly, it is *defective;* when it is missing a necessary part, it is *deficient.*

Defferre, Gaston. (1910–1986) French Socialist politician and journalist.

defibrillator.

definite, definitive. *Definite* means precise and unmistakable. *Definitive* means final and conclusive. A definite offer is a clear one; a definitive offer is one that permits of no haggling.

Defoe, Daniel. (1659–1731) British author.

defuse, diffuse. Occasionally confused. *Defuse* means to make less harmful; *diffuse* means to spread thinly.

de Gaulle, Charles. (1890–1970) President of France (1944–1946, 1959–1969).

de haut en bas. (Fr.) "With contempt."

De Havilland. Aircraft.

Deirdre of the Sorrows. Play by J. M. Synge.

déjà vu.

de jure. (Lat.) According to law; see also DE FACTO.

Dekker, Thomas. (c. 1570–c. 1640) English playwright.

de Klerk, F. W. (for Frederik Willem) (1936–) President of South Africa (1989–1994); co-winner with Nelson Mandela of the Nobel Peace Prize in 1993.

de Kooning, Willem. (1904–1997) Dutch-born American painter.

Delacroix, Eugène. (1789–1863) French painter.

de La Tour, Georges. (1593–1652) French painter.

De Laurentiis, Dino. (1919–) Italian film producer; his formal first name is Agostino.

delectable. Not *-ible.*

Deledda, Grazia. (1871–1936) Italian novelist, awarded Nobel Prize for Literature in 1926.

deleterious.

delftware. (No cap.)

Delilah.

DeLillo, Don. (1936–) American novelist.

Delius, Frederick. (1862–1934) British composer.

Deloitte Touche Tohmatsu. (No commas.) International accountancy company.

DeLorean. Automobile named for John Z. DeLorean (1925–2005).

de los Angeles, Victoria. (1924–2005) Spanish soprano.

Delta Air Lines. Note *Air Lines* two words.

Del Toro, Benicio. (1967–) Puerto Rican actor.

De Lucchi, Michele. (1951–) Italian architect and designer.

demagogue is the preferred spelling, though some authorities also accept *demagog.*

de mal en pis, de pis en pis. (Fr.) Both mean "from bad to worse."

de Maupassant, (Henri René Albert) Guy. (1850–1893) French writer of short stories and novels.

Dementieva, Elena. (1981–) Russian tennis player.

Demerol. (Cap.) Type of medication.

Demeter. Greek goddess of agriculture and fertility; the Roman equivalent is Ceres.

De Mille, Cecil B(lount). (1881–1959) American film producer and director, noted for epics.

demimonde. (In French, demi-monde.) Term loosely applied to prostitutes, kept women, or anyone else living on the wrong side of respectability.

demise does not mean decline; it means death.

de mortuis de nil nisi bonum. (Lat.) Say nothing but good of the dead.

Demosthenes. (384–322 BC) Athenian orator and statesman.

Denali National Park and Preserve, Alaska; Denali is also an alternative name for Mount McKinley, North America's highest peak (20,320 feet; 6,194 meters), which stands within the park.

Deng Xiaoping. (1904–1997) Chinese elder statesman.

De Niro, Robert. (1943–) American actor.

dénouement. Outcome or solution.

deodorant.

Deo gratias. (Lat.) "Thanks to God."

Deo volente. (Lat.) "God willing."

De Palma, Brian. (1941–) American film director.

dependant, dependent. The first refers to a person, the second to a situation.

deplete, reduce. Though their meanings are roughly the same, *deplete* has the additional connotation of injurious reduction. As the Evanses note, a garrison may be reduced by administrative order, but depleted by sickness.

deplore. Strictly, you may *deplore* a thing, but not a person. I may deplore your behavior, but I cannot deplore you.

deprecate does not mean to play down or show modesty, as is often intended. It means to disapprove of strongly or to protest against.

de profundis. (Lat.) "From the depths"; a heartfelt cry.

De Quincy, Thomas. (1785–1859) English writer.

de rigueur. Often misspelled. Note the second *u*.

derisive, derisory. Something that is *derisive* conveys ridicule or contempt. Something that is *derisory* invites it. A derisory offer is likely to provoke a derisive response.

descendible.

Deschanel, Zooey. (1980–) American actress.

Deschutes River, Oregon.

déshabillé (Fr.) Untidily or incompletely dressed; usually rendered in English as **dishabille.**

De Sica, Vittorio. (1902–1974) Italian film actor and director.

desiccate.

de Soto, Hernando. (c. 1496–1542) Spanish explorer.

desperate.

despite, in spite of. There is no distinction between the two. A common construction is seen here: "But despite the cold weather the game went ahead." Because *despite* and *in spite of* indicate a change of emphasis, "but" is generally superfluous with either. It is enough to say "Despite the cold weather the game went ahead."

destroy is an incomparable—almost. If a house is consumed by fire, it is enough to say that it was destroyed, not that it was "completely destroyed" or "totally destroyed." However, and illogical as it may seem, it is all right to speak of a house that has been partly destroyed. There is simply no other way of putting it without resorting to more circuitous descriptions. That is perhaps absurd and inconsistent, but ever thus was English.

destructible.

detestable.

de trop. (Fr.) Excessive.

Deukmejian, George. (1928–) Republican governor of California (1983–1991).

deus ex machina. In drama, a character or event that arrives late in the action and provides a solution.

Deuteronomy. The last book of the Pentateuch in the Old Testament.

Deutsche mark. (Two words.) Former currency of Germany. The euro is now used.

Deutsches Museum, Munich.

de Valera, Éamon. (1882–1975) U.S.-born prime minister (1919–1921, 1932–1948, and 1957–1959) and president (1959–1973) of Ireland.

devilry, deviltry. Either is acceptable.

Devil's Island, French Guiana; site of infamous prison; in French, île du Diable.

Devils Playground. (No apos.) Desert in California.

Devils Tower National Monument, Wyoming. (No apos.)

DeVoto, Bernard. (1897–1955) American historian and biographer. Note *DeVoto* is one word.

De Vries, Peter. (1910–1993) American novelist.

dexterous is preferred, but **dextrous** is acceptable.

Dhaulagiri. Himalayan mountain, seventh highest in the world (26,810 feet; 8,172 meters).

dhow. Arab boat.

DHTML. Short for Dynamic Hypertext Markup Language; computer terminology.

Diaghilev, Sergei (Pavlovich). (1872–1929) Russian ballet impresario, founder of Ballets Russes.

diagnosis, prognosis. To make a *diagnosis* is to identify and define a problem, usually a disease. A *prognosis* is a projection of the course and likely outcome of a problem. *Diagnosis* applies only to conditions, not to people. Thus, "Asbestos victims were not diagnosed in large numbers until the 1960s" (*Time*) is not quite right. It was the victims' conditions that were not diagnosed, not the victims themselves.

dialect, patois. Both describe the form of language prevailing in a region and can be used interchangeably, though *patois* is normally better reserved for contexts involving French or its variants. "He spoke in the patois of Yorkshire" is at best jocular. The plural of *patois*, incidentally, is also *patois*.

Dial "M" for Murder. Note quotation marks around *M*. Drama by Frederick Knott and film by Alfred Hitchcock.

dialysis.

Diana. Roman goddess of the moon and the hunt; identified with the Greek goddess Artemis.

diaphragm.

diarrhea.

Dickinson, Emily (Elizabeth). (1830–1886) American poet.

Diderot, Denis. (1713–1784) French encyclopedist and philosopher.

Didrikson, Babe. (1913–1956) American golfer and athlete. Real name **Mildred Didrikson**; last name later **Didrikson Zaharias.**

Diefenbaker, John George. (1895–1979) Prime minister of Canada (1957–1963).

Dien Bien Phu. Battle in 1954 that led the French to pull out of Indochina (later Vietnam).

Dieppe. French port.

dieresis, not *dia-*, for the punctuation mark consisting of two dots above a vowel, as in Brontë or Chloë, which is used to indicate that a vowel that could be silent should in fact be sounded. (It is a curiosity of English that the word *dieresis* is entitled to, but never given, the mark it describes.) The dieresis mark always goes above the second vowel in a pair. It should not be confused with the German *umlaut*, which also consists of two dots, as in Göring or Müller, but which signifies a phonetic shift rather than an elaboration into separate sounds.

diesel. Not *deisel*.

Diet. Japanese parliament.

dietitian.

Dietrich, Marlene. (1904–1992) German-born actress and singer; born Maria Magdalene von Losch.

Dieu et mon droit. (Fr.) "God and my right," motto of the British royal family.

different. Often used unnecessarily, as in "It is found in more than 250 different types of plants." In such constructions it can nearly always be deleted without loss.

different from, to, than. Among the more tenacious beliefs among many writers and editors is that *different* may be followed only by *from*. In fact, the belief has no real basis. *Different from* is, to be sure, the usual form in most sentences and the only acceptable form in some, as when it precedes a noun or pronoun ("My car is different from his"; "Men are different from women"). But when *different* introduces a clause, there can be no valid objection to following it with a *to* (though this usage is chiefly British) or *than*, as in this sentence by John Maynard Keynes: "How different things appear in Washington than in London." You may, if you insist, change it to "How different things appear in Washington from how they appear in London," but all it gives you is more words, not better grammar.

diffuse. To spread out; not to be confused with *defuse*, meaning to make safe.

digestible.

dike, dyke. Either is acceptable.

dilapidated, dilapidation.

dilatory. Not *-tary.*

dildos.

dilemma refers to a situation involving two courses of action, both unsatisfactory. A person who cannot decide what he wants for breakfast is not in a dilemma.

dilettante. A lover of, or dabbler in, the fine arts; most often used with a hint of condescension; pl. *dilettantes* or *dilettanti.*

diligence, diligent.

dilly-dally.

DiMaggio (no space) for the baseball players (and brothers) Joe (1914–1999) and Dom (1917–).

Diners Club International. (No apos.)

Dinesen, Isak. Pen name of Karen Blixen (1885–1962), Danish writer and baroness.

dingo. Wild Australian dog; pl. *dingoes.*

Dione. Moon of Saturn.

Dionysius the Elder. (c. 430–367 BC) Tyrant of Syracuse who suspended the famous sword above the head of Damocles.

Dionysus (or **Dionysos**). Not -*ius*; Greek god of wine and revelry, corresponding to the Roman god Bacchus; the adjective is *Dionysian* or *Dionysiac.*

diphtheria. Note that the first syllable is spelled *diph-*, not *dipth-*, and is pronounced accordingly.

dirigible.

dirigisme. (Fr.) Dominance of the economy by the state; adjective is *dirigiste.*

dirndl. Alpine dress.

disassemble, dissemble. The first means to take apart; the second means to conceal.

disassociate, dissociate. The first is not incorrect, but the second has the virtue of brevity.

disastrous.

disc, disk. There is no special logic to which it is used in American English. *Disc* generally is used for contexts involving music and entertainment (*compact disc, disc jockey, video disc*) and in the contexts of machinery (*disc brakes, disc harrow*). *Disk* is preferred in anatomy (*slipped disk*) and computer storage (*hard disk, floppy disk*). In most situations, the best advice is to strive for consistency.

discernible. Not -*able*.

discomfit, discomfort. "In this she is greatly assisted by her husband . . . who enjoys spreading discomfiture in a good cause as much as she does" (*Observer*). The writer here, like many before him, clearly meant *discomfort*, which has nothing in common with *discomfiture* beyond a superficial resemblance. *Discomfit* means to rout, overwhelm, or completely disconcert. Some dictionaries now accept the newer sense of to perplex or induce uneasiness, but I would submit that the distinction is very much worth preserving. If *discomfort* is the condition you have in mind, why not use that word and leave *discomfiture* for less discriminating users?

discothèque.

discreet, discrete. The first means circumspect, careful, showing good judgment ("He promised to be discreet in his inquiries"). The second means unattached or unrelated ("The compound was composed of discrete particles").

dishabille. To be untidily or incompletely dressed; in French, déshabillé.

disheveled.

disinterested, uninterested. The first means neutral, the second not caring. A *disinterested* person is one who has no stake in the outcome of an event; an *uninterested* person is one who doesn't care. As with DISCOMFIT, DISCOMFORT (see above), the distinction is an important one and worth observing.

dismissible.

dispensable.

disposal, disposition. If you are talking about getting rid of, use *disposal* ("the disposal of nuclear weapons"). If you mean arranging, use *disposition* ("the disposition of troops on the battlefield").

dissatisfy, dissatisfied, dissatisfaction. Note -*ss*-.

dissect, dissection.

dissemble, disassemble. The first means to conceal; the second means to take apart.

dissent, but **dissension.**

dissimilar.

dissipate.

dissociate, disassociate. The first is preferred, but either is acceptable.

dissolvable.

distrait, distraught. The first means abstracted in thought, absent-minded. The second means deeply agitated.

disturb, perturb. They can often be used interchangeably, but generally the first is better applied to physical agitation, the second to mental agitation.

dived, dove. Either is acceptable.

diverge. When two things diverge, they move farther apart (just as when they converge they come together). It is not a word that should be applied freely to any difference of opinion, but only to those in which a rift is widening.

divergences. Not -*ies.*

divertissement. Light diversion.

Divina Commedia, La. Dante's *Divine Comedy.*

divvy. To divide, especially equally, as with a jackpot.

Djakarta. Use **Jakarta.**

Djibouti. African republic, formerly French Somaliland and, briefly, French Territory of Afars and Issas; the capital is also called Djibouti.

Djokovic, Novak. (1987–) Serbian tennis player.

DNA. Deoxyribonucleic acid.

Dnieper. River in Russia, Belarus, and Ukraine.

Dniester. River in Ukraine and Moldova.

Dobbs Ferry, New York.

Doberman pinscher for the breed of dog, but **Ludwig Dobermann** for the breeder for whom the dogs are named.

Dodecanese. Chain of twelve Greek islands, including Rhodes and Kos.

Dodgson, Charles Lutwidge. (1832–1898) Real name of Lewis Carroll.

Dodoma. Capital of Tanzania.

Dodsworth. Novel by Sinclair Lewis (1929).

doggerel.

dogsbody. A person given menial tasks to perform for a superior.

doily, pl. *doilies.*

Dolce & Gabbana. Italian fashion firm.

Dollfuss, Engelbert. (1892–1934) Austrian chancellor (1932–1934), assassinated by Austrian Nazis.

Domenichino. (1581–1641) Italian painter.

Domesday Book. Census of England carried out in 1086; pronounced *doomsday.*

Dominica. Small (pop. 69,000) Caribbean island state; capital Roseau. Not to be confused with nearby **Dominican Republic;** capital Santo Domingo.

dominoes.

Dom Pérignon. Champagne.

Donatello. (c. 1386–1466) Italian sculptor, real name Donato di Niccolò di Betto Bardi.

Donegal. Irish county, but **Marquess of Donegall.**

Don Giovanni. Opera by Mozart (1787).

Donizetti, Gaetano. (1797–1848) Italian composer.

doorjamb.

doppelganger. (Ger.) A person's ghostly double.

Doppler effect. The change that occurs in sound waves as the source and the observer move closer together or farther apart, named after **Christian Johann Doppler** (1803–1853), Austrian physicist.

dormouse for the small rodent, which isn't actually a mouse at all. The name is thought to be a corruption of the Norman French *dormeus,* meaning "sleepy." The plural is *dormice.*

dos and don'ts. Not *do's*.

Dosewallips River, Washington.

Dos Passos, John. (1896–1970) American writer.

Dostoyevsky, Fyodor, is the commonest spelling of the name of the Russian novelist (1821–1881), but there are many possible variants for both names.

double meanings. Anyone who has written headlines for a living will know the embarrassment that comes from causing hilarity to a large group of people by writing an inadvertently two-faced headline. I have no doubt that someone at the *Toronto Globe and Mail* is still cringing at having written "Upturns May Indicate Some Bottoms Touched" (cited in *Punch*), as must earlier have been the author of the oft-quoted and variously attributed "MacArthur Flies Back to Front." It is always worth remembering that many words carry a range of meanings, or function as both nouns and verbs, and consequently offer unexpected opportunities for mischief.

double negatives. Most people know you shouldn't say "I haven't had no dinner," but some writers, doubtless more out of haste than ignorance, sometimes perpetrate sentences that are scarcely less jarring, as here: "Stranded and uncertain of their location, the survivors endured for six days without hardly a trace of food" (*Chicago Tribune*). Since *hardly*, like *scarcely*, has the grammatical effect of a negative, it requires no further negation. Make it "with hardly."

Some usage guides flatly condemn all double negatives, but there is one kind, in which a negative in the main clause is paralleled in a subordinate construction, that we might view more tolerantly. Evans cites this sentence from Jane Austen: "There was none too poor or remote not to feel an interest." And Shakespeare wrote: "Nor what he said, though it lacked form a little, was not like madness." But such constructions must be considered exceptional. More often the intrusion of a second negative is merely a sign of fuzzy writing. At best it will force the reader to pause and perform some verbal arithmetic, adding negative to negative, as here: "The plan is now thought unlikely not to go ahead" (*London Times*). At worst it may leave the reader darkly baffled, as in this memorably convoluted sentence from a leading authority: "Moreover . . . our sense of linguistic tact will not urge us not to use words that may offend or irritate" (Quirk, *The Use of English*).

Double Top Mountain, New York, but **Doubletop Peak,** Wyoming.

doubt if, that, whether. Idiom demands some selectivity in the choice of conjunction to introduce a clause after *doubt* and *doubtful.* The rule is simple: *Doubt that* should be reserved for negative contexts ("There is no doubt that . . ."; "It was never doubtful that . . .") and interrogative ones ("Do you have any doubt that . . . ?"; "Was it ever doubtful that . . . ?"). *Whether* or *if* should be used in all others ("I doubt if he will come"; "It is doubtful whether the rain will stop").

doubtless, undoubtedly, indubitably. "Tonight he faces what is doubtlessly the toughest and loneliest choice of his 13-year stewardship of the Palestine Liberation Organization" (*Washington Post*). Since *doubtless* can be an adverb as well as an adjective, there is no need to add -*ly* to it. *Undoubtedly* would have been a better choice still because, as the Evanses note, it has a less concessive air. *Doubtless* usually suggests a tone of reluctance or resignation: "You are doubtless right." *Undoubtedly* carries more conviction: "You are undoubtedly right." *Indubitably* is a somewhat jocular synonym for either.

Douglass, Frederick. (1817–1895) Escaped American slave who became a leading abolitionist and statesman; born Frederick Augustus Washington Bailey.

douse, dowse. The first means to drench; the second means to search for water.

Dow Jones industrial average. (No hyphen, last two words no caps.)

Downers Grove (no apos.), Illinois.

Down House. Charles Darwin's home; located in **Downe**, Kent.

Down syndrome. Congenital condition, formerly called mongolism; named after the British physician J. L. H. Down (1828–1896). Sometimes still called **Down's syndrome**, but increasingly the convention in medical circles is to abandon the possessive in the names of diseases (so Parkinson disease, Hodgkin disease).

D.Phil. British equivalent of the American Ph.D.

dramatis personae. Cast of characters.

Drechsler, Heike. (1964–) German sprinter and long jumper.

Dreiser, Theodore. (1871–1945) American writer.

Dresdner Kleinwort Wasserstein. Investment bank.

Drexel Burnham Lambert. (No commas.) Defunct U.S. investment bank.

Dreyfus, Alfred. (1859–1935) French officer whose wrongful imprisonment on Devil's Island became a celebrated controversy.

Dreyfuss, Richard. (1949–) American actor.

drier, dryer. *Drier* is the condition of being more dry; a *dryer* is an appliance for drying clothes or hair.

droit de/du seigneur. A feudal lord's supposed right to spend the first night with a vassal's bride.

drunkenness. Note *-nn-*.

dual, duel. *Dual* means twofold; *duel* describes a fight between two parties.

du Barry, Marie Jeanne Bécu, Comtesse. (1743–1793) Mistress of Louis XV, beheaded during the French Revolution.

Dubček, Alexander. (1921–1992) First secretary of the Communist Party (i.e., head of state) in Czechoslovakia (1968–69); his reforms led to the Soviet invasion of the country in 1968.

dubiety. The state of being dubious.

Du Bois, W(illiam) E(dward) B(urghardt). (1868–1963) American political activist and civil rights leader.

Duchamp, Marcel. (1887–1968) French painter.

dudgeon. Feeling of resentment.

duenna. Governess or chaperon; in Spanish, *dueña*.

due to. Most authorities continue to accept that *due* is an adjective only and must always modify a noun. Thus, "He was absent due to illness" would be wrong. Make it either "He was absent because of [or owing to] illness" or recast the sentence to give *due* a noun to modify, e.g., "His absence was due to illness." The rule is mystifyingly inconsistent—no one has ever really explained why "owing to" used prepositionally is acceptable while "due to" used prepositionally is not—but it should perhaps still be observed, at least in formal writing, if only to avoid a charge of ignorance.

duffel bag, duffel coat. After Belgian town **Duffel.**

Dufy, Raoul. (1877–1953) French painter.

Duisburg, Germany; pronounced *doos-boork.*

Dukakis, Michael (Stanley). (1933–) U.S. presidential candidate (1988); governor of Massachusetts (1975–1979, 1983–1990).

Duma. Russian parliament.

Dumas, Alexandre. (1802–1870) French novelist and dramatist.

Dumbarton Oaks, Washington, D.C.

dumdum bullet.

dumfound (pref.), **dumbfound** (alt.).

dummkopf. (Ger.) Not *dumb-.* A stupid person.

Dum spiro, spero. (Lat.) "While I breathe, there is hope."

Dun & Bradstreet Corporation.

Dunkin' Donuts.

Dunkirk. French port; in French, Dunkerque.

Dun Laoghaire. Irish port near Dublin; pronounced *dun-leery.* In the Gaelic spelling *Dún* has an accent.

Duns Scotus, Johannes. (c. 1270–1308) Scottish philosopher and theologian.

duomo. (It.) Cathedral; pl. *duomi.*

Du Pont. U.S. chemicals business; formally E.I. du Pont de Nemours & Company. But on second or informal references it is normally spelled *DuPont* (one word). The place in Washington, D.C., is **Dupont Circle.**

du Pré, Jacqueline. (1945–1987) British cellist.

Dürer, Albrecht. (1471–1528) German artist and engraver.

duress.

durum. A type of wheat.

Dushanbe. Capital of Tajikistan.

Düsseldorf. Capital of North Rhine-Westphalia, Germany.

Dutchess County, New York State.

Dutch Guiana. Former name of Surinam.

Dvořák, Antonin. (1841–1904) Czech composer.

dwarfs is generally preferred to *dwarves.*

dyeing, dying. The first means adding color; the second means becoming dead.

dysentery.

dyslexia.

dysprosium. Chemical element.

dystrophy. Lacking adequate nutrition.

Dzibilchaltún National Park, Mexico.

Ee

each. When *each* precedes the noun or pronoun to which it refers, the verb should be singular: "Each of us was . . ." When it follows the noun or pronoun, the verb should be plural: "They each were . . ." *Each* not only influences the number of the verb, it also influences the number of later nouns and pronouns. In simpler terms, if *each* precedes the verb, subsequent nouns and pronouns should be plural (e.g., "They each are subject to sentences of five years"), but if *each* follows the verb, the subsequent nouns and pronouns should be singular ("They are each subject to a sentence of five years").

each and every is hopelessly tautological. Choose one or the other.

each other, one another. A few arbiters of usage continue to insist on *each other* for two things and *one another* for more than two. There is no harm in observing such a distinction, but also little to be gained from it, and, as Fowler long ago noted, the practice has no basis in historical usage. The possessive form is *each other's,* not *each others'.*

EADS. Short for European Aeronautic Defense and Space Company, maker of Airbus planes.

Eagels, Jeanne. (1890–1929) American actress.

Earhart, Amelia. (1897–1937) Female aviator who disappeared while trying to circumnavigate the globe.

Earl's Court, London.

Earnhardt, Dale. (1951–2001) Racecar driver.

earring. Note *-rr-*.

Earth, earth. When considering it as a planet, particularly in apposition to other cosmic features, *Earth* is normally capitalized. In more general senses ("He shot the arrow and it fell to earth") lowercase is usually favored.

East Chester, New York, and **Eastchester,** New York (separate places).

eau-de-vie. The French term for brandy; pl. *eaux-de-vie.*

eBay.

Ebbets Field, Brooklyn, New York; home of the Brooklyn Dodgers, 1913–1957.

EBITDA. Short for *earnings before interest, taxes, depreciation, and amortization*; in finance, it is a measure of a company's profits before various deductions.

Ecclesiastes, Ecclesiasticus. The first is a book in the Old Testament; the second a book in the Old Testament Apocrypha.

ECG. Electrocardiogram.

éclat. Brilliant display or effect, notable success, renown.

Eco, Umberto. (1932–) Italian academic and novelist.

economic, economical. If what you mean is cheap and thrifty, use *economical.* For every other sense use *economic.* An economic rent is one that is not too cheap for the landlord. An economical rent is one that is not too expensive for the tenant.

ecstasy.

Ecuadorean is generally the preferred spelling for a person or product from Ecuador.

Eddy, Mary Baker. (1821–1910) American religious leader, founder of the Christian Science church, formally the Church of Christ, Scientist.

edema. Swelling of body tissue as a result of abnormal retention of fluid.

Edgware Road. Street and Underground station in London.

Edmonton. Capital of Alberta, Canada.

Eduskunta. Parliament of Finland.

EEG. Electroencephalogram.

eerie.

effect, affect. As a verb, *effect* means to accomplish ("The prisoners effected an escape"); *affect* means to influence ("Smoking may affect your health") or to adopt a pose or manner ("He affected ignorance"). As a noun, the word needed is almost always *effect* (as in "personal effects" or "the damaging effects of war"). *Affect* as a noun has a narrow psychological meaning to do with emotional states (by way of which it is related to *affection*).

effete does not mean effeminate and weak, as it is often used. It means exhausted and barren. An *effete* poet is not necessarily foppish, but rather someone whose creative impulses are spent.

e.g., i.e. (Lat.) The first is an abbreviation of *exempli gratia* and means "for example," as in "Some words are homonyms, e.g., *blew* and *blue*." The second is the abbreviation for *id est* and means "that is" or "that is to say," as in "He is pusillanimous, i.e., lacking in courage."

eggplant. Commonly known elsewhere as *aubergine*.

Eglin Air Force Base, Florida.

egoism, egotism. The first pertains to the philosophical notion that a person can prove nothing beyond the existence of his own mind. It is the opposite of altruism and is better left to contexts involving metaphysics and ethics. If all you wish to suggest is inflated vanity or preoccupation with the self, use *egotism*.

Eichmann, Adolf. (1906–1962) Notorious Nazi war criminal, head of Gestapo; captured in Argentina by Israeli agents in 1960 and tried and executed in Israel.

Eiffel Tower, Paris, but **Eifel Mountains,** Germany.

Eileithyia. Greek goddess of childbirth.

Eindhoven, Netherlands.

Eisenbahn (Ger.) Railroad.

Eisenhower, Dwight David. (1890–1969) U.S. general and president (1953–1961).

Eisenstaedt, Alfred. (1898–1995) German-born American photographer.

Eisenstein, Sergei. (1898–1948) Russian filmmaker.

eisteddfod. Welsh festival or competition of music or literature; pl. *eisteddfods* or (in Welsh) *eisteddfodau*.

either. *Either* suggests a duality and is almost always better avoided when the context involves quantities of more than two, as in "Decisions on Mansfield's economy are now made in either Detroit, Pittsburgh, or New York." Often in such constructions, *either* is unnecessary anyway; delete it and the sentence says no less. A separate problem with *either* is seen here: "But in every case the facts either proved too elusive or the explanations too arcane to be satisfactory." *Either* should be placed before "the facts" or deleted; for a further discussion, see BOTH . . . AND. For a discussion of errors of number involving *either,* see NEITHER.

eke means to add to something in a meager way or with difficulty, not to gain a close but favorable result. A hungry person might *eke* out a supply of food, but a football team does not eke out a victory.

El Alamein/Al Alamayn. Egyptian village that gave its name to two battles in World War II.

El Dorado. Legendary city of gold.

Electra. In Greek mythology, the daughter of Agamemnon and Clytemnestra, and the subject of plays by Sophocles, Euripedes, and Aeschylus. An Electra complex is an unnatural attachment to a father by a daughter.

electrolyte. A solution that conducts electricity.

elegy, eulogy. The first is a mournful poem; the second is a tribute to the dead.

elemental, elementary. *Elemental* refers to things that are basic or primary: "Physiology is an elemental part of a medical student's studies." *Elementary* means simple or introductory: "This phrase book provides an elementary guide to Spanish."

elephantiasis. Condition of abnormal swelling caused by disease of the lymph nodes.

Elgin Marbles, British Museum, is pronounced with a hard *g*: *el-gin*, not *el-jin.*

elicit, extract, extort. These three are broadly synonymous, but are distinguished by the degree of force that they imply. *Elicit*, the mildest of the three, means to draw or coax out, and can additionally suggest an element of craftiness: you can elicit information without the informant being aware that he has divulged it. *Extract* suggests a stronger and more persistent effort, possibly involving threats or importuning. *Extort* is stronger still and suggests clear threats of violence or harm.

Eli Lilly. Not *Lilley.* U.S. pharmaceuticals company.

Eliot, George. Pen name of Mary Ann (later Marian) Evans (1819–1880), English author.

Eliot, T. S. (for Thomas Stearns) (1888–1965) American-born British poet, critic, and playwright; awarded Nobel Prize for Literature (1948).

Ellice Islands. Pacific island group; now called Tuvalu.

Elliott Bay, Seattle.

Elliott, Denholm. (1922–1992) British actor.

Ellis Island. Site of former immigration center in New York.

El Salvador. Central American country; capital San Salvador. The people are Salvadorans.

Elstree. Film studios, England.

Élysée Palace, Paris. Official home of French presidents. Not *the.*

Elysium, Elysian Fields. In Greek mythology, paradise.

embalmment. Note *-mm-.*

embarrass, embarrassment. Both are misspelled more often than they should be. Note, however, that the French spelling is *embarras*, as in *embarras de richesses* ("an embarrassment of riches") and *embarras du choix* ("an embarrassment of choice").

Emerson, Ralph Waldo. (1803–1882) American poet and essayist.

émigré. An emigrant, particularly a political refugee.

Emilia-Romagna. Region of Italy; capital Bologna.

Emmanuel College, Cambridge University, England.

Emmental. A type of cheese.

empathy, sympathy. *Empathy* denotes a close emotional understanding of the feelings or problems of another. It is thus close in meaning to *compassion*. *Sympathy* is more general. It can denote a closeness of understanding, but it can equally suggest no more than an abstract or intellectual awareness of another's misfortune. *Empathy* generally applies only to serious misfortunes; *sympathy* can apply to any small annoyance or setback.

Empedocles. (c. 495–c. 435 BC) Greek philosopher and poet.

emphysema.

empower. Not *en-*.

EMU. In the context of the European Union, it stands for Economic (not *European*) and Monetary Union.

encomium. A lavish tribute or eulogy; pl. *encomiums*.

encumbrance. Not *-erance*.

encyclopedia, encyclopedist, but *Encyclopaedia Britannica*.

endemic. See EPIDEMIC.

Endymion. In Greek mythology, a young man loved by the moon and condemned to eternal sleep.

enfant terrible. (Fr.) Troublesome young person; anyone of embarrassingly indiscreet or unruly behavior.

Engels, Friedrich. (1820–1895) German socialist.

Englischer Garten, Munich, Germany.

Enniskillen, Northern Ireland, site of infamous IRA bombing in 1987.

ennoble.

ennui.

enormity does not, as is frequently thought, indicate size, but rather refers to something that is wicked, monstrous, and outrageous ("The enormity of Hitler's crimes will never be forgotten"). If what you require is a word denoting large scale, try "immensity" or "vastness."

en passant. (Fr.) "In passing."

enroll, enrollment.

entelechy. The act of changing from potential to actual, or a kind of vital force for living things.

entente cordiale. Term used to describe a long-standing amity between countries.

Entertaining Mr. Sloane. Not *Sloan.* Comedy by Joe Orton (1964).

enthrall.

entomology. The study of insects.

entr'acte. Interval between acts or an entertainment performed then.

entrecôte. Tenderloin.

entrepôt. A trading place or storehouse.

envelop. (Verb.) To wrap up.

envelope. (Noun.) Container for letters, or anything that envelops.

envisage, envision. Both words suggest the calling up of a mental image. *Envision* is slightly the loftier of the two. You might envision a better life for yourself, but if all you are thinking about is how the dining room will look when the walls have been repainted, *envisage* is probably the better word. If no mental image is involved, neither word is correct. A rough rule is that if you find yourself following either word with *that,* you are using it incorrectly, as here: "He envisaged that there would be no access to the school from the main road" (cited by Gowers).

EOKA. Ethniki Organosis Kypriakou Agonos (National Organization for Cypriot Struggle), Greek Cypriot underground movement.

E.On. German utility company.

epaulet. A decoration worn on the shoulder of a uniform; in French, *épaulette.*

EPCOT. Environmental Prototype Community of Tomorrow, Disney World, Florida.

épée. Thin, flexible sword used in fencing.

ephemera, pl. *ephemeras/ephemerae.*

epicene. Of uncertain sex.

epicurean. Person devoted to the pursuit of pleasure; when capitalized it refers to the philosophy of Epicurus.

epidemic. Strictly speaking, only people can suffer an epidemic (the word means "in or among people"). An outbreak of disease among animals is *epizoötic.* It is also worth noting that *epidemic* refers only to outbreaks. When a disease or other problem is of long standing, it is *endemic.*

epiglottis.

epigram, epigraph. The first is a short, witty saying or poem. The second is an inscription, as on a monument or statue, or an introductory quotation at the beginning of a book or substantial block of text.

Epiphany. January 6, or the twelfth day of Christmas on the Christian calendar.

"Epipsychidion." Poem by Shelley (1821).

epistemology. The theory of knowledge.

epithet, strictly speaking, describes a word or phrase that is used in place of a name. Calling Tarzan "King of the Jungle" is to employ an epithet. More commonly nowadays, however, *epithet* is used to describe an abusive or contemptuous utterance. A few authorities disdain this looser usage, but it is accepted now by most dictionaries. *Epithet* should not be confused with *epitaph,* which is an inscription on a gravestone or other written memorial to a dead person.

E pluribus unum. (Lat.) "Out of many, one"; the motto on the official seal of the United States.

equable, equitable. Most dictionaries define *equable* as meaning steady and unvarying, but it should also convey the sense of being remote from extremes. A consistently hot climate is not equable, no matter how unvarying the temperature. Similarly, someone whose outlook is invariably sunny cannot properly be described as having an equable temperament. *Equitable*, with which *equable* is sometimes confused, means fair and impartial. An equitable settlement is a just one.

equally as is always wrong; a thing is equally good, not equally as good.

Equatorial Guinea. Formerly Spanish Guinea; West African country; capital Malabo.

equerry. Royal attendant.

equivocator.

Equuleus. Constellation near Pegasus.

equus. Latin for "horse."

Erasmus, Desiderius. (1466–1536) Dutch philosopher.

Eratosthenes. (c. 276–c. 194 BC) Greek mathematician, astronomer, and geographer; calculated Earth's circumference.

Erdoğan, Recep Tayyip. (1954–) Prime minister of Turkey (2003–).

Ericson (or **Ericsson** or **Eriksson**), **Leif.** (c. tenth c.) Norse explorer. The Swedish electrical group is **Ericsson.**

Erie Lackawanna Railway.

Erving, Julius. (1950–) American basketball player, known as "Dr. J."

escutcheon. A shield bearing a coat of arms.

Eskimos is the plural of *Eskimo*, but the preferred term is **Inuit** (sing. and pl.).

esophagus, esophageal.

especially, specially. *Specially* means for a specific purpose or occasion, as in "a specially designed wedding dress." *Especially* means particularly or exceptionally, as in "an especially talented singer." A simple guide is to ask yourself whether you could substitute *particularly*. If so, the word you want is *especially*.

esthetic is acceptable, but **aesthetic** is generally preferred.

estimated at about, as in "The crowd was estimated at about 50,000," is wrong. Because *estimated* contains the idea of an approximation, *about* is superfluous. Delete it.

Eszterhas, Joe. (1944–) Hungarian-born American screenwriter.

ETA. Euzkadi ta Azkatasuna (Basque Nation and Liberty), Basque separatist organization. (ETA can also mean "estimated time of arrival.")

et al. An abbreviation of the Latin *et alia, et alibi,* and *et alii,* meaning, respectively, "of other things," "of other places," and "of other persons"; note period (full stop) after *al* only.

et cetera when spelled out, but **etc.** (closed up) when abbreviated.

Ethernet. (Cap.)

etiology, etiolate.

Etobicoke. Toronto suburb.

Étoile, L'. Area around the Arc de Triomphe in Paris.

"Et tu, Brute?" (Lat.) "You too, Brutus?" Julius Caesar's dying words in Shakespeare's play *Julius Caesar* (3.1.77).

etymology. The study of the origin and development of words.

eucalyptus, pl. *eucalyptuses.*

Euclidean.

eukaryotes.

Eumenides. In Greek mythology, another name for the Furies.

euonymus. Any tree or shrub of the genus *Euonymous.*

euphemism. A mild expression substituted for another more objectionable or indelicate one.

euphuism and **euphuistic** describe a pretentiously elevated style of writing, after John Lyly's *Euphues: The Anatomy of Wit* (1578).

Euratom. European Atomic Energy Community.

Euripides. (c. 484–406 BC) Greek dramatist.

euro (lowercase) for the unit of currency used by most, but not all, of the nations of the European Union since early 2002.

European Court of Human Rights, based in Strasbourg, deals with issues of civil liberties arising out of the European Convention on Human Rights; it has no connection with the European Union or the UN.

European Court of Justice, in Luxembourg, is a European Union institution dealing exclusively with disputes involving member states.

European Organization for Nuclear Research is more commonly called CERN (from Conseil Européen pour la Recherche Nucléaire).

European Union was formed in 1967 with a formal merger between the European Economic Community, the European Coal and Steel Community, and the European Atomic Energy Community. As of 2007, it had twenty-seven members: Austria, Belgium, Bulgaria, Cyprus, Czech Republic, Denmark, Estonia, Finland, France, Germany, Greece, Hungary, Ireland, Italy, Latvia, Lithuania, Luxembourg, Malta, Netherlands, Poland, Portugal, Romania, Slovakia, Slovenia, Spain, Sweden, United Kingdom.

Eurydice. In Greek mythology, wife of Orpheus.

Eustachian tube. (Cap. E.) Passage connecting middle ear to nasopharynx.

euthanasia.

evangelical, evangelistic. Generally, *evangelical* is better reserved for contexts pertaining to adherence to the Christian gospel. If you need a word to describe militant zeal or the like, *evangelistic* is almost always better (e.g., "the evangelistic fervor of the Campaign for Nuclear Disarmament").

eventuate. "Competition for economic interest, power and social esteem can eventuate in community formation only if . . ." (*British Journal of Sociology*, cited by Hudson). A pompous synonym for *result.*

everyday (adj.), **every day** (adverb). "He was wearing everyday clothes" but "We come here every day."

exaggerate.

exasperate.

Excalibur. Not -*er.* King Arthur's sword.

ex cathedra. (Lat.) With authority.

excavator.

exception proves the rule, the. A widely misunderstood expression. As a moment's thought should confirm, it isn't possible for an exception to confirm a rule—but then, that isn't the sense that was originally intended. *Prove* here is a "fossil"—that is, a word or phrase that is now meaningless except within the confines of certain sayings (*hem and haw, rank and file,* and *to and fro* are other fossil expressions). Originally *prove* meant test (it comes from the Latin *probo,* "I test"), so "the exception proves the rule" meant—and really still ought to mean—that the exception tests the rule. The original meaning of *prove* is preserved more clearly in two other expressions: *proving ground* and *the proof of the pudding is in the eating.*

exchangeable.

excisable.

excitable.

exhalation.

exhaustible.

exhilarate.

exhort, exhortation.

exigent, exiguous. The first means urgent and pressing or exacting and demanding; the second means scanty and slender. But both have a number of synonyms that may spare the reader a trip to the dictionary.

ex officio (Lat.) By virtue of one's office or position.

exorbitant.

exorcise.

expatriate. One who lives abroad. Not to be confused in spelling or meaning with *compatriot*.

expectorate, spit. The distinction between these two is not, it must be conceded, often a matter of great moment, but still it is worth noting that there is a distinction. To *spit* means to expel saliva; to *expectorate* is to dredge up and expel phlegm from the lungs. *Expectorate* therefore is not just an unnecessary euphemism for *spit*, but it is usually an incorrect one.

Expedition of Humphry Clinker, The. Not *Humphrey*. Novel by Tobias Smollett (1771).

ex post facto. (Lat.) "After the fact."

expressible. Not *-able*.

extempore, impromptu. Although both words describe unrehearsed remarks or performances, their meanings are slightly different in that *impromptu* can apply only to acts that are improvised at the time of performance, whereas *extempore* suggests only that the actions were undertaken without the benefit of notes or other formal props. *Impromptu*, in other words, conveys a greater element of surprise on the part of the speaker or performer.

extraneous. Not *exter-*.

extrovert. Not *extra-*.

ExxonMobil Corporation. U.S. oil company.

eyeing.

Ezeiza Airport, Buenos Aires.

E-ZPass. Trademarked toll collection system.

Ff

FAA. Federal Aviation Administration.

fable, parable, allegory, myth. *Fables* and *parables* are both stories intended to have instructional value. They differ in that parables are always concerned with religious or ethical themes, while fables are usually concerned with more practical considerations (and frequently have animals as the characters). An *allegory* is an extended metaphor—that is, a narrative in which the principal characters represent things that are not explicitly stated. Orwell's *Animal Farm* is an allegory. *Myths* originally were stories designed to explain some belief or phenomenon, usually the exploits of superhuman beings. Today the word can signify any popular misconception or invented story.

facile is usually defined as easy, smooth, without much effort. But the word should contain at least a suggestion of derision. Facile writing isn't just easily read or written; it is also lacking in substance or import.

facsimile. An exact copy.

factious, factitious. *Factious* applies to factions; it is something that promotes internal bickering or disharmony. *Factitious* applies to that which is artificial or a sham; applause for a despotic ruler may be factitious. Neither should be confused with *fractious,* a term for something that is unruly or disorderly, as in "a fractious crowd."

Faerie Queene, The. Epic poem by Edmund Spenser (1589–1596).

Faeroe Islands/The Faroes. Danish islands in the North Atlantic between Scotland and Iceland; in Danish, Faeröerne.

Fahd bin Abdul Aziz. (1923–2005) King of Saudi Arabia (1982–2005).

Fahrenheit. (Cap.) Temperature scale that sets freezing at 32 degrees and boiling at 212; named after the German physicist **Gabriel Daniel Fahrenheit** (1686–1736). To convert Celsius to Fahrenheit, multiply the Celsius temperature by 1.8 and add 32, or use the table in the Appendix.

faience. A kind of glazed pottery.

Fairleigh Dickinson University.

fairway, not *fare-*, in golf.

fait accompli. (Fr.) An accomplished fact; pl. *faits accomplis*.

Falange, Phalange. The first is a political party in Spain; the second a political party in Lebanon.

fallible.

Fallujah. Sunni Muslim stronghold in central Iraq besieged by American troops in 2004.

fandango. Lively Spanish dance; pl. *fandangoes/fandangos*.

Faneuil Hall, Boston; pronounced *fan-yull*.

Fannie Mae/Fannie May. The first is the nickname for the Federal National Mortgage Association and the bonds it issues; the second is a long-established candy company. See also FREDDIE MAC.

FAO. Food and Agriculture (not Agricultural) Organization, a UN body.

Farabundo Martí National Liberation Front. Salvadoran revolutionary movement.

Faraday, Michael. (1791–1867) British chemist and physicist.

FARC. Short for Fuerzas Armadas Revolucionarias de Colombia (Revolutionary Armed Forces of Colombia), guerrilla group.

Far from the Madding Crowd. Not *Maddening*. Novel by Thomas Hardy (1874).

Farne Islands, Northumberland, England.

farrago. A confused mixture; pl. *farragoes*.

Farrar, Straus & Giroux. Not *Strauss*. U.S. publisher.

Farrell, James T(homas). (1904–1979) American novelist.

farther, further. Insofar as the two are distinguished, *farther* usually appears in contexts involving literal distance ("New York is farther from Sydney than from London") and *further* in contexts involving figurative distance ("I can take this plan no further").

fascia.

fascism, fascist.

Fassbinder, Rainer Werner. (1946–1982) German filmmaker.

Fates, the. In Greek mythology, the three daughters of Nyx: Clotho, Lachesis, and Atropos; they are known as the Moerae in Greek and Parcae in Latin.

Father's Day. (Sing.)

fatwa. Islamic decree.

Faubourg St.-Honoré, Rue du, Paris. Note *du.*

fauna, flora. The first means animals; the second, plants.

faute de mieux. (Fr.) "For lack of anything better."

fauvism. (No cap.) Short-lived school of expressionist art in France. Proponents, known as Les Fauves, included Matisse, Dufy, Braque, and Rouault.

faux bonhomme. (Fr.) A person whose superficial good nature disguises a darker side.

faux pas. (Fr.) An error or blunder; pl. same.

favela. (Port.) A Brazilian shantytown.

Fawkes, Guy. (1570–1606) Catholic rebel caught up in England's unsuccessful Gunpowder Plot. Guy Fawkes' (note apos.) Day is November 5 and marks the date of his capture, not execution.

faze. To disturb or worry; not to be confused with *phase.*

FCC. Federal Communications Commission, authority responsible for regulating television and radio.

FDIC. Federal Deposit Insurance Corporation, authority that steps in when banks fail. .

feasible. Not *-able.* The word does not mean probable or plausible, as is sometimes thought, but simply capable of being done. An action can be feasible without being either desirable or likely.

FedEx Corporation.

feet, foot. An occasional error is seen here: "Accompanied by Interior Secretary Gale Norton, the president also stopped at the 275-feet-high General Sherman Tree, a sequoia thought to be one of the largest living things on Earth." When one noun qualifies another, the first is normally singular. That is why we talk about toothbrushes rather than teethbrushes and horse races rather than horses races. Exceptions can be found—*systems analyst, singles bar*—but usually these appear only when the normal form would produce ambiguity. When a noun is not being made to function as an adjective, the plural is the usual form. Thus a wall that is six feet high is a six-foot-high wall. (For a discussion of the punctuation distinction, see HYPHEN in the Appendix.)

Fehn, Sverre. (1924–) Norwegian architect.

feijoada. Brazilian national dish.

Feininger, Lyonel. (1871–1956) American artist; note unusual spelling of first name.

Feinstein, Dianne. (1933–) Democratic senator from California.

feisty.

feldspar.

Fellini, Federico. (1920–1993) Italian film director.

FEMA. Federal Emergency Management Agency.

femto-. Prefix meaning one-quadrillionth.

Ferlinghetti, Lawrence. (1920–) American poet and writer.

Fermanagh, Northern Ireland county.

Ferrara. City in Emilia-Romagna, Italy.

Ferrari. Italian car.

Ferraro, Geraldine (Anne). (1935–) American Democratic politician, ran as vice presidential candidate with Walter Mondale in 1984.

ferrule, ferule. A *ferrule* is a metal cap or band used to strengthen a tool, as with the metal piece that attaches the brush to the handle of a paintbrush. A *ferule* is a ruler or stick used for punishment.

fervid means intense; not to be confused with *fetid*, meaning foul-smelling.

fettuccine.

Feuchtwanger, Lion. (1884–1958) German writer.

feu de joie. (Fr.) Ceremonial salute with gunfire; pl. *feux de joie.*

Feuerbach, Ludwig. (1804–1872) German philosopher.

feuilleton. Section of French newspaper containing literary reviews, fiction serializations, or other pieces of light journalism.

fever, temperature. You often hear sentences like "John had a temperature yesterday" when in fact John has a temperature every day. Strictly speaking, what he had yesterday was a fever.

fewer, less. Use *less* with singular nouns (less money, less sugar) and *fewer* with plural nouns (fewer houses, fewer cars).

Feydeau, Georges. (1862–1921) French playwright known for farces.

Feynman, Richard. (1918–1988) American physicist.

fiancé (masc.), **fiancée** (fem.).

Fianna Fáil. Irish political party; pronounced *fee-yan'-a foil.*

Fiat. Abbreviation of Fabbrica Italiana Automobile Torino, Italian car manufacturer.

fiddle-de-dee.

FIDE. Fédération Internationale des Échecs, world governing body of chess.

Fidei Defensor. (Lat.) "Defender of the Faith."

FIFA. Fédération Internationale de Football Associations, world governing body of soccer.

fifth column. Enemy sympathizers working within their own country; the term comes from the Spanish Civil War when General Emilio Mola boasted that he had four columns of soldiers marching on Madrid and a *fifth column* of sympathizers waiting in the city.

Fifth Third Bancorp. U.S. banking group.

filament.

filet, fillet. Use the first when the phrase or context is distinctly French (*filet mignon*), but otherwise use *fillet*.

filial.

filibuster.

filigree.

Filipino (masc.)/**Filipina** (fem.). A native of the Philippines.

fille de joie. (Fr.) A prostitute.

Fillmore, Millard. (1800–1874) Thirteenth U.S. president (1850–1853).

finagle. To secure by cajoling; to use trickery.

finalize is still objected to by many as an ungainly and unnecessary word, and there is no arguing that several other verbs—*finish, complete, conclude*—do the job as well without raising hackles.

fin de siècle. (Fr.) "End of the century"; normally applied to the end of the nineteenth century.

Fine Gael. Irish political party; pronounced *feen gayle*.

finial. Ornament on the pinnacle of a roof or similar.

finical, finicky. Both mean fussy, overprecise.

Finisterre, Cape. Westernmost point of Spanish mainland.

Finnegans Wake. (No apos.) Novel by James Joyce (1939).

fiord, fjord. Either is correct.

Firenze. The Italian for Florence.

first and foremost. Choose one.

first come first served. (No comma.)

first floor. Depending on context, it may be pertinent to remember that in Britain and elsewhere in the English-speaking world, the first floor is not the ground floor but the floor above it.

First Man in the Moon, The. H. G. Wells novel (1901); note *in*, not *on*.

Fischer, Bobby. (1943–2008) American chess player; world champion (1972–1975).

Fischer-Dieskau, Dietrich. (1925–) German baritone.

fish, fishes. Either is correct as a plural.

Fishburne, Laurence. (1961–) American actor.

Fisherman's Wharf, San Francisco. Not -*men's*.

fission, fusion. In physics, ways of producing nuclear energy: *fission* by splitting the nucleus of an atom, *fusion* by fusing two light nuclei into a single, heavier nucleus.

fisticuffs.

Fittipaldi, Emerson. (1946–) Brazilian racing car driver.

FitzGerald, Edward. (1809–1883) English scholar and poet, translator of Omar Khayyám's *Rubáiyát*.

Fitzwilliam Museum, Cambridge, England.

Fiumicino Airport, Rome. Formally it is Aeroporto Intercontinentale Leonardo da Vinci, but it is more commonly known by the name of its locality.

fjord, fiord. Either is correct.

fl. Floruit (Lat.), meaning "flourished"; used to indicate the productive period of a person ("fl. second century BC") for whom more specific dates are lacking.

flack, flak. The first is a slightly pejorative term for a publicist. The second, a contraction of the German *Fliegerabwehrkanonen*, is antiaircraft fire and by extension criticism or abuse.

flagon. A drinking vessel.

flair, flare. *Flair* is a knack for doing something well; *flare* describes a burst of flame or other phenomenon involving light.

flak. See FLACK, FLAK.

flaky.

flamingoes.

flammable, inflammable. *Inflammable* means capable of burning but has so often been taken to mean the opposite that most authorities now suggest it be avoided. It is generally better to use *flammable* for materials that will burn and *nonflammable* for those that will not.

flaunt, flout. To *flaunt* means to display ostentatiously, to show off. To *flout* means to treat with contempt, to disregard in a smug manner.

flautist. Person who plays a flute.

Fledermaus, Die. Operetta by Johann Strauss the Younger (1874).

Fleming. A native of Flanders, the Dutch-speaking part of Belgium; the adjective is *Flemish.*

Fleming, Sir Alexander. (1881–1955) British bacteriologist, discoverer of penicillin; shared Nobel Prize for Physiology or Medicine in 1945.

fleugelhorn (or **flügelhorn**). Brass musical instrument.

fleur-de-lis, pl. *fleurs-de-lis.*

flexible.

flibbertigibbet. A scatterbrain.

floccinaucinihilipilification. The act of estimating as worthless; sometimes cited as the longest word in English.

flora, fauna. The first means plants, the second animals.

florescent, fluorescent. The first means in flower, the second radiating light.

floruit. (Lat.) Abbr. *fl.;* "flourished"; used when the exact dates lived are not known. E.g., "Caedmon (fl. seventh c.)."

flotsam and jetsam. *Jetsam* is that part of a shipwreck that has been thrown overboard (think of *jettison*) and *flotsam* that which has floated off of its own accord. (A third type, wreckage found on the sea floor, is called *lagan.*) There was a time when the distinction was important: flotsam went to the crown and jetsam to the lord of the manor on whose land it washed up.

flounder, founder. *Founder* means to sink, either literally (as with a ship) or figuratively (as with a project). *Flounder* means to flail helplessly. It too can be used literally (as with someone struggling in deep water) or figuratively (as with a nervous person making an extemporaneous speech).

flourish.

flout, flaunt. The first means to disregard; the second to show off.

flügelhorn. Alt. spelling of *fleugelhorn*.

flummox.

flunky, flunkies.

fluorescent light.

fluoridate, fluoridation.

fluoroscope.

focaccia. An Italian bread.

fo'c'sle. Forecastle.

foehn. Type of warm mountain wind.

Fogg, Phileas. Not *Phogg*, not *Phineas*, for the character in Jules Verne's *Around the World in Eighty Days*.

Fogg Art Museum, Cambridge, Massachusetts.

fogy (or **fogey**). An old-fashioned person; pl. *fogies* (or *fogeys*).

föhn. See FOEHN.

foie gras. Fattened goose liver.

foley artist. (Not cap.) A specialist in dubbing sounds on film; named for **Jack Foley** (1891–1967), Hollywood sound effects editor.

Folger Shakespeare Library, Washington, D.C.

folie à deux. (Fr.) A delusion shared by two people.

Folies-Bergère. Parisian music hall.

Folketing. Danish parliament.

Fond du Lac, Wisconsin.

Fontainebleau. Château, town, and forest on the Seine near Paris; also a hotel in Miami, Florida.

Foochow. Use **Fuzhou** for the capital of Fujian Province, China. (It is pronounced *foo-jo'*.)

foot-and-mouth disease. (Hyphens.) Not *hoof-and-mouth*.

forbear, forebear. The first is a verb meaning to avoid or refrain from. The second is a noun and means ancestor.

forbid, prohibit. The words have the same meaning, but the construction of sentences often dictates which should be used. *Forbid* may be followed only by *to* ("I forbid you to go"). *Prohibit* may not be followed by *to*, but only by *from* ("He was prohibited from going") or by an object noun ("The law prohibits the construction of houses without planning consent"). Thus the following is wrong: "They are forbidden from uttering any public comments." Make it either "They are prohibited from uttering . . ." or "They are forbidden to utter . . ." A small additional point is that *forbid*'s past tense form, *forbade*, has the preferred pronunciation *for-bad*, not *for-bade*.

forceful, forcible, forced. *Forcible* indicates the use of brute force ("forcible entry"). *Forceful* suggests a potential for force ("forceful argument," "forceful personality"). *Forced* can be used for *forcible* (as in "forced entry"), but more often is reserved for actions that are involuntary ("forced march") or occurring under strain ("forced laughter," "forced landing").

force majeur. (Fr.) An uncontrollable event.

forcible.

forego, forgo. The first means to precede; the second means to do without. One of the most common spelling errors in English is to write *forego* when *forgo* is intended.

Forester, C. S. (for Cecil Scott) (1899–1966) English writer, chiefly remembered for naval adventures involving Horatio Hornblower; not to be confused with E. M. Forster.

foreword. An introduction to a book written by someone other than the book's author.

forgather. Not *fore-*. The need for the word is doubtful since *gather* says as much and says it more quickly.

formaldehyde. (Not cap.)

former, latter. *Former*, properly used, should refer only to the first of two things and *latter* to the second of two things. Both words, since they require the reader to hark back to an earlier reference, should be used sparingly and only when what they refer to is immediately evident. Few editing shortcomings are more annoying and less excusable than requiring a reader to re-cover old ground.

Formica is a trademark.

Formosa. Former name of Taiwan.

Fornebu Airport, Oslo, Norway.

Forster, E. M. (for Edward Morgan) (1879–1970) English novelist.

forswear.

forsythia.

forte. (Abbr. *f.*) In music, loud; also, a person's strong point.

fortissimo, fortississimo. The first (abbr. *ff.*) means very loud; the second (abbr. *fff.*) means as loud as possible.

Fort-Lamy. Former name of N'djamena, capital of Chad.

Fort Sumter, Charleston, South Carolina, site of first action in the Civil War.

fortuitous means by chance; it is not a synonym for *fortunate.* A fortuitous event may be fortunate, but equally it may not.

forty-niner. (No cap.) Participant in the 1849 California gold rush. The San Francisco football team is the **49ers** (no apos.).

For Whom the Bell Tolls. Not *Bells Toll.* Novel by Ernest Hemingway (1940).

Foucault pendulum. For the device (pronounced *foo-ko*), but ***Foucault's Pendulum*** (1988) for the novel by Umberto Eco.

founder, flounder. *Founder* means to sink, break down, or fail; *flounder* means only to struggle. A drowning person flounders; ships founder.

foundry. Not *-ery.*

Four Horsemen of the Apocalypse represent Conquest, Slaughter, Famine, and Death.

fourth estate. In Britain, the press. The other three estates are the Lords, the Commons, and the Church of England.

Fowler's. Common name for *A Dictionary of Modern English Usage* by **H. W. Fowler.**

Foxe, John. (1516–1587) English clergyman, most remembered for the book commonly known as *Foxe's Book of Martyrs*; not to be confused with **George Fox** (1624–1691), founder of the Society of Friends, or Quakers.

fraction. A few authorities continue to maintain that *fraction* in the sense of a small part is ambiguous: 99/100 is also a fraction but hardly a negligible part. The looser usage, however, has been around for at least three hundred years. Even so, it would be more precise to say "a small part" or "a tiny part." (See also PER-CENT, PERCENTAGE POINT.)

fractious. Disorderly.

France is divided into the following twenty-two regions (English version in parentheses where appropriate): Alsace, Aquitaine, Auvergne, Basse-Normandie, Bretagne (Brittany), Bourgogne (Burgundy), Centre, Champagne-Ardennes, Corse (Corsica), Franche-Comté, Haute-Normandie, Île-de-France, Languedoc-Roussillon, Limousin, Lorraine, Midi-Pyrénées, Nord-Pas-de-Calais, Pays-de-la-Loire, Picardie (Picardy), Poitou-Charentes, Provence-Alpes-Côte d'Azur, Rhône-Alpes.

Franche-Comté. Region of France.

Francis of Assisi, St. (1182–1226) Born Giovanni Francesco Bernardone; founder of Franciscan order of monks.

Frankenstein. The full title of the novel by Mary Wollstonecraft Shelley (1797–1851) is *Frankenstein, or the Modern Prometheus* (1818). Frankenstein is the scientist, not the monster.

Frankfurt am Main, western Germany, is not to be confused with **Frankfurt an der Oder,** eastern Germany, on the border with Poland. The towns in Indiana, Kentucky, Michigan, Ohio, and several other U.S. states are all **Frankfort.**

Frankfurter, Felix. (1882–1965) American jurist.

Franz Josef Land. Archipelago in the Barents Sea.

frappé. (Fr.) Iced, artificially chilled.

Frau. (Ger.) Married woman, pl. *Frauen.*

Fräulein. (Ger.) Sing. and pl., unmarried woman/women.

Frayn, Michael. (1933–) English writer.

Frazer-Nash. Not *Fraser-.* British sports car.

Freddie Mac. Nickname of U.S. Federal Home Loan Mortgage Corporation. See also FANNIE MAE/FANNIE MAY.

Fredericksburg, Virginia; site of battle in Civil War.

Fredericton. Capital of New Brunswick, Canada.

Frederiksberg. Suburb of Copenhagen.

freesia. Flowering plant.

Freiburg (im Breisgau) for the ancient university town in Baden-Württemberg, Germany, but **Freiberg** for its near namesake in Saxony.

Frelinghuysen, Rodney. (1946–) U.S. representative from New Jersey, one in a long line of politicians of that name in New Jersey.

Fremantle, Western Australia.

French Guiana. An overseas region of France on the South American mainland; capital Cayenne.

Frenchman Flat, Nevada; site of atomic bomb tests in 1950s.

French Somaliland. Former name of Djibouti.

fresh. Usually the word serves as an unobjectionable synonym for *new,* but it has additional connotations that make it inappropriate in some contexts, as the following vividly demonstrates: "Three weeks after the earthquake, fresh bodies have been found in the wreckage" (cited by Spiegl in *The Joy of Words*).

fricassee, pl. *fricassees.*

fricative. A type of consonant.

Friedan, Betty. (1921–2006) American feminist; born Elizabeth Naomi Goldstein.

Friedman, Milton. (1912–2006) American economist, awarded Nobel Prize for Economics (1976).

Friedrichshafen, Germany.

Friesian/Frisian. *Friesian* is a breed of cattle; *Frisian* is the name of a north Germanic language and of a chain of islands lying off, and politically divided between, the Netherlands, Denmark, and Germany. Friesian cattle in the United States are normally called Holsteins. *Frisian* is also sometimes applied to people from Friesland, the Dutch province that partly encompasses the Frisian islands.

frieze.

Friml, Rudolf. (1879–1972) Czech-born American pianist and composer of light operas.

Frisbee. (Cap.)

frisson. "A slight frisson went through the nation yesterday" (*London Times*). There is no other kind of frisson than a slight one. The word means shiver or shudder.

Friuli-Venezia Giulia. Region of Italy.

frontispiece. Illustration facing the title page of a book.

frowsty, frowzy. The first means musty or stale; the second, untidy or dingy.

Frühstück. (Ger.) Breakfast.

FTC. Federal Trade Commission.

Führer (pref.)**/Fuehrer** (alt.). German leader, particularly Adolf Hitler.

Fujiyama means Mount Fuji, so "Mount Fujiyama" is redundant. Make it either Fujiyama or Mount Fuji. The Japanese also call it Fujisan and Fuki-no-Yama.

fulfill, fulfillment, fulfilled, fulfilling.

fulsome means odiously insincere. "Fulsome praise," properly used, isn't a lavish tribute; it is unctuous and insincere toadying.

furor.

further, farther. Insofar as the two are distinguished, *farther* usually appears in contexts involving literal distance ("New York is farther from Sydney than from London") and *further* in contexts involving figurative distance ("I can take this plan no further").

Fusaichi Pegasus. Racehorse, winner of 2000 Kentucky Derby.

fusion, fission. Both describe ways of producing nuclear energy: *fu-sion* by fusing two light nuclei into a single, heavier nucleus; *fission* by splitting the nucleus of an atom.

future plans and similar locutions are nearly always redundant. If a person makes plans, it would follow that they are for the future.

Fuzhou. Formerly often written Foochow or Fouchou, capital of Fujian Province, China; pronounced *foo-jo'*.

Gg

gabardine, gaberdine. The first is a type of worsted cloth, the second a long cloak.

Gaborone. Capital of Botswana.

Gaddafi/Qaddafi, Muammar al-. (1942–) Libyan head of state (1969–). He has no official title or position.

Gadsden Purchase. Large purchase of territory by the United States from Mexico in 1853.

Gaeltacht. Any region of Ireland where Gaelic is the vernacular.

Gagarin, Yuri. (1934–1968) Soviet cosmonaut, first man in space (1961).

gage, gauge. The first is a pledge or a type of plum (as in *greengage*); the second is to do with scales and measurements.

Gaia (also, but rarely, **Gaea** or **Ge**). In early Greek mythology, the earth personified; later, goddess of the earth.

gaiety.

gaijin. (Jap.) "Outsider"; used of foreigners.

gaillardia. (Lowercase.) Type of flower of the genus *Gaillardia* (cap.).

Gainsborough, Thomas. (1727–1788) English painter.

Galahad, Sir. The purest and noblest knight in the Arthurian legend.

Galápagos Islands. Pacific islands belonging to Ecuador; their Spanish name is Archipiélago de Colón.

Galeries Lafayette. Paris department store.

Galileo. (1564–1642) Italian astronomer and mathematician; full name **Galileo Galilei.**

Gallaudet College, Washington, D.C.

gallimaufry. A jumble; pl. *gallimaufries.*

Gallipoli. Turkish peninsula and site of World War I campaign; in Turkish, Gelibolu.

gallivant. To wander.

Galsworthy, John. (1867–1933) English novelist, awarded Nobel Prize for Literature in 1932.

Gama, Vasco da. (Not *de.*) (c. 1469–1524) Portuguese explorer.

Gambia. (Not *the.*) African country, capital Banjul.

gambit. Properly, a gambit is an opening move that involves some strategic sacrifice or concession. All gambits are opening moves, but not all opening moves are gambits.

gamy. Not *-ey.*

Gandhi, Mohandas Karamchand. (1869–1948) Indian leader; called Mahatma, "great soul."

ganef/gonof. (Yid.) A thief or disreputable person.

gangrene. Not *-green.*

Gannett Company. Newspaper group.

Gannett Peak, Wyoming.

gantlet, gauntlet. For the sense of running between two lines of aggressors (whether literally or metaphorically) the normal spelling is *gantlet,* though *gauntlet* is usually also accepted. For the idea of a glove thrown down in challenge, the invariable spelling is *gauntlet.*

Ganymede. Fourth moon of Jupiter; in Greek mythology, the young Trojan who was made cupbearer to the gods.

García Lorca, Federico. (1899–1936) Spanish poet and playwright.

García Márquez, Gabriel. (1928–) Colombian novelist; awarded Nobel Prize for Literature in 1982.

Garda Síochána. Formal name of the police force in the Republic of Ireland, usually shortened to Garda; a member of the force is called a **garda** (not cap.), pl. *gardai.*

Gardner, Erle Stanley. (1889–1970) American writer of crime and courtroom fiction. Note unusual spelling of first name.

Garibaldi, Giuseppe. (1807–1882) Italian leader; played a central role in national unification.

garish. Gaudy.

Garmisch-Partenkirchen. German skiing resort.

Garonne. French river.

garote (or **garrote**). To strangle with an object.

gas, gases, gaseous, gasify, gasification, but **gassed** and **gassing.**

gasoline.

Gasthaus, Gasthof. The first is German for an inn or guesthouse; the second is German for a hotel. The plurals are *Gasthäuser* and *Gasthöfe.*

gastronome. A connoisseur of food.

GATT. General Agreement on Tariffs and Trade; UN agency that attempts to regulate world trade.

Gaudier-Brzeska, Henri. (1891–1915) French sculptor.

gauge, gage. The first is to do with scales and measurements; the second is a pledge or a type of plum (as in *greengage*).

Gaugin, (Eugène Henri) Paul. (1848–1903) French painter.

Gauloise. Brand of French cigarettes.

gauntlet. A form of punishment or severe criticism, as in "run the gauntlet"; to challenge, as in "throw down the gauntlet." See also GANTLET.

Gauthier-Villars. French publisher.

gauzy.

Gawain, Sir. One of the knights of Arthurian legend.

Gay-Lussac, Joseph Louis. (1778–1850) French chemist and physicist.

gazetteer.

gazpacho. Cold Spanish soup.

Gdańsk, Poland; formerly Danzig.

GDP, GNP. *GNP,* gross national product, is the total worth of everything produced by a nation during a given period, including earnings from abroad. *GDP,* gross domestic product, is everything produced by a nation during a given period, except earnings from abroad.

GDR. German Democratic Republic; the former East Germany.

geezer. An old man.

Geffrye Museum, London.

gefilte fish. (Yid.) Chopped-fish dish.

Gehrig, Lou. (1903–1941) Baseball player, full name Henry Louis Gehrig.

Gehry, Frank. (1929–) Canadian-American architect; born Ephraim Owen Goldberg.

Geiger counter. (Cap.) Measures radioactivity; devised by the German physicist Hans Geiger (1882–1945).

Geisenheimer wine.

gelatin is the usual spelling, but *gelatine* is also accepted.

Gell-Mann, Murray. (1929–) American physicist, awarded Nobel Prize for Physics in 1969.

gemütlich. (Ger.) Agreeable, comfortable, good-natured.

Gemütlichkeit. (Ger.) Congeniality, friendliness.

gendarmes are not policemen; they are soldiers employed in police duties, principally in the countryside. Police officers in French cities and towns are just that—police officers.

genealogy.

General Agreement on Tariffs and Trade. (Abbr. GATT.) UN body set up to promote world trade.

generalissimo, pl. *generalissimos.* But note in Spanish it is *generalisimo* (one *s*).

Geneva, Switzerland; it is Genève in French, Genf in German, and Ginevra in Italian; Lake Geneva is Lac Léman in French and Genfersee in German.

Geneva Convention. (1864; rev. 1950, 1978) International agreement on the conduct of war and treatment of wounded and captured soldiers.

Geneviève, Sainte. (c. 422–c. 512) Patron saint of Paris.

Genghis Khan. (1162–1227) Mongol conqueror.

genie, pl. *genies* or *genii*.

Genova. Italian for Genoa.

gentilhomme. (Fr.) Gentleman or nobleman; pl. *gentilshommes*.

Gentlemen's Quarterly. Not *-man's*. U.S. magazine, now called *GQ*.

gentoo. Breed of penguin.

genus, species. The second is a subgroup of the first. The convention is to capitalize the genus but not the species, as in *Homo sapiens*. The plurals are *genera* and *species*. The traditional order of divisions in taxonomy is phylum, class, order, family, genus, species.

Geographic Names, U.S. Board on. Not *Geographical*, not *of*.

George Town, Georgetown. *George Town* is the spelling for the capital of the Cayman Islands and the principal city of the island and state of Penang in Malaysia. Almost all others, including the capital of the South American country Guyana and the district and university in Washington, D.C., use the spelling *Georgetown*.

Gephardt, Richard Andrew "Dick." (1941–) Democratic politician, U.S. representative from Missouri (1977–2005).

gerbil. Not *jer-*.

Géricault, Jean Louis André Théodore. (1791–1824) French painter.

germane, relevant, material. *Germane* and *relevant* are synonymous. Both indicate a pertinence to the matter under discussion. *Material* has the additional connotation of being necessary. A material point is one without which an argument would be incomplete. A germane or relevant point will be worth noting but may not be essential to the argument.

Germany was partitioned into East Germany (Deutsche Demokratische Republik), with its capital in East Berlin, and West

Germany (Bundesrepublik Deutschland), with its capital at Bonn, in 1949. The two Germanys (not *-ies*) were reunited on October 3, 1990. The sixteen states, or Länder, are Baden-Württemberg, Bavaria, Berlin, Brandenburg, Bremen, Hamburg, Hesse, Lower Saxony, Mecklenburg–West Pomerania, North Rhine–Westphalia, Rhineland Palatinate, Saarland, Saxony, Saxony-Anhalt, Schleswig-Holstein, and Thuringia.

gerrymander means to distort or redraw to one's advantage, especially a political boundary. Not to be confused with JERRY-BUILT.

gerunds are verbs made to function as nouns, as with the italicized words in "I don't like *dancing*" and "*Cooking* is an art." Two problems commonly arise with gerunds:

1. Sometimes the gerund is unnecessarily set off by an article and preposition, as here: "They said that *the* valuing *of* the paintings could take several weeks." Deleting the italicized words would make the sentence shorter and more forceful.

2. Problems also occur when a possessive noun or pronoun (called a *genitive*) qualifies a gerund. A common type of construction is seen here: "They objected to him coming." Properly it should be: "They objected to his coming." Similarly, "There is little hope of Smith gaining admittance to the club" should be "There is little hope of Smith's gaining admittance . . ."

Gestapo. Short for *Geheime Staatspolizei*, German secret police during the Third Reich.

Gesundheit! Interjection made in response to a sneeze.

Gethsemane. Olive grove at Jerusalem where Jesus was betrayed.

gettable.

Getty, J(ean) Paul. (1892–1976) Not *John*. U.S. oil man and benefactor; his son **Jean Paul Getty II** (1932–) is also often given wrongly as John.

Gettysburg, Pennsylvania, is the site of a decisive (but not the final) battle of the Civil War (July 1863); locally pronounced *gettiz-burg*.

gewgaw. Worthless bauble.

Ghanaian for a person or thing from Ghana.

ghettos. Not *-oes*.

ghillie (or gillie). Scottish hunting or fishing assistant; also a type of shoe.

Ghirardelli Square, San Francisco.

ghiribizzoso. Musical term for whimsical playing.

Ghirlandaio, Il. (1449–1494) Florentine painter; real name Domenico di Tommaso Bigordi.

Giacometti, Alberto. (1901–1966) Swiss sculptor and painter.

Giannini, A. P. (1870–1949) American banker, founded Bank of America; full name Amadeo Peter Giannini.

Giant's Causeway, Northern Ireland. Not *Giants'*.

Gibbon, Edward. (1737–1794) Not *Gibbons*. English historian.

Gibbons, Grinling. (1648–1721) Dutch-born English sculptor and woodcarver.

gibe, jibe. The first means to taunt or ridicule; the second means to agree or be in accord. *Jibe* is also a nautical term.

giga-. Prefix meaning one billion.

gigolo, pl. *gigolos*.

Gilbert and Ellice Islands. Equatorial islands in Pacific Ocean; part of the Republic of Kiribati.

gild the lily. The passage from Shakespeare's *King John* is: "To gild refined gold, to paint the lily . . . Is wasteful and ridiculous excess." Thus it is both wrong and hackneyed to speak of "gilding the lily" in the sense of overdoing something.

Gilgamesh Epic. Babylonian epic poem.

Gillette. Brand of razors.

Gillray, James. (1757–1815) British caricaturist.

Gimbel Brothers. Former New York department store; commonly referred to as Gimbels (no apos.).

gingivitis. Not -*us*. Inflammation of the gums.

ginkgo. Not *gingko*. Asian tree; pl. *ginkgoes*.

Ginsberg, Allen. (1926–1997) American Beat poet.

Gioconda, La. Alternative name for the *Mona Lisa*.

Giorgione, Il. (1478–1510) Italian painter; full name Giorgio Barbarelli da Castelfranco.

Giotto. (c. 1266–1337) Italian painter and architect; full name Giotto di Bondone.

girlfriend, boyfriend. (Each one word.)

Giuliani, Rudolph ("Rudy") W. (1944–) Republican mayor of New York City (1994–2001).

giveable.

gizmo, pl. *gizmos.*

gladiolus, pl. *gladioli.*

glamour, but **glamorous, glamorize.**

glasnost. (Rus.) Literally "publicity"; the effort to make Soviet government and life more open.

glassful, pl. *glassfuls.*

Glaswegian. A person from Glasgow.

GlaxoSmithKline. (All one word.) Anglo-U.S. pharmaceuticals company.

Glenlivet. Whiskey.

Glens Falls, New York.

Gloria in excelsis Deo. (Lat.) "Glory be to God on high."

Gloucestershire. English county.

GmbH, for *Gesellschaft mit beschränkter Haftung.* (Ger.) Limited liability company.

GMT. Greenwich Mean Time.

gneiss. A kind of rock, similar to granite; pronounced *nice*.

gnocchi, for a type of Italian dumplings, is plural; a single dumpling is a *gnocco* (no *h*).

GNP, GDP. *GNP,* gross national product, is the total worth of everything produced by a nation during a given period, including earnings from abroad. *GDP,* gross domestic product, is everything produced by a nation during a given period, except earnings from abroad.

gobbledygook.

Gobelin tapestry. Named for a textile works in Paris.

Gobi Desert.

Godard, Jean-Luc. (1930–) French film director.

Goddard, Robert Hutchings. (1882–1945) American rocket scientist.

godsend, godforsaken, godhead (no caps.), but **God-awful, God-fearing,** and **Godspeed** (caps.).

Godthaab. Former name of the capital of Greenland; now called **Nuuk.**

Godwin Austen. Not *Austin*; no hyphen. More commonly called K2, the highest mountain in the Karakoram Range of the Himalayas.

Goebbels, Joseph. (1897–1945) German Nazi propaganda chief.

Goering/Göring, Hermann. (1893–1946) Leading Nazi, second in command to Hitler.

Goethe, Johann Wolfgang von. (1749–1832) German poet and dramatist.

Gogol, Nikolai. (1809–1852) Russian novelist and playwright.

Golgi body. Structure found within cells.

Gomorrah. Ancient city in Palestine.

Goneril. One of Lear's daughters in Shakespeare's *King Lear.*

gonof (or **ganef**). (Yid.) A thief or disreputable person.

gonorrhea.

Gonville and Caius College, Cambridge University, England; normally referred to as just Caius; pronounced *keys.*

goodbye. (One word.)

Good-natur'd Man, The. Comedy by Oliver Goldsmith (1768).

good will is the usual spelling, though **goodwill** is acceptable, particularly when referring to the reputation and trading value of a business.

Good Woman of Setzuan, The. Play by Bertolt Brecht (1941).

Google for the search engine, but **googol** for the very large number: a 1 followed by 100 zeroes.

GOP. Abbreviation of Grand Old Party, nickname of Republican Party.

Gorbachev, Mikhail (Sergeyevich). (1931–) General secretary of the Communist Party of the Soviet Union (1985–1991), president of the Supreme Soviet (1988–1991), president of the USSR (1990–1991).

Gordian knot. A complex problem. According to legend, King Gordius of Phrygia tied the knot and it was said that anyone who could undo it would rule Asia; Alexander the Great cut it with his sword. "To cut the Gordian knot" is to solve a difficult problem by a decisive action.

gorgheggio. Musical term for a trill.

Gorgons. In Greek mythology, three creatures (Medusa, Stheno, and Euryale) so ugly that anyone gazing at them turned to stone.

Gorgonzola (cap.) for the cheese and the village in Italy in which it originated.

gorilla.

Göring, Hermann. Use **Goering.**

Gorky, Maxim. Pseudonym of **Aleksei Maksimovich Peshkov** (1868–1936), Russian writer. The Russian city named for him has reverted to its original name of **Nizhny Novgorod.**

Gothenburg, Sweden; in Swedish, Göteborg.

Götterdämmerung. (Ger.) "Twilight of the gods." Last part of Wagner's *Ring* cycle; figuratively, a complete downfall.

gouache. A kind of opaque watercolor paint mixed with a gluelike preparation; a picture painted in this way or with such a pigment.

Gould, Elliott. (1938–) American film actor; note unusual spelling of first name; born Elliot Goldstein.

gourmand is a word to be used carefully. Some dictionaries now define it only as a person who likes to eat well, but others equate it with gluttony. Unless you mean to convey a pejorative sense, it would be better to use *gourmet, gastronome, epicure,* or some other more flattering term.

goy. (Yid.) A gentile; pl. *goyim.*

gracias. (Sp.) Thank you.

Gradgrind. (Cap.) A cold, emotionless person, after a character in Charles Dickens's *Hard Times.*

Graeae. In Greek mythology, three sisters who guard the Gorgons.

Graf, Steffi. (1969–) German tennis player.

graffiti is, strictly speaking, a plural. If all you mean is a single embellishment, the proper term is *graffito.* However, it must also be noted that fewer and fewer authorities insist on the distinction.

graham cracker. (Not cap.)

Grahame, Kenneth. (1859–1932) British writer, author of *The Wind in the Willows.*

Graian Alps. Stretch of alps along French-Italian border.

Gramm-Rudman Act. Law intended to reduce and eliminate U.S. federal deficit; formally, it is the Gramm-Rudman-Hollings Act.

Grammy, pl. *Grammys.* Musical awards formally known as the National Academy of Recording Arts and Sciences Awards.

gramophone. Not *grama-.*

Granada, Grenada. The first is the historic city in Spain, the second the Caribbean island state; capital St. George's. They are pronounced respectively *grə-nah-də* and *grə-nay-də.*

Grand Coulee Dam, Columbia River, Washington.

granddad, granddaughter. Note *-dd-.*

Grand Guignol. High drama, constructed around a sensational theme. The term comes from the Théâtre du Grand Guignol in Paris, where such plays were in vogue in the last years of the nineteenth century.

grandiloquence, not -*eloquence*, for inflated speech.

grand jury. In U.S. law, a jury of up to twenty-three people empowered to decide whether enough evidence exists for a case to proceed against an accused person.

Grand Ole Opry.

Grasmere, Cumbria, England; site of Dove Cottage, home of the poet William Wordsworth.

gratia Dei. (Lat.) "By God's grace."

grazie. (It.) Thank you.

Great American Ball Park. Cincinnati baseball stadium, home of the Reds. Note *Ball Park* is two words.

Greater London, Greater Paris, etc. Cap. *Greater.*

Great Smoky Mountains National Park, North Carolina and Tennessee.

Greco, El. (1541–1614) Cretan-born Spanish painter; real name Domenikos Theotokopoulos.

Greeley, Horace. (1811–1872) American politician and journalist, founder of the *New York Tribune* (1841). The expression "Go west, young man" is frequently attributed to him, probably wrongly.

Greene, Graham. (1904–1991) British writer.

Greene, Nathanael. (1742–1786) American Revolutionary War general.

Greenstreet, Sydney. (1879–1954) British character actor.

Gregorian calendar is the type now in use in most of the world; named for Pope Gregory XII.

Grenada. Small island state in the Caribbean, capital St. George's. Not to be confused with the Spanish city of **Granada.**

grenadier.

grenadine (lowercase) for the fabric and flavoring, but **Grenadines** (cap.) for the Caribbean island chain.

Grendel. Monster in *Beowulf.*

Gresham's Law is that "bad money drives out good"; attributed to Sir Thomas Gresham (1519–1579), British financier.

Greuze, Jean-Baptiste. (1725–1805) French painter.

Grey, Lady Jane. (1537–1554) Queen of England for ten days in 1553.

Grey, Zane. (1875–1939) American author.

Grey Friars for the Franciscan monks, but **Greyfriars College,** Oxford University.

greyhound.

Greylock, Mount. Massachusetts mountain.

Grieg, Edvard. (1843–1907) Norwegian composer.

grievous. Not *-ious.*

griffin is the usual spelling for a creature with an eagle's head and wings and a lion's body, but most dictionaries also accept **gryphon.**

Griffith-Joyner, Florence. (1959–1998) American sprinter.

grille is the usual spelling for the front part of a car or other metal grating, though **grill** is also acceptable.

Grimm, Brothers. Jacob Ludwig Carl Grimm (1785–1863) and **Wilhelm Carl Grimm** (1786–1859), German writers and philologists.

grisly, gristly, grizzly. Occasionally and variously confused. The first means horrifying or gruesome. The second applies to meat that is full of gristle. The third means gray, especially gray-haired, and is a cliché when applied to old men.

Grisons, Graubünden are respectively the French and German names for a single Swiss canton.

grosbeak. Species of finch.

groschen. Former Austrian coin.

gros rouge. (Fr.) Ordinary red table wine.

gross domestic product, gross national product. *Gross domestic product* is everything produced by a nation during a given period except earnings from overseas. *Gross national product* is everything produced by a nation during a given period including earnings from overseas. In most contexts, the reader is entitled to an explanation of the difference.

Grosse Pointe, Michigan.

Grosz, George. (1893–1959) German-born American artist.

Grósz, Karoly. (1930–1996) Prime minister of Hungary (1987–1988).

grotto, pl. *grottoes.*

Group of Eight, or **G8.** Leading industrial nations that meet regularly to discuss economic and trading issues. They are Canada, France, Germany, Italy, Japan, Russia, the United Kingdom, and the United States.

Grudzielanek, Mark. (1970–) American baseball player.

grueling.

gruesome.

Gruner + Jahr. German magazine publisher, part of Bertelsmann. Note the use of a plus sign instead of an ampersand.

gruyère cheese. But the Swiss town from which it takes its name is **Gruyères.**

GT. Gran Turismo.

Guadalajara. Cities in Spain and Mexico.

Guadalcanal, Solomon Islands; site of ferocious fighting in World War II.

Guadalupe, Guadeloupe. The cluster of islands in the Caribbean, which together form an overseas department of France, is *Guadeloupe.* Most other geographical features bearing the name, including a river and range of mountains in the southwestern United States, and towns or cities in California, Spain, Peru, and the Azores, spell it *Guadalupe.*

Guadalupe Hidalgo, Treaty of. 1848 treaty in which Mexico ceded to the United States what would become the states of Arizona, California, Colorado, Nevada, Texas, and Utah.

Guangdong, Guangzhou. *Guangdong* is the Chinese province formerly known as Kwantung. Its capital is *Guangzhou,* formerly Canton.

Guantánamo Bay, Cuba, site of U.S. naval base.

Guaragigna. African language.

guarantee, guaranty. *Guarantee* is generally used for the verb ("I guarantee a positive result") and *guaranty* for the noun ("The TV is still under guaranty"), but most dictionaries allow a wide overlap of definitions. If in doubt, use *guarantee.*

Guatemala. Central American country; capital Guatemala City.

Guayaquil, Santiago de. Largest city in Ecuador.

Guernica. Spanish town near Bilbao, ancient capital of the Basques; its bombing by German aircraft in April 1937 during the Spanish Civil War was the subject of a celebrated painting by Picasso. The town's full, formal name is **Guernica y Luno,** but this is seldom used and not necessary in most contexts.

guerrilla.

guesstimate is much overused and generally unnecessary in serious writing; all estimates are fundamentally guesses.

gueuze. Type of Belgian beer.

Guggenheim. The New York museum is formally the **Solomon R. Guggenheim Museum. Guggenheim Fellowships** are awarded by the **John S. Guggenheim Memorial Foundation.**

Guiana, Guyana. Some scope for confusion here, particularly if using old references. The name *Guiana* has at various times been attached to three contiguous territories on the Atlantic coast of northern South America. The westernmost, British Guiana, is now called *Guyana.* The central territory, Dutch Guiana, is now Suriname. The easternmost, an overseas department of France, remains French Guiana.

guillemet, guillemot. The first is the word for the chevron-like quotation marks [« »] used primarily in French and Spanish; pronounced *gee-yuh-meh'*. Not to be confused with the type of seabird known as a *guillemot*, pronounced *gill'-a-mot*.

guillotine.

guinea. (Not cap.) In Britain, a sum equivalent to one pound and one shilling or a coin of that value; no longer used.

Guinea, Guinea-Bissau, Equatorial Guinea. They are separate countries, all in West Africa. *Guinea* was formerly French Guinea. *Guinea-Bissau* was formerly Portuguese Guinea. *Equatorial Guinea* was formerly Spanish Guinea.

Guinevere. Wife of King Arthur.

Guinness stout, Sir Alec Guinness (1914–2000), **Guinness Book of World Records,** etc.

Guizhou. Chinese province; formerly spelled *Kweichow.*

Gujurat. Indian state; capital Gandhinagar.

gunny sack.

Gunpowder Plot. Conspiracy among a group of English Catholics to blow up the Houses of Parliament in 1605.

gunwale. Not *-whale*. The topmost edge of the side of a ship; pronounced *gunnel* and sometimes so spelled.

Guomindang. Chinese Nationalist Party, founded by Sun Yat-sen; formerly spelled **Kuomintang.** The syllable *-dang* contains the notion of party, so refer only to the Guomindang, not Guomindang Party.

Gurkha. (Cap.) Nepalese soldier in the British army.

guten Abend, but *gute Nacht.* German for "good evening" and "good night." (The daytime salutations are *guten Morgen* for "good morning" and *guten Tag* for "good day.")

Gutenberg, Johann. (c. 1400–1468) Born Johannes Gensfleisch; German credited with the invention of movable type.

Gutiérrez, Luis Vicente. (1953–) Democratic politician, U.S. representative from Illinois.

gutta-percha. Hard, rubbery substance produced from the latex of various tropical trees.

guttural. Not -*er*-.

Guyana. Formerly British Guiana. South American country; capital Georgetown.

Gwynedd. County of Wales; pronounced *gwin'-neth*.

Gwynn, Nell. (1605–1687) Born Eleanor Gwynne; actress and mistress of Charles II of England.

gynecology.

gypsy, pl. *gypsies.*

Hh

ha. is the abbreviation of **hectare.**

Häagen-Dazs. Ice cream.

Haakon VII. (1872–1957) King of Norway (1905–1957).

Haarlem, Netherlands, but **Harlem,** New York.

Haas, Ernst. (1921–1986) Austrian-born photographer.

Haas-Lilienthal House, San Francisco.

habeas corpus. (Lat.) "Deliver the body"; writ requiring that a person be brought before a court. Its purpose is to ensure that prisoners are not unlawfully detained.

habits. Take care not to write of someone's "customary habits" or "usual habits" and the like. Habits are always customary and always usual. That is, of course, what makes them habitual.

habitué (masc.), **habituée** (fem.).

Habsburg. Use **Hapsburg.**

Hadid, Zaha. (1950–) Iraqi-born British architect.

Haeckel, Ernst. (1834–1919) German naturalist.

Hågatña. Capital of Guam; formerly Agana.

Haggai. (fl. sixth c. BC) Hebrew prophet; also the book of his prophecies in the Old Testament.

haggis. Scottish dish.

Hague, The. (Cap. *T.*) In Dutch, Den Haag or 's Gravenhage; seat of government of the Netherlands (though Amsterdam is the capital).

hail, hale. *Hale* means robust and vigorous, or to drag or forcibly draw (as in "haled into court"), in which sense it is related to *haul. Hail* describes a greeting, a salute, or a downpour (as in "hailstorm" or "hail of bullets"). The expressions are *hale and hearty* and *hail-fellow-well-met*.

Haile Selassie. (1892–1975) Emperor of Ethiopia (1930–1936, 1941–1974).

Hainault. District of London.

hair's breadth, hairbreadth. Either is fine.

hajj. A pilgrimage to Mecca; one who has made the pilgrimage is a **hajji.**

haka. Maori war dance widely associated with New Zealand rugby appearances.

Hakluyt, Richard. (c. 1553–1616) English geographer; pronounced *hak'-loot.*

halberd. A combined spear and battle-ax, carried by a **halberdier.**

Halberstam, David. (1934–2007) American author and journalist.

Haleakala National Park, Maui, Hawaii.

halibut.

halitosis.

hallelujah.

Hallé Orchestra, Manchester, England.

Halley, Edmond. (1655–1742) Not *Edmund.* English astronomer; he did not discover the comet named after him, but rather predicted its return.

Halloween, in preference to *Hallowe'en.*

halo, pl. *halos.*

Hamelin. City in Germany (in German, Hameln), source of the legend of the Pied Piper of Hamelin.

Hamlisch, Marvin. (1944–) American composer.

Hammarskjöld, Dag. (1905–1961) Swedish statesman, secretary-general of the United Nations (1953–1961), awarded Nobel Peace Prize posthumously (1961).

Hammerstein, Oscar, II. (1895–1960) American dramatist and lyric writer, known for his collaborations with Jerome Kern and Richard Rodgers.

Hammett, (Samuel) Dashiell. (1894–1961) American writer of detective fiction.

Hammonasset River, Connecticut.

Hammurabi. (fl. eighteenth c. BC) Babylonian king, codifier of laws.

Hamtramck. Suburb of Detroit; pronounced *ham-tram-ick.*

Handel, George Frideric. (1685–1759) German composer, born Georg Friedrich Händel.

handicraft, handiwork. Not *handy-.*

Haneda Airport, Tokyo.

hangar, not *-er,* for the place where aircraft are stored.

hanged, hung. People are hanged; objects are hung.

Hangzhou. Chinese city, capital of Zhejiang Province, formerly Hangchow.

Hannover. German spelling for *Hanover.*

Hansard, not *Hansard's,* is the unofficial name of the record of proceedings in Britain's parliament, equivalent to America's *Congressional Record.* Formally, it is *The Official Report of Parliamentary Debates,* but that title is almost never used even on first reference.

Hansen's disease. Alternate name for leprosy.

hansom cab.

Hantuchova, Daniela. (1983–) Czech tennis player.

Hanukkah is the most widely used spelling.

haole. Hawaiian term for a Caucasian person.

Hapsburg. Austrian imperial family; in German, Habsburg.

hara-kiri is the correct spelling for the ritual form of suicide involving disembowelment. In Japan, it is normally known as *seppuku.*

Harald V. (1937–) King of Norway (1991–).

harangue, tirade. Each is sometimes used when the other is intended. A *tirade* is always abusive and can be directed at one person or at several. A *harangue,* however, need not be vituperative, but may merely be prolonged and tedious. It does, however, require at least two listeners. One person cannot, properly speaking, harangue another.

Harare. Capital of Zimbabwe, formerly called Salisbury.

harass, harassment. Note one *r*, two *s*'s.

Harcourt Brace Jovanovich. (No commas.) Former name of U.S. publisher now known as **Harcourt Inc.**

Hardie, Keir. (1856–1915) British socialist politician, one of the founders of the Labour Party.

hardiness.

Harding, Warren G(amaliel). (1865–1923) Twenty-ninth U.S. president (1921–1923).

harebrained, harelipped. Not *hair-*.

Hare Krishna. Religious movement.

Hargreaves, James. (c. 1720–1778) English inventor of the spinning jenny.

hark, but **hearken.**

Harland and Wolff. Northern Irish shipbuilding company.

HarperCollins Publishers. Formerly Harper & Row.

Harper's Bazaar. Fashion magazine.

Harpers Ferry, West Virginia (no apos.).

Harper's Magazine.

harridan. Bad-tempered old woman.

Harriman, Averell. (1891–1986) Politician and diplomat; full name William Averell Harriman.

Harrods.' (No apos.) London department store.

Harte, Bret. (1836–1902) American writer and editor; born Francis Brett Harte.

hartebeest, not *beast*, for the African antelope.

Hartsfield-Jackson Atlanta International Airport, Atlanta.

harum-scarum.

Harvard Business School is formally the Harvard Graduate School of Business Administration, though in most contexts the formal title is unnecessary.

Harvard University, but **Harvard College Observatory.**

Harz Mountains, Germany. Not *Hartz.*

Hasid, pl. *Hasidim; Hasidic* (adj.). Jewish sect.

Hasselblad for the Swedish cameras.

hausfrau. (Ger.) Housewife; pl. *hausfrauen.*

Haussmann, Boulevard, Paris; named after **Baron Georges Eugène Haussmann** (1809–1891), who led the rebuilding of the city.

haute couture. (Fr.) High fashion.

Havel, Václav. (1936–) Czech playwright and reformist politician.

Havre de Grace, Maryland.

Hawaiian Islands. The eight principal islands are Hawaii, Maui, Oahu, Kauai, Molokai, Lanai, Niihau, and Kahoolawe.

Haw-Haw, Lord. Nickname of William Joyce (1906–1946), American who made propaganda broadcasts for Germany in World War II.

Hawker Siddeley (no hyphen) for the British aviation company.

Hawksmoor, Nicholas. (1661–1736) English architect.

Hawthorne, Nathaniel. (1804–1864) American writer. (But **hawthorn** for the tree or shrub.)

Haydn, Franz Joseph. (1732–1809) Austrian composer.

Hazlitt, William. (1778–1830) English essayist and critic.

healthy, healthful, salutary. Some authorities maintain that *healthy* should apply only to those things that possess health and *healthful* to those that promote it. Thus we would have "healthy children," but "healthful food" and "healthful exercise." There is no harm in observing the distinction, but also little to be gained from insisting on it. *Salutary* has a wider meaning than the other two words. It too means conducive to health, but can also apply to anything that is demonstrably beneficial ("a salutary lesson in etiquette").

"Hear, hear!" is the exclamation of British parliamentarians, not "Here, here!"

Hebrew, Yiddish. The two languages have almost nothing in common except that they are spoken primarily by Jewish people.

Yiddish (from the German *jüdisch*, "Jewish") is a modified German dialect and thus a part of the Indo-European family of languages. *Hebrew* is a Semitic tongue and therefore is more closely related to Arabic. Yiddish writers use the Hebrew alphabet, but the two languages are no more closely related than, say, English and Swahili.

Hebrides. Group of islands off the west coast of Scotland, divided between the Inner Hebrides and Outer Hebrides; also called Western Isles. Pronounced *heb'-rid-eez.*

hectare. (Abbr. ha.) 10,000 square meters; equivalent to 2.47 acres.

hecto-. Prefix meaning 100.

Hedda Gabler. Not *-bb-*. Play by Henrik Ibsen (1890).

Heeger, Alan J. (1936–) American scientist, awarded Nobel Prize for Chemistry (2000).

Heep, Uriah. Character in Dickens's *David Copperfield.*

Hegel, Georg Wilhelm Friedrich. (1770–1831) German philosopher.

hegira. (In Arabic, *hijrah.*) The flight of Muhammad from Mecca to Medina on July 16, 622, used as the starting point for the Muslim era.

Heian. Former name of Kyoto, Japan.

Heidegger, Martin. (1889–1976) German philosopher.

Heidelberg. German university city.

Heidsieck champagne.

heifer. Not *-ff-*. A young cow.

Heifetz, Jascha. (1901–1987) Russian-born American violinist.

Heilbroner, Robert L. (1920–2005) American economist.

Heineken. Dutch beer.

Heinemann, William. British publisher.

heinous. Wicked.

heir apparent, heir presumptive. The first inherits no matter what; the second inherits only if a nearer relation is not born first.

Heisenberg, Werner. (1901–1976) German physicist, formulator of the uncertainty principle; awarded the Nobel Prize in Physics in 1932.

Heisman Trophy. Annual award to outstanding U.S. college football player; named for **John W. Heisman** (1869–1936), director of athletics at the New York Downtown Athletics Club.

Hekmatyar. See HIKMATYAR.

Helens, Mount St. (No apos.) for the volcanic mountain in Washington State.

Hellespont. Former name of Dardanelles, the strait connecting the Sea of Marmara to the Aegean.

Hellman, Lillian. (1905–1984) American playwright.

Hello! Magazine. Note exclamation mark.

Héloïse. (1101–1164) Lover of Pierre Abelard; but the poem of Alexander Pope is "Eloisa to Abelard."

Helsingør. Danish name for the Danish port known in English as Elsinore; setting of Shakespeare's *Hamlet.*

hematology, hematoma, hematemesis.

hemoglobin.

hemophilia.

hemorrhage. Note *-rr-.*

hemorrhoids. Note *-rr-.*

Hendrix, Jimi. (1942–1970) Born **Johnny Allen Hendrix;** American rock musician.

Hennes & Mauritz. Clothing retailer.

Hennessy cognac.

Henry, O. Pen name of William Sydney Porter (1862–1910), American short story writer. The candy bar is **Oh Henry!**

hepatitis.

Hephaestus. Greek god of fire and metalworking; analogous to Roman god Vulcan.

Hephaesteion/Temple of Hephaestus, Athens, Greece.

Hepplewhite. Eighteenth-century style of furniture, named after English cabinetmaker **George Hepplewhite** (d. 1786).

Hera. Greek goddess and wife of Zeus; identified with the Roman goddess Juno.

Heracles, Hercules. The first was a Greek demigod; the second was a Roman god derived from Heracles.

herbaceous.

Herculaneum. Roman city destroyed with Pompeii in AD 79.

herculean.

Heriot-Watt University, Edinburgh, Scotland.

hermaphrodite. Plant or animal having male and female characteristics; from the Greek god **Hermaphroditus.**

hermeneutics. (Sing.) The science of interpretation, especially of biblical texts.

Hermes. In Greek mythology, the messenger to the gods and guide to souls of the dead, as well as god of science, commerce, oratory, and travel; identified with the Roman god Mercury.

Hero and Leander. Tragic lovers in Greek legend; Hero drowned herself in despair after Leander perished while swimming the Hellespont to see her.

heroin, heroine. The first is a dangerous drug; the second is a female hero.

herpetology. The study of reptiles.

Herschbach, Dudley R. (1932–) American scientist, awarded Nobel Prize for Chemistry (1986).

Herschel, Sir William. (1738–1822) German-born English astronomer, discoverer of Uranus.

Hershko, Avram. (1932–) Hungarian-born Israeli scientist, awarded Nobel Prize for Chemistry (2004).

Herzog & de Meuron. Swiss architectural firm named for **Jacques Herzog** (1950–) and **Pierre de Meuron** (1950–).

Hess, Rudolf. (1894–1987) German Nazi politician.

Hesse, Hermann. (1877–1972) German writer.

heterogeneous. Made of unrelated parts.

heureusement. (Fr.) "Happily."

heuristics. The solving of problems through trial and error; it is singular.

Hewitt, Lleyton. (1981–) Australian tennis player. Note unusual spelling of first name.

Hewlett-Packard Company. (Hyphen.)

Heyerdahl, Thor. (1914–2002) Norwegian anthropologist.

Hezbollah (or **Hizbollah**). Militant Lebanese Shiite Muslim group.

HI. Postal abbreviation of Hawaii. The traditional abbreviation is **Ha.**, with period.

Hiawatha, The Song of. Epic poem by Henry Wadsworth Longfellow (1855).

hiccup, hiccough. The first is now generally the preferred spelling.

hic et nunc. (Lat.) "Here and now."

Hicpochee, Lake, Florida.

hierarchy, hierarchies, hierarchical.

hieroglyphics.

higgledy-piggledy.

highfalutin (no apos.) is the standard spelling, though many dictionaries also accept **highfaluting, highfaluten,** and **hifalutin.** It is still considered informal by most sources. Its origin is uncertain.

high-flier.

high jinks (two words) is the usual spelling, though some dictionaries also accept **hijinks.** The derivation is unknown, but it is not related to (or to be confused with) *jinx* as in bad luck. The word can be used as either singular or plural.

hijab. Scarf or head cover for Muslim women and, by extension, the system of modesty that goes with it.

Hikmatyar (or **Hekmatyar**), **Gulbuddin.** (1947–) Afghan warlord, leader of Hizb-e-Islami faction; prime minister of Afghanistan (1993–1994).

Hillary, Sir Edmund. (1919–2008) New Zealand explorer and mountaineer, first person to scale Everest (1953).

Himmler, Heinrich. (1900–1945) Nazi leader.

Hindenburg. Dirigible that exploded at Lakehurst, New Jersey, in 1937.

Hindi, Hindu, Hinduism, Hindustani. *Hindi* is the main language of India and *Hindustani* is its main dialect. *Hinduism* is the main religious and social system of India. *Hindu* describes a follower of Hinduism.

hindrance. Not *-erance.*

Hindu Kush. Mountain range in Afghanistan.

hippie. Not *-ppy.*

Hippocrates. (c. 460–377 BC) Greek physician, considered the father of medicine.

hippopotamus, pl. *hippopotamuses.*

hireable.

Hirschfeld, Al. (1903–2003) American caricaturist.

Hirshhorn Museum, Washington, D.C. Note *-hh-.*

HIS, HJS. *Hic iacet sepultus/sepulta, hic jacet sepulta* (Lat.), "here lies buried." Often seen on gravestones.

Hispaniola. Caribbean island on which Haiti and Dominican Republic are located.

historic, historical. Something that makes history or is part of history is *historic.* Something that is based on history or describes history is *historical* ("a historical novel"). A historic judicial ruling is one that makes history; a historical ruling is based on precedent. There are, however, at least two exceptions to the rule—in accountancy ("historic costs") and, curiously, in grammar ("historic tenses").

histrionics is plural.

hitchhike, hitchhiker. Note -*hh*-.

hitherto. "In 1962, the regime took the hitherto unthinkable step of appropriating land" (*Daily Telegraph*). *Hitherto* means "until now," so in the example cited it is out of step with the sentence's tense. The writer meant *thitherto* ("until then"), but *theretofore* would have been better and *previously* better still.

Hitler, Adolf. (1889–1945) Not *Adolph*. The German Nazi leader.

Hittites. Ancient people of Asia Minor.

HIV. Human immunodeficiency virus, the virus associated with AIDS. "HIV virus" is redundant.

Hizbollah. Alternative spelling of **Hezbollah.**

hoagie. Type of sandwich.

hoard, horde. An accumulation of valuables, often hidden, is a *hoard*. *Horde* applies to any crowd, but particularly to a thronging and disorganized one ("hordes of Christmas shoppers").

hoary. Not -*ey*. Gray or aged.

Hobbema, Meindert. (1638–1709) Dutch artist.

Hobbes, Thomas. (1588–1679) English philosopher.

hobo, pl. *hoboes.*

Hobson's choice is sometimes taken to signify a dilemma or difficult decision, but in fact means having no choice at all. It is said to derive from a sixteenth-century stable-keeper in Cambridge, England, named Thomas Hobson, who hired out horses in strict rotation. The customer was allowed to take the one nearest the stable door or none at all.

Hochhuth, Rolf. (1931–) German playwright.

Ho Chi Minh City, Vietnam; formerly Saigon.

Hodder & Stoughton. British publisher.

Hodgkin disease (or **Hodgkin's disease**). A cancer of the lymphatic system first described by the British physician **Thomas Hodgkin.**

Hoffman, Dustin. (1937–) American actor.

Hoffmann, The Tales of. 1881 opera by Jacques Offenbach. Note *-ff-*, *-nn-*.

Hoffmann-La Roche. Swiss pharmaceuticals company.

Hofheinz Pavilion, Houston, Texas.

Hofstadter, Richard. (1916–1970) American historian.

Hogmanay. Scottish name for New Year's Eve.

Hohenzollern. German royal family and a former province of Prussia.

hoi polloi means "the masses, the common populace," and not "the elite" as is often thought. A second problem is that in Greek *hoi* means *the*, so to speak of "the hoi polloi" is redundant.

Hokkaido. Japanese island; capital Sapporo.

Hokusai, Katsushika. (1760–1849) Japanese artist and wood engraver.

Holbein, Hans, the Elder. (c. 1460–1524) German painter and father of **Hans Holbein the Younger** (1497–1543), court painter to Henry VIII of England.

Holiday, Billie. (1915–1959) American singer; born Eleanora Fagan Holiday.

Holinshed, Raphael. (d. c. 1580) English historian, known for *The Chronicles of England, Scotland and Ireland* (1577), which was popularly known as *Holinshed's Chronicles.*

hollandaise sauce. (Not cap.)

Holland America Line. (No hyphen.) Cruise ship company.

Holman-Hunt, William. (1827–1910) English painter.

Holmegaard. Danish crystal.

Holmes, Oliver Wendell. (1809–1894) Physician, professor at Harvard, poet, essayist, and novelist, father of **Oliver Wendell Holmes Jr.** (1841–1935), associate justice of the U.S. Supreme Court (1902–1932).

holocaust. In Greek the word means "burnt whole" and, generally speaking, it is better reserved for disasters involving fiery destruction. You should not, for instance, use the word to describe the devastation wrought by a hurricane or mudslide. However, a clear exception is in references to the slaughter of Jews by Germany during World War II, when it describes the entire extermination process. In such contexts, the word is capitalized.

Holyroodhouse, Palace of, Edinburgh, Scotland; pronounced *holly-*.

Home Counties. In British usage, the counties immediately around London.

homely. If writing for an international audience, you should be aware (or beware) that the word has strikingly different connotations between America and elsewhere. In Britain and most of its former dominions *homely* means comfortable and appealing, having the warm and familiar qualities associated with a home. In America, for obscure reasons, it has long signified something that is unattractive, particularly in respect to the human face. If the audience is international and confusion likely to follow, clearly a more neutral term is advised. In any case, to describe someone as homely, in the American sense, is inescapably subjective, generally uncharitable, and may cause needless hurt.

homogeneous, homogenous. *Homogeneous* means consistent and uniform; *homogenous* is almost always restricted to biological contexts, where it describes organisms having common ancestry.

homonym, homophone. Both describe words that have strong similarities of sound or spelling, but different meanings. A *homophone* is a word that sounds like another but has a different meaning or spelling, or both. A *homonym* is a word that also has a different meaning, but the same spelling or sound. Thus *blue* and *blew* are both homonyms and homophones. However, *bow* as in a ship and *bow* as in a tie are homonyms (because they are spelled the same) but not homophones (because they have different pronunciations). In short, unless the intention is to emphasize the equivalence of pronunciations, *homonym* is generally the better word.

Honecker, Erich. (1912–1994) Chairman of East German Communist Party (i.e., head of state) (1977–1989).

Honiara. Capital of the Solomon Islands.

Honi soit qui mal y pense. (Fr.) Usually translated as "Evil to him who evil thinks"; motto of the Royal Order of the Garter in Britain.

honnête homme. (Fr.) An honest man.

honorificabilitudinitatibus. Nonsense word in Shakespeare's *Love's Labour's Lost.*

Honshu. Main island of Japan, site of Tokyo and Yokohama.

Hooch/Hoogh, Pieter de. (c. 1629–c. 1684) Dutch painter; pronounced *hoke* for either spelling.

Hook of Holland. In Dutch, Hoek van Holland.

Hoosick Falls, New York.

hopefully. Much ink has been expended arguing whether the word is acceptable when used in an absolute sense, as in "Hopefully the sun will shine tomorrow." Many usage authorities argue that that sentence should be recast as "It is to be hoped that the sun will shine tomorrow" or something similar. However, other authorities say that such a stand is pedantic and inconsistent, since no one objects to other *-ly* words, such as *apparently*, *sadly*, *thankfully*, and *mercifully*, being used absolutely. I side with the second group, but you should be aware that the use of *hopefully* in an absolute sense is still widely, and often hotly, objected to.

Hopkins, Gerard Manley. (1844–1889) British poet and Jesuit priest. His poetry was published posthumously.

Hopkins, Johns. (1795–1873) Not *John*. American financier who endowed now-famous hospital and university, both in Baltimore.

Horae. Greek goddesses who presided over the weather and seasons.

horde, hoard. The first is a swarm of people; the second, a cache.

Hornsby, Rogers. (1896–1963) Not *Roger*. American baseball player and manager.

Hornung, Paul. (1935–) American football player.

Horowitz, Vladimir. (1904–1989) Russian-born American concert pianist.

hors de combat. (Fr.) "Out of action."

hors d'oeuvre. An appetizer; pl. *hors d'oeuvres.*

"Horst Wessel Lied." Nazi song.

hosanna. A shout of praise.

Hosokawa, Morihiro. (1938–) Japanese prime minister (1993–1994).

hot dog (two words) for the food, but **hotdog** as a verb meaning to show off and for associated words such as **hotdogging** and **hotdogger.**

Hôtel des Invalides, Paris, site of Napoleon's tomb.

hôtel de ville. (Fr.) Town hall.

Houellebecq, Michel. (1958–) French novelist.

Houston, Whitney. (1963–) American singer. (But note, it is **Anjelica Huston.**)

Houyhnhnms. In *Gulliver's Travels,* a race of horses with the finer qualities of humans; pronounced *win-ums.*

Hovenweep National Monument, Utah.

hovercraft. (No cap.) The name is no longer a trademark.

Howards End. (No apos.) Novel by E. M. Forster (1910).

Howells, William Dean. (1837–1920) American critic, editor, and writer.

howitzer. A cannon.

Hoxha, Enver. (1908–1985) Head of state of Albania (1944–1985); pronounced *hod'-juh.*

Hrvastska. Croatian name for Croatia.

HTML. Short for Hypertext Markup Language; language used for communicating on World Wide Web.

HTTP. Short for Hypertext Transfer Protocol; governing standard for World Wide Web information transfers.

Hua Guofeng. (1920–) Chinese Communist leader, premier (1976–1980); formerly Hua Kuo-feng.

Huanghe. Pinyin name for the **Hwang-Ho** or **Yellow River**, China. In most contexts a reference to one or both of the older names would be helpful.

hudibrastic, in a mock-heroic manner, from the epic satirical poem *Hudibras* (1663–1678) by Samuel Butler.

Hudson Bay, Hudson Strait, Hudson River, but **Hudson's Bay Company.**

hue and cry, not *hew*, for an uproar.

Huguenots. Sixteenth-to-seventeenth-century French Protestants.

Hu Jintao. (1942–) President of China (2003–).

hullabaloo.

human immunodeficiency virus. HIV, virus associated with AIDS.

humerus. Bone between the elbow and shoulder; pl. *humeri.*

Humperdinck, Engelbert. (1854–1921) German composer; also the stage name of a popular British singer, born Arnold Dorsey (1935–).

Humphry Clinker, The Expedition of. Not *Humphrey*. Novel by Tobias Smollett (1771).

humus, hummus. The first is broken-down plant material in soil; the second is a dish made from mashed chickpeas.

Humvee. Name derived from the initials HMMWV (short for high mobility multipurpose wheeled vehicle); general-purpose military vehicle.

Hundred Years' War. Series of wars (1337–1453) in which France wrested back all its territory from England except Calais.

hurdy-gurdy. Musical instrument activated by a crank.

hurly-burly.

Hurston, Zora Neale. (1891–1960) American writer, associated with the movement known as the Harlem Renaissance.

Hussein, Saddam. (1937–2006) President of Iraq (1979–2003). His name in full was Saddam Hussein Abd al-Majid al-Tikrit.

Huston, Anjelica. (1951–) American actress, daughter of film director John Huston (1906–1987) and granddaughter of actor **Walter Huston** (1884–1950).

Huxley, Aldous. (1894–1963) English novelist and brother of **Sir Julian Huxley** (1887–1975), biologist and writer; their grandfather was **T. H. Huxley** (1825–1895), scientist and champion of Charles Darwin.

Huygens, Christiaan. (1629–1695) Dutch mathematician and scientist. Note *-aa-* in first name.

Huysmans, Joris-Karl. (1848–1907) French novelist.

Hwang Ho. Chinese river now more commonly known as **Huanghe.**

hyacinth. Flower.

Hyannis Port, but **West Hyannisport,** Cape Cod, Massachusetts.

Hyderabad. Capital of Andhra Pradesh, India. There is also a city in Pakistan of the same name, which is sometimes spelled **Haidarabad.**

Hydra. In Greek mythology, a many-headed monster.

hydrangea.

hydrography. The study and mapping of oceans, rivers, and lakes.

hyena.

Hygeia. Greek goddess of health.

hygiene, hygienic.

hymen. Not *-man*. Vaginal membrane, named after Hymen, Greek god of marriage.

Hynes Convention Center, Boston, Massachusetts; formally it is the John B. Hynes Veterans Memorial Convention Center.

hyperbole. Exaggeration.

hypertension. High blood pressure.

hypochondria.

hypocrite, hypocrisy.

hypotenuse. On a right-angled triangle, the side opposite the right angle.

hypothermia. Lack of body warmth.

hypothesis, pl. *hypotheses.*

hysterectomy.

hysterics is plural.

Hywel. Welsh forename; pronounced *howl.*

Iacocca, Lee. (1924–) American businessman.

IAEA. International Atomic Energy Agency, UN nuclear watchdog.

IATA. International Air Transport Association.

Iberia Airlines. Not *Iberian*.

ibex. A mountain goat; pl. *ibexes*.

ibid., the abbreviation of *ibidem* (Lat.), "in the same place," is used in reference notes to indicate that a source is the same as the previous one in the note. See also OP. CIT.

-ible, -able. No reliable rules exist for when a word ends in *-ible* and when in *-able;* see Appendix for a list of some of the more frequently confused spellings.

Ibsen, Henrik. (1828–1906) Norwegian playwright.

ICBM. Intercontinental ballistic missile.

iceberg.

iced tea. Not *ice*.

Icelandair. Icelandic airline.

Iceni. British tribe that revolted against Rome under the leadership of Boudicca in the first century AD.

Ich dien. (Ger.) "I serve"; motto of the Prince of Wales in the United Kingdom.

ichthyology. The study of fishes.

ichthyosaur, ichthyosaurus. Prehistoric marine reptile.

ici on parle français. (Fr.) "French spoken here." Note lowercase *français*.

I, Claudius. Novel by Robert Graves (1934). Note comma.

Ictinus. (fl. fifth c. BC) Greek architect, co-designer with Callicrates of the Parthenon.

idée fixe. (Fr.) for an obsession or fixation. The plural is *idées fixes*.

ideology, ideological, ideologue.

ides of March. March 15, the day on which Julius Caesar was assassinated. In the Roman calendar, the ides was the fifteenth of March, May, July, and October, and the thirteenth of the other months.

idiosyncrasy. One of the most commonly misspelled of all words. Note that the ending is *-sy*, not *-cy*.

idyll. Poem or prose depicting rural bliss.

i.e. *Id est* (Lat.) "that is to say." Used to introduce an elaboration, as in "He is pusillanimous, i.e., lacking in courage."

if. Problems often arise in deciding whether *if* is introducing a subjunctive clause ("If I were . . .") or an indicative one ("If I was . . ."). The distinction is straightforward. When *if* introduces a notion that is hypothetical or improbable or clearly untrue, the verb should be in the subjunctive: "If I were king . . ."; "If he were in your shoes . . ." But when the *if* is introducing a thought that is true or could well be true, the mood should be indicative: "If I was happy then, I certainly am not now." One small hint: if the sentence contains *would* or *wouldn't*, the mood is subjunctive, as in "If I were you, I wouldn't take the job."

if and when. Almost always unnecessary. Choose one or the other.

igneous rock.

ignominy, ignominious.

ignotum per ignotius. (Lat.) "The unknown by the even less known"; used of an explanation that is more confusing than what it is meant to explain.

iguanodon. Not *iguana-*. Dinosaur.

Iguassu (or **Iguaçu**) **Falls.** Waterfall on the Argentina-Brazil border; in Portuguese, Saltos do Iguaçu; in Spanish, Cataratas del Iguazú.

IJsselmeer, the Netherlands; freshwater lake created by damming part of the Zuider Zee. Note double caps.

Île-de-France. Region of France that includes Paris.

ileum, ilium. The *ileum* is part of the small intestine; the *ilium* is part of the pelvis and, when capitalized, is also the Latin name for Troy.

Iliad. Epic poem attributed to Homer.

illegitimate, illegitimize.

Illinoian, not *Illinoisian*, for something or someone from Illinois.

illuminati. (Always plural.) Enlightened people.

illustrator.

imbroglio. A predicament, a complicated situation; pl. *imbroglios*.

immanent, imminent. The first means inherent, the second, impending. Neither should be confused with *eminent*, which means outstanding.

immaterial.

immeasurable.

immoral, amoral. *Immoral* applies to things that are evil; *amoral* describes matters in which questions of morality do not arise or are disregarded.

Immortels, Les. Nickname of members of the Académie Française.

immovable, immovability.

immutable.

impala. Not *-ll-*.

impassable, impassible. The first means impossible to negotiate; the second means impervious to pain.

impazientemente. (It.) In music, to perform in an impatient manner.

imperative.

imperceptible.

impermeable.

impertinent.

implacable.

imply, infer. *Imply* means to suggest: "He implied that I was a fool." *Infer* means to deduce: "After three hours of waiting, we inferred that they weren't coming."

imports, exports. It is implicit in *imports* that their source is foreign, so it is tautological to write "imports from abroad." Similar phrases involving *exports*, such as "exports to overseas fell slightly last month," equally cry out for pruning.

impostor. Not *-er.*

impractical, impracticable, unpractical. If a thing could be done but isn't worth doing, it is *impractical* or *unpractical* (the words mean the same). If it can't be done at all, it's *impracticable* (the word means "incapable of being put into practice").

impresario.

impressible.

imprimatur. Official authorization.

improvable.

improvvisata. (It.) In music, improvisation. Note *-vv-.*

impugn, impunity. The first is to criticize or attack; the second means to enjoy freedom from punishment.

in, into, in to. Generally, *in* indicates a fixed position ("He was in the house") while *into* indicates movement toward a fixed position ("He went into the house"). There are, however, many exceptions (e.g., "He put the money in his pocket"). As so often with idiom, there is no describable pattern to these exceptions; it is just the way it is.

Whether to write *into* as one word or two also sometimes causes problems. The simple rule is that *in to* is correct when *in* is an adverb, but the distinction can perhaps best be seen in paired examples: "He turned himself into [one word] an accomplished artist" but "The criminal turned himself in to [two words] the police."

in absentia. (Lat.) "While absent."

inadmissible. Not *-able.*

inadvertent.

inadvisable.

innamorata (fem.), *innamorato* (masc.). Lover; pl. *innamorati.*

inasmuch.

in camera. Behind closed doors, not in open court.

incessant.

inchoate. Undeveloped, just starting out.

incidentally.

incisor.

include indicates that what is to follow is only part of a greater whole. To use it when you are describing a totality (as in "The 350 layoffs include 200 in Michigan and 150 in Indiana") is sloppy and possibly misleading.

incognito.

incombustible. Cannot be burned.

incommodious.

incommunicado. Unable or unwilling to communicate.

incomparable.

incompatible.

incomprehensible. Not *-able.*

incongruous, incongruity.

incorrigible.

incubus. An evil spirit that has intercourse with sleeping women; a nightmare or something that oppresses like a nightmare. See also SUCCUBUS.

inculcate means to persistently impress a habit upon or belief into another person. You inculcate an idea, not a person. "My father inculcated me with a belief in democracy" should be "My father inculcated in me a belief in democracy."

incunabulum. A book printed at an early date, especially before 1501, and by extension, the early stages of development of something; pl. *incunabula.*

in curia. (Lat.) "In open court."

indefatigable. Tireless.

indefeasible. Permanent, cannot be made void.

indefensible.

indefinitely means only "without prescribed limits," not "lasting forever." To say that a process will last indefinitely doesn't necessarily mean that it will last for a very long time, but simply that its durability is unknown.

indelible.

indescribable.

indestructible.

indexes/indices. Either is acceptable, depending on how much of an air of formality you wish to convey.

Index Librorum Prohibitorum. Catalogue of books forbidden to Roman Catholics by their church. Not to be confused with **Index Expurgatorius,** a catalogue of books in which only certain passages are forbidden.

india ink. (Not cap.)

indices/indexes. Either is acceptable, though some dictionaries favor *indices* for technical applications.

indict, indite. The first means to accuse formally of a crime; the second means to set down in writing, but in fact is rare almost to the point of obsolescence.

indigenous.

indigent.

indigestible.

indiscreet, indiscrete. The first means lacking discretion; the second means not composed of separate parts.

indispensable. Not *-ible.*

individual is unexceptionable when you are contrasting one person with an organization or body of people ("How can one individual hope to rectify the evils of society?"). But as a simple synonym for *person* ("Do you see that individual standing over there?"), it is still frowned upon by many authorities as casual and inelegant.

indivisible.

indomitable.

indubitable, indubitably.

Induráin, Miguel. (1964–) Spanish cyclist.

Industrial Workers of the World. (Abbr. IWW.) A radical trade union movement from 1905 to 1925, often called Wobblies, particularly by detractors.

inebriate, inebriety.

inedible.

ineffaceable. Indelible (which in most cases is to be preferred).

inefficacious. A longer way of saying *ineffective.*

ineligible.

ineluctable. Inevitable, unavoidable.

inequable, inequitable. The first means not even or uniform; the second means unfair.

ineradicable.

inevitable.

in excelsis. (Lat.) "To the highest degree."

inexcusable.

inexplicable.

inexpressible.

in extenso. (Lat.) "At full length."

inextinguishable.

in extremis. (Lat.) "At the point of death"; in dire circumstances.

infallible.

infer, imply. *Imply* means to suggest: "He implied that I was a fool." *Infer* means to deduce: "After three hours of waiting, we inferred that they weren't coming." The condition of being able to make an inference is *inferable.*

infinitesimal.

infinitude.

in flagrante delicto. (Lat.) In the act of commiting an offense.

inflammable, flammable, nonflammable. Although *inflammable* means "capable of being burned," it has so often been taken to mean the opposite that most authorities now suggest that it be avoided. It is deemed generally better to use *flammable* for materials that will burn and *nonflammable* for those that will not.

inflammation, inflammatory. Not *im-*.

inflation has become so agreeably quiescent in recent years that the word and its several variant forms are much less troublesome than they were when this book first appeared. However (and just in case), it is worth noting a few definitions. *Inflation* itself means that the money supply and prices are rising. *Hyperinflation* means that they are rising rapidly (at an annual rate of at least 20 percent). *Deflation* means that they are falling, and *reflation* that they are being pushed up again after a period of deflation. *Stagflation* means that prices are rising while output is stagnant. *Disinflation*, a word so vague in sense to most readers that it is almost always better avoided, means that prices are rising but at a rate slower than before. Finally, bear in mind that if the rate of inflation was 4.5 percent last month and 3.5 percent this month, it does not mean that prices are falling; they are still rising, but at a slower rate.

inflexible.

infra dig is the abbreviation of **infra dignitatem**, which translates to "without (or beneath) dignity."

ingenious, ingenuous. The first means to be clever or inventive; the second means innocent, unsophisticated, guileless.

ingénue.

Ingushetia (or **Ingushetiya**). Russian republic.

inimical. Harmful, antagonistic.

iniquitous. Wicked.

Inkatha Freedom Party, South Africa.

In loco parentis. (Lat.) "In place of the parent."

in media res. (Lat.) "In the middle of things."

in memoriam. Not *-um*.

Innes, George. (1825–1894) American landscape painter of the Hudson River school.

innocent. It is pedantic to insist on it too rigorously on all occasions, but it is worth noting that people do not actually plead *innocent* (since one of the hallmarks of our legal system is that innocence is presumed). Strictly, they plead guilty or not guilty.

innocuous.

innuendoes.

inoculate.

in order to. A wordy locution. In nearly every instance, removing *in order* tightens the sentence without altering the sense. See also IN, INTO, IN TO.

Inouye, Daniel K. (1924–) U.S. senator from Hawaii.

inscrutable.

insects. It is always worth remembering that the term does not apply to spiders, mites, and ticks, which are arachnids, a different class of creature altogether. Although some dictionaries (*American Heritage*, for one) allow the looser usage in informal or in nontechnical writing, it is unquestionably incorrect and thus better avoided almost always. If you need a term to describe insects and spiders together, the word is *arthropods*.

inshallah. (Arab.) "If Allah wills it."

insidious, invidious. *Insidious* indicates the stealthy or tardily detected spread of something undesirable ("an insidious leak in the pipe"). *Invidious* means offensive or inviting animosity ("I was angered by his invidious remarks").

insignia. (Sing. and pl.) Historically, *insigne* is the correct singular, but almost no authority insists on it now.

in situ. (Lat.) "In place."

insofar. (One word.)

insouciance, insouciant. Lack of concern, carefree.

install, installment.

instantaneous.

instill.

Institut de France. Not *-tute.* Umbrella organization for the five French academies: Académie des Beaux-Arts, Académie Française, Académie des Inscriptions et Belles-Lettres, Académie des Sciences, and the Académie des Sciences Morales et Politiques.

insuperable.

insuppressible.

insurer. Not *-or.*

intelligentsia. The intellectual elite of a society.

intelligible.

in tenebris. (Lat.) "In the dark," in doubt.

intense, intensive. *Intense* should describe things that are heavy or extreme or occur to a high degree ("intense sunlight," "intense downpour"). *Intensive* implies a concentrated focus ("intensive care," "an intensive search"). Although the two words often come to the same thing, they needn't. An intense bombardment, as Fowler pointed out, is a severe one. An intensive bombardment is one directed at a small (or relatively small) area.

inter alia. (Lat.) "Among other things."

intermezzo. In music, a short piece between longer ones; pl. *intermezzi/intermezzos.*

interminable.

International Atomic Energy Agency. Not *Authority.*

international courts. Understandably, these sometimes cause confusion. The International Court of Justice, or World Court, in The Hague, Netherlands, is an offspring of the United Nations and deals with disputes between or among UN member states. The

European Court of Justice, in Luxembourg, is a European Union institution dealing exclusively with disputes involving EU member states. The European Court of Human Rights, in Strasbourg, France, addresses issues of civil liberties arising from the European Convention on Human Rights. It has no connection with the United Nations or European Union.

International Olympic Committee. Not *Olympics*.

internecine. For more than two hundred years writers have used *internecine* in the sense of a costly or self-destructive conflict, even though etymologically the word signifies only a slaughter or massacre without any explicit sense of cost to the victor. It has been misused for so long that it would be pedantic and wildly optimistic to try to enforce its original meaning, but it should at least be reserved for bloody and violent disputes and not mere squabblings.

interpolate. To insert.

interregnum. Period between reigns; pl. *interregnums*.

interrelated. Note -*rr*-.

in toto. (Lat.) "In total."

intransitive verbs are those that do not require a direct object, as with *sleep* in the sentence "He sleeps all night."

intrauterine device.

intra vires. (Lat.) "Within one's powers."

intrigue. Originally *intrigue* signified underhanded plotting and nothing else. The looser meaning of arousing or fascinating ("We found the lecture intriguing") is now established. It is, however, greatly overworked and almost always better replaced by a more telling word.

in utero. (Lat.) "In the uterus."

in vacuo. (Lat.) "In a vacuum."

invariably does not mean *frequently* or *usually*. It means fixed, constant, not subject to change—in short, without variance.

inveigh, inveigle. Occasionally confused. The first means to speak strongly against ("He inveighed against the rise in taxes"). The second means to entice or cajole ("They inveigled an invitation to the party").

invidious, insidious. *Invidious* means unfair or likely to cause offense; *insidious* describes the stealthy spread of something undesirable.

in vino veritas. (Lat.) "In wine there is truth."

in vitro. (Lat.) Literally "in glass," i.e., in a test tube, as with in vitro fertilization.

in vivo. (Lat.) "In a living organism."

ipissima verba. (Lat.) "The very words."

IPO. Short for *initial public offering*, the term for stock issued on a company's market debut.

ipso facto. (Lat.) "By the very fact."

IQ. Intelligence quotient.

Iraqi, Iraqis.

Ireland, Republic of (in Gaelic, Eire), consists of the following provinces (and their counties): Connacht (Galway, Leitrim, Mayo, Roscommon, Sligo), Leinster (Carlow, Dublin, Kildare, Kilkenny, Laois, Longford, Louth, Meath, Offaly, Westmeath, Wexford, Wicklow), Munster (Clare, Cork, Kerry, Limerick, Tipperary, Waterford), and Ulster (Cavan, Donegal, Monaghan).

Irgun Zvai Leumi. Jewish guerrilla organization whose aim was to establish a state in Israel.

iridescence, iridescent.

irony, sarcasm. *Irony* is the use of words to convey a contradiction between the literal and intended meanings. *Sarcasm* is very like irony except that it is more stinging. Where the primary intent behind irony is to amuse, with sarcasm it is to wound or score points.

Iroquois. Native American group consisting of Cayuga, Mohawk, Oneida, Onondaga, Seneca, and Tuscarora peoples; pl. same.

Irrawaddy. Principal river of Burma.

Irreconcilable.

irrefragable, irrefrangible. The first means indisputable, the second indestructible, but both are inescapably pretentious when such useful synonyms are available.

irregardless is not a real word; make it *regardless*.

irrelevance, irrelevant.

irreparable.

irreplaceable.

irrepressible.

irresistible.

irreversible.

Isaiah. Book of the Old Testament.

Isakson, Johnny. (1944–) U.S. senator from Georgia.

ISBN. International Standard Book Number, an identifying number on books.

Ischia. Volcanic island in the Bay of Naples, Italy.

-ise/-ize. Since about the time of Noah Webster, American users have been strongly inclined to use *-ize* terminations on verbs such as *recognize* and *conceptualize*, while in Britain *-ise* endings remain more common. However, it is worth noting that even under the *-ize* system, certain verbs continue always to end in *-ise*, of which the following are the main ones: *advertise, apprise, chastise, circumcise, comprise, compromise, demise, despise, devise, disguise, excise, exercise, franchise, improvise, incise, merchandise, reprise, supervise, surmise, surprise, televise.*

Iseult/Isolde/Isolt/Ysolt. In Arthurian legend, an Irish princess who falls tragically in love with Tristan, the nephew of a Cornish king. Wagner's opera is *Tristan und Isolde.*

Ishiguro, Kazuo. (1954–) British novelist.

isosceles triangle. One with two equal sides.

Isozaki, Arata. (1931–) Japanese architect.

Issigonis, Sir Alec. (1906–1988) Turkish-born British car designer.

Italy is divided into twenty regions: Abruzzi, Basilicata, Calabria, Campania, Emilia-Romagna, Friuli–Venezia Giulia, Lazio, Liguria, Lombardia (Lombardy), Marche (Marches), Molise, Piemonte (Piedmont), Puglia (Apulia), Sardegna (Sardinia), Sicilia (Sicily), Trentino–Alto Adige, Toscana (Tuscany), Umbria, Valle d'Aosta, Veneto.

ITAR-TASS. Russian news agency; formerly just called TASS.

its, it's. *Its* is the possessive form of *it*: "Put each book in its place." *It's* is the contraction of *it is*: "The beauty of solar power is that it's environmentally friendly."

Iverson, Allen. (1975–) American basketball player.

Ivy League. Group of eight universities in the eastern United States noted for high academic standards: Brown, Columbia, Cornell, Dartmouth, Harvard, Princeton, University of Pennsylvania, and Yale.

IWW. Industrial Workers of the World, called Wobblies.

Izmir, Turkey; formerly Smyrna.

Izvestia (or ***Izvestiya***). Russian newspaper.

Jj

ja, jawohl. (Ger.) "Yes."

"Jabberwocky." Poem by Lewis Carroll in *Through the Looking-Glass* (1872), and (no cap.) any kind of nonsense writing.

jacana. Tropical bird.

jacaranda. Tropical tree.

jackal.

jackanapes. A cocky person.

Jacobean, Jacobin, Jacobite. *Jacobean* describes the period of the reign of James I of England (1603–1625). *Jacobins* were radical republicans during the French Revolution. *Jacobites* were supporters of James II of England and his heirs following the Glorious Revolution.

Jacobi, Derek. (1938–) English actor.

Jacobs Field. Cleveland baseball stadium, home of the Indians.

Jacobs Suchard. Swiss chocolate company.

jactitation of marriage. Note *-ctit-*. Falsely claiming to be someone's wife or husband.

Jacuzzi. (Cap.) Whirlpool bath.

Jaeger clothing.

jai alai. Also called *pelota*. Fast-paced ball game popular in Spain and Latin America.

Jakarta. Not *Djakarta*. Capital of Indonesia; formerly Batavia.

jalopy. Old car.

jalousie. Type of slatted shutter.

jamb. Not *jam*. A doorpost or similar.

James's, St., not James', for the palace, park, and square in London.

Janáček, Leoš. (1854–1928) Czech composer.

Jane Eyre. Novel by Charlotte Brontë (1847).

Jankovic, Jelena. (1985–) Serbian tennis player.

Janus. Roman god of the gate of Heaven, depicted as having two faces—one at the front and one at the back—because every door or gate looks two ways; also god of beginnings and of the first month, January.

Japan Air Lines. Not *Airlines.*

Jaques, not *Jacques,* for the character in William Shakespeare's *As You Like It.*

jardinière. Ornamental pot or stand for plants; garnish of mixed vegetables.

Jaruzelski, General Wojciech. (1923–) Polish general, prime minister (1981–1985), head of state (1985–1989), president (1989–1990).

Jarvik-7. Artificial heart invented by Robert Jarvik (1946–).

javelin.

JCPenney. (One word.) Venerable U.S. retailer.

Jeanne d'Arc. French for Joan of Arc.

Jeddah/Jidda, Saudi Arabia.

jeep, Jeep. Use *jeep* generally for army vehicles, but *Jeep* specifically for the brand name of cars produced by DaimlerChrysler.

Jeffreys, George, Baron. (1648–1689) British "hanging" judge, infamous for severity of his punishments handed down after Monmouth's rebellion (1685).

Jehovah's Witness.

jejune. Insubstantial.

Jekyll and Hyde. The full title of the book by Robert Louis Stevenson is *The Strange Case of Dr. Jekyll and Mr. Hyde* (1886).

Jelinek, Elfriede. (1946–) Austrian writer, awarded Nobel Prize for Literature in 2004.

Jellicoe, John Rushworth, Earl. (1859–1935) British admiral.

Jell-O. Venerable dessert.

Jemaah Islamiah. Islamist group responsible for several bombings in Indonesia.

je ne sais pas. (Fr.) "I don't know."

je ne sais quoi. (Fr.) "I don't know what"; applied to the indescribable.

Jenkins' Ear, War of. (1739–48) War between Britain and Spain over trade with South America, ostensibly provoked by an incident in which Spanish sailors boarded a British vessel in the Caribbean and cut off the ear of the captain, Robert Jenkins, but this happened seven years before the hostilities began.

jeopardy, jeopardize.

jeremiad. Elaborate lamentation.

jeroboam. Wine bottle that contains four ordinary wine bottles' worth of wine.

jerry-built, jury-rigged. Occasionally confused. The first applies to things that are built cheaply and sloppily without regard to quality. The second describes things made in haste, with whatever materials are at hand, as a temporary or emergency measure.

Jervaulx Abbey, England; pronounced *jer-vo'*.

jetsam, flotsam. *Jetsam* applies to goods that have been thrown overboard (jettisoned) at sea; *flotsam* describes goods that have floated free from wreckage. Historically flotsam went to the Crown and jetsam to the lord of the manor on whose land it washed up.

Jeu de Paume, Galerie Nationale du, Paris.

jeune fille. (Fr.) A girl.

jew's harp. (No caps.)

Jhabvala, Ruth Prawer. (1927–) German-born British novelist and screenwriter.

jibe means to be in agreement and is also a nautical term for the act of changing course. See also GIBE.

jihad. A Muslim holy war.

Jinnah, Mohammed Ali. (1876–1948) Founder of Pakistan, governor-general (1947–1948).

Jobs, Steven. (1955–) Not *-ph-*. Computer entrepreneur, co-founder of Apple Computer Inc.

jodhpurs. Riding breeches, named after the Indian city of Jodhpur.

Johannesburg, South Africa, but the German wine is **Johannisberger.**

John Newbery Medal. Award for outstanding children's literature.

John o' Groat's. House and ferry site in Scotland traditionally (but incorrectly) given as the northernmost point on the British mainland.

Johns Hopkins (note *s* on both) is the name of the university and medical center in Baltimore.

Johnson, Lady Bird. (1912–2007) Wife of Lyndon Baines Johnson; her real name was Claudia Alta Johnson.

Johnson, Lyndon Baines. (1908–1973) U.S. president (1963–1969).

Johnson, Magic. (1959–) Basketball player; his real name is Earvin Johnson Jr.

Johnson, Nunnally. (1897–1977) American screenwriter, film director, and producer.

joie de vivre. (Fr.) State of being carefree, full of joy.

Joiners' and Ceilers' Company. London livery company. *Ceiler* is an old term for a wood carver.

Joliet, Illinois.

Joliet (or **Jolliet**), **Louis.** (1645–1700) French-Canadian explorer.

Joliette County, Quebec.

Jones, Inigo. (1573–1652) English architect and designer.

Joneses, keeping up with the. Not *Jones'* or *Jones's* or other common variants.

jonquil. Species of narcissus.

Jonson, Ben. (1572–1637) Not *John-*. English dramatist and poet.

Jordaens, Jakob. (1593–1678) Flemish painter.

Joslyn Art Museum, Omaha.

joss stick.

Jove. Alternative name for the Roman god Jupiter.

JPMorgan Chase & Co. Financial services company.

Juan de Fuca Strait. Passage in Puget Sound between Washington and British Columbia.

Juárez, Mexico; formally it is **Ciudad de Juárez.**

Judas Iscariot. Apostle who betrayed Jesus for thirty pieces of silver.

jugular vein.

Juilliard School of Music, New York City. Note *Jui-*.

jujitsu. Japanese form of unarmed combat.

julienne. To slice vegetables into strips; a soup containing such vegetables.

Juno and the Paycock. Play by Sean O'Casey (1924).

Jurgensen, Sonny. (1934–) American football quarterback; real name Christian Adolph Jurgensen III.

just deserts. Not *desserts*. The expression has nothing to do with the sweet course after dinner. It comes from the French for *deserve*, which may help you to remember that it has just one middle *s*.

Juvenal. (c. 60–c. 140) Roman poet; full name **Decimus Junius Juvenalis.**

j'y suis, j'y reste. (Fr.) "Here I am, here I stay."

Kk

Kaaba. Sacred shrine at Mecca.

Kabardino-Balkariya. Russian republic.

kabuki. Japanese theater.

Kaczyński, Lech, and **Jaroslaw.** (1949–) Identical twin brothers, respectively president (2005–) and prime minister (2006–2007) of Poland.

Kádár, János. (1912–1989) Hungarian politician.

Kaddish. (Cap.) Type of Jewish prayer.

kaffeeklatsch. (Ger.) A gathering for coffee and conversation.

Kahlúa. Coffee liqueur.

Kahneman, Daniel. (1934–) Israeli-American academic; awarded Nobel Prize in Economics (2002).

Kahoolawe. Smallest of the main Hawaiian islands.

Kakadu National Park, Northern Territory, Australia.

kakapo. Endangered flightless bird from New Zealand.

Kalamazoo, Michigan.

Kalashnikov. Rifle.

kaleidoscope.

Kalgoorlie. Mining town in Western Australia.

Kamchatka Peninsula, Russia.

kamikaze.

Kampuchea. Official name for Cambodia, 1975–1989.

Kandinsky, Wassily (or **Vasily**). (1866–1944) Russian-born French artist.

Kaneohe. City and bay on Oahu, Hawaii.

Kant, Immanuel. (1724–1804) German philosopher.

Kaohsiung. Second-largest city in Taiwan.

Kapuściński, Ryszard. (1932–2007) Polish writer.

Karachayevo-Cherkesiya. Russian republic.

Karadžić, Radovan. (1945–) Bosnian Serb politician accused of genocide and war crimes.

Karajan, Herbert von. (1908–1989) Austrian conductor.

Karamanlis, Kostas (or **Costas**). (1956–) Prime minister of Greece (2004–); formally **Konstantinos Karamanlis.**

Karl-Marx-Stadt. (Hyphens.) Name of Chemnitz, Germany, during Communist era.

Karlovy Vary. Czech spa formerly known as Carlsbad.

Kármán, Theodor von. (1881–1963) Hungarian-born American physicist.

Karolinska Institute, Stockholm.

Kaskaskia River, Illinois.

Kasparov, Garry. (1963–) Note -*rr*-. Russian chess player; born Harry Weinstein.

Kassel, Germany.

Katharina. Character in *The Taming of the Shrew* by William Shakespeare.

Katharine's Docks, St., London. Note the unusual spelling of *Katharine.*

Katmandu (or **Kathmandu**). Capital of Nepal.

Kattegatt. The strait between Denmark and Sweden; in Danish Kattegat.

Kauai. Hawaiian island.

Kauffman Stadium. Kansas City baseball stadium, home of the Royals.

Kaufman, George S(imon). (1889–1961) American dramatist.

Kazakhstan. Central Asian republic, formerly part of the Soviet Union; capital Astana.

keelhaul.

keenness, but **keenest.**

keeshond. Breed of dog; pl. *keeshonden.*

Kefauver, (Carey) Estes. (1909–1963) American politician.

Keino, Kip. (1940–) Kenyan runner; full name **Kipchoge Keine.**

Keneally, Thomas. (1935–) Australian writer.

Kenyatta, Jomo. (c. 1897–1978) Born Kamau Ngengi; president of Kenya (1964–1978).

Kerensky, Alexander (Feodorovich). (1881–1970) Russian revolutionary, briefly prime minister (1917).

kerfuffle. Disorder, commotion.

Kerguelen Islands. Group of islands in the southern Indian Ocean.

Kerkyra. Greek for Corfu.

Kern, Jerome. (1885–1945) American composer.

kerosene.

Kerouac, Jack. (1922–1969) American novelist, a spokesman for the "beat generation"; born Jean-Louis Kerouac.

Kerrey, Bob. (1943–) U.S. politician and academic; president of the New School.

Kerry, John. (1943–) U.S. Democratic senator from Massachusetts; ran for president in 2004.

Kertész, Imre. (1929–) Hungarian writer; awarded Nobel Prize for Literature in 2002.

kewpie doll.

Key, Francis Scott. (1780–1843) Author of "The Star-Spangled Banner."

KGB. Komitet Gosudarstvennoi Bezopasnosti, "Commission of State Security"; the secret service of the former Soviet Union. The name ceased to be used after 1991.

khaki, pl. *khakis.*

Khalilzad, Zalmay. (1951–) Afghan-born American academic and diplomat; U.S. ambassador to United Nations (2007–).

Khamenei, Ayatollah Sayyid Ali. (1939–) Supreme Leader of Iran (1989–). Note that *Sayyid* has many variant spellings, among them *Seyyed, Seyed,* and *Said.*

Khartoum. Capital of Sudan.

Khayyám, Omar. Omar is not a first name, so alphabetically this Persian poet and mathematician (c. 1050–c. 1125) should be listed under *O*.

Khomeini, Ayatollah Ruhollah. (1908–1989) Iranian religious and political leader, head of state (1979–1989).

Khrushchev, Nikita. Few errors make a publication look more careless than misspelling the name of a world leader, and few leaders' names have been misspelled more frequently or variously than that of the late Soviet leader Nikita Khrushchev. Note that the surname has three *h*'s.

Kibaki, Mwai. (1931–) President of Kenya (2002–).

kibbutz, kibitz. The first refers to Israeli communal settlements (pl. *kibbutzim*). The second is to watch at cards or some other such activity, often in an interfering manner.

kibosh.

kidnapped, kidnapper, kidnapping.

kielbasa. Polish sausage.

Kierkegaard, Søren (Aabye). (1813–1855) Danish philosopher.

Kigali. Capital of Rwanda.

Kiick, Jim. (1946–) American football player.

Kilauea. Active volcano on the island of Hawaii.

Kilimanjaro. Mountain in Tanzania, the highest point in Africa (19,340 feet; 5,895 meters). At the end of a line the name should be divided *Kilima-njaro*.

Kill Van Kull. Strait between Staten Island and New Jersey.

kiloton. (Abbr. kT.) An explosive force equal to 1,000 tons of TNT.

kilowatt. (Abbr. kW.) 1,000 watts.

Kimberley, South Africa and Australia.

Kimberly-Clark. U.S. paper and forest products group.

Kim Il Sung. (1912–1994) North Korean prime minister (1948–1972) and president (1972–1994), succeeded by his son, **Kim Jong Il** (1942–).

kimono, pl. *kimonos.*

kind, kinds. There should always be agreement between *kind* or *kinds* and its antecedents. "These kind of mistakes" should be either "This kind of mistake" or "These kinds of mistakes."

kindergarten, but **kindergartner.**

kinesiology. The study of body movement.

kinetics is singular.

King, (William Lyon) Mackenzie. (1874–1950) Prime minister of Canada (1921–1926, 1926–1930, 1935–1948).

Kings Canyon National Park, California (no apos.).

Kingsford-Smith (hyphen) for the airport in Sydney, Australia, but **Sir Charles Kingsford Smith** (no hyphen) for the aviator after whom it was named.

Kinshasa. Formerly Léopoldville; capital of the Democratic Republic of Congo.

Kirghizia. Now called **Kyrgyzstan.**

Kirgizstan. Use **Kyrgyzstan.**

Kiribati. Remote coral-islands state in Pacific Ocean; capital Tarawa.

Kirin/Jilin. (Pinyin.) Chinese province.

Kirkpatrick, Jeane. (1926–2006) American diplomat and academic. Note irregular spelling of first name.

Kissimmee, Florida.

Kitakyushu, Japan.

kith and kin. Your kin are your relatives. Your kith are your relatives and acquaintances.

kittiwake. Type of gull.

Kitty Litter is a trademark.

Kitzbühel. Austrian resort.

Klein, Calvin (Richard). (1942–) American fashion designer.

klieg light.

Klinefelter syndrome. Not *-felter's.* Genetic disease that causes language difficulties.

KLM. Abbreviation of Koninklijke Luchtvaart Maatschappij, national airline of the Netherlands. It merged with Air France in 2004 to form **Air France–KLM.**

Klöckner-Werke. German steel manufacturer.

Kmart for the stores group. The formal name is **Kmart Corporation.**

knackwurst (or **knockwurst**). Sausage.

knead. To manipulate, as with bread dough.

Knesset. Israeli parliament.

knick knack.

Knight Commander of the Order of the Bath for the British honorary title. Note the second *the.*

knockwurst. Alternative spelling of **knackwurst.**

Knossos is generally the preferred spelling in American English for the ancient capital of Crete; alternative spellings are **Cnossos** and **Cnossus.**

knot. A speed of one nautical mile an hour. A ship does eight knots or it does eight nautical miles an hour, but not eight knots an hour. A nautical mile equals 1.15 land miles, and in most contexts the reader will appreciate having that difference elucidated.

koala bears is wrong. *Koalas* are marsupials and have no relation to bears. Just call them **koalas.**

København. Danish spelling of Copenhagen.

Kohinoor/Koh-i-noor. Famous Indian diamond, now part of the British crown jewels.

Kohlberg Kravis Roberts. (No commas.) American investment firm.

Köhler, Horst. (1943–) President of Germany (2004–).

kohlrabi. Edible plant, pl. *kohlrabies.*

Kohn Pedersen Fox. (No commas.) U.S. architectural firm.

Kokoschka, Oskar. (1886–1980) Austrian-born British artist and writer.

Kolkata is the new official name for the Indian city traditionally known as Calcutta; until the new name is fully established, both should be used on first reference.

Köln. German spelling of Cologne.

Komunyakaa, Yusef. (1947–) American poet.

Konditorei. (Ger.) Bakery.

kookaburra. Australian kingfisher.

Koolhaas, Rem. (1944–) Dutch architect; full name **Remment Koolhaas.**

kopek (or **kopeck**). Small Russian coin.

Kopit, Arthur. (1937–) American playwright.

Koppel, Ted. (1940–) American television journalist.

Koran (or **Quran**). Muslim holy book.

Korea was partitioned in 1948 into **South Korea** (officially **Republic of Korea**), capital Seoul; and **North Korea** (officially **People's Democratic Republic of Korea**), capital Pyongyang.

Korean names are similar to Chinese in that the family name comes first; thus, after the first reference, Park Chung Hee becomes Mr. Park. Koreans tend not to hyphenate their given names, and neither as a rule do they write the second given name without caps, as in the old Chinese system.

Korematsu v. United States. 1944 Supreme Court case that upheld the internment of Japanese-American citizens on grounds of national security.

Korsakoff's syndrome. Dementia associated with chronic alcoholism or vitamin deficiency.

koruna. Basic unit of currency in Czech Republic and Slovakia.

Kosciusko, Thaddeus. (1746–1817) In Polish, Tadeusz Kościuszko. Polish general who fought on the American side in the Revolutionary War. But note that it is the **Kosciuszko Bridge** in New York.

Kosinski, Jerzy. (1933–1991) Polish-born American novelist.

Kosovar. Of or from Kosovo (e.g., Kosovar Albanians).

Kosygin, Alexei (Nikolayevich). (1904–1980) Prime minister of Soviet Union (1964–1980).

Kournikova, Anna. (1981–) Russian tennis player.

Krafft-Ebing, Baron, Richard von. (1840–1902) German psychiatrist.

Kraków, Poland; in English, Cracow.

Krapp's Last Tape. One-act play by Samuel Beckett (1958).

Kreuger, Ivar. (1880–1932) Not *Ivan*. Swedish financier who perpetrated $500 million fraud on investors.

Kriss Kringle. Alternative name for Santa Claus.

Kristallnacht. (Ger.) "Crystal night"; so called because of all the glass broken during looting and destruction of Jewish businesses and synagogues in Germany and Austria on November 9–10, 1938.

krona, krone, kronor, etc. The currencies of Scandinavia are easily confused. In Sweden, the basic unit of currency is a *krona* (pl. *kronor*); in Denmark and Norway it is a *krone* (pl. *kroner*); in Iceland it is a *króna* (pl. *krónur*).

Krugerrand for the South African gold coin (used as an investment vehicle and not as a currency). Note *-rr-*.

Krung Thep. Thai name for Bangkok.

Krusenstern, Cape, Alaska.

Krzyzewski, Mike. (1947–) American basketball coach.

Kuala Lumpur. Capital of Malaysia.

Kublai Khan. (1216–1294) Mongol emperor of China (1279–1294); but **"Kubla Khan"** for the unfinished poem by Samuel Taylor Coleridge (1797).

kudos is a Greek word meaning fame or glory. Though often treated as a plural, it is in fact singular. Thus, it should be "the kudos that was his due."

Kuiper belt. Band of comets in outer solar system, named for **Gerard Kuiper** (1905–1973), Dutch-born American astronomer who posited their existence.

Ku Klux Klan. (No hyphens.)

kulak. Russian peasant.

Kumagai Gumi Company Limited. Japanese construction company.

kumquat.

Kuomintang/Guomindang. The first is the former spelling, the second the preferred current spelling for the Chinese Nationalist Party, founded by Sun Yat-sen. The syllable *-tang/-dang* contains the notion of party, so refer only to the Kuomintang, not Kuomintang Party.

Kurile Islands. Island chain between Russia and Japan.

Kurosawa, Akira. (1910–1998) Japanese film director.

Kuwaiti, pl. *Kuwaitis.*

Kuybyshev. Russian city; formerly Samara.

Kuznetsov, Anatoly. (1930–1979) Russian novelist.

Kuznetsova, Svetlana. (1985–) Russian tennis player.

kW. Kilowatt.

KwaNdebele. Former South African homeland, now part of Mpumalanga Province.

kwashiorkor. Nutritional disorder in young children.

KwaZulu-Natal. Province of South Africa.

Kyd, Thomas. (1558–1594) English playwright.

Kydland, Finn E. (1943–) Norwegian-American academic, awarded Nobel Prize for Economics (2004).

Kyrgyzstan, or **Kyrgyz Republic.** Formerly **Kirghizia.** Central Asia republic, formerly part of Soviet Union; capital Bishkek.

Kyzyl-Kum. Desert in Kazakhstan and Uzbekistan.

Ll

labyrinth.

lackadaisical for something done without enthusiasm. Not *lacks-*.

Lackawanna, New York.

Lackawaxen River, Pennsylvania.

lacquer.

La Crosse, Wisconsin. But **lacrosse** for the sport.

lacuna. A missing part; pl. *lacunas/lacunae.*

lacy. Not *-ey.*

laddie. Not *-dy.*

Ladies' Home Journal.

Ladies Professional Golf Association. (No apos.)

Lady Chatterley's Lover. Novel by D. H. Lawrence (1928).

Lafayette, Marie Joseph Paul Yves Roch Gilbert du Motier, Marquis de. (1757–1834) French general who played a leading role in both the American and French revolutions.

Laffitte, Jacques. (1767–1844) French statesman.

Lafite, Château. Celebrated wine from Bordeaux.

Lafitte/Laffitte, Jean. (c. 1780–c. 1826) French pirate.

La Follette, Robert M(arion). (1855–1925) American politician; ran for president as a Progressive in 1924.

Lag b'Omer. Jewish holiday.

lagniappe. A small, unexpected gift; pronounced *lan-yap.*

La Guardia Airport, New York. Some users make the name one word, as in Fiorello H. LaGuardia Community College in Queens, but the two-word form is more general for both the man and any entities named for him, particularly the airport. For the record, **Fiorello Henry La Guardia** (1882–1947) was a New York congressman from 1917–1921 and 1923–1933 and mayor of New York City from 1934–1945.

laissez-faire. (Hyphen.) Policy of noninterference by government in trade and industry.

Laius. In Greek mythology, the king of Thebes and father of Oedipus.

La Jolla, California.

Lake Wobegon. Fictional town in stories by Garrison Keillor.

lama, Lammas, llama. A *lama* is a Buddhist monk from Tibet or Mongolia (his dwelling place is a lamasery). *Lammas* is a type of harvest festival. The *llama* is a wool-bearing animal from South America.

lambaste. Not *-bast.* To criticize sharply.

Lambeau Field. Home of the Green Bay Packers.

Lamborghini. Italian sports car.

lamb's wool. Not *lambswool.*

LAN Airlines. Principal airline of Chile; formerly LanChile.

Lancelot/Launcelot. Both spellings have been used for the Arthurian knight, the first notably by Tennyson and the second notably by Malory.

Land Rover, Range Rover (two words, no hyphen) for the British cars.

Land's End, Cornwall, England, but **Lands' End** for the clothing company.

Langtry, Lillie. (1853–1929) British actress; but her nickname was "The Jersey Lily."

Languedoc-Roussillon. Region of France; capital Montpellier.

languid, limpid. Not to be confused. *Limpid* means clear, calm, untroubled ("a limpid stream"). It has nothing to do with being limp or listless—meanings that are covered by *languid.*

languor, languorous.

lanyard. Not -*lard*. Short rope or cord.

Lanzhou. Capital of Gansu Province, China; formerly known in English as Lanchow.

Laois. Irish county (pronounced *lay-ish.*); in Gaelic, Laoighis. Formerly called Leix (pronounced *laix*) and Queen's.

Laomedon. In Greek mythology, the founder of Troy.

Lao-tze (or **Lao-tzu**); in Pinyin **Lao Zi.** (c. 600–530 BC) Chinese philosopher, reputed founder of Taoism. On first reference it is probably best to give both the traditional and Pinyin spellings of the name.

laparotomy. Surgical incision into the abdominal wall.

La Paz. Administrative capital and main city of Bolivia; the official capital is Sucre.

Laphroaig. Whiskey; pronounced *la-froyg*.

lapis lazuli. Type of gemstone.

La Plata, Argentina, but **Río de la Plata.**

Lapp, Lappish, but **Lapland, Laplander.** The correct name for the people is *Sami.*

lapsus memoriae. (Lat.) A lapse of memory.

largess.

La Rochefoucauld, François, Duc de. (1613–1680) French writer known for his maxims.

Larousse. French publisher of reference books.

larrikin. Australian term for an uncultured or ill-behaved person.

larynx, pl. *larynges/larynxes. Larynges* should be the preferred term for medical or academic writings, but *larynxes* is probably better, and certainly more immediately understood, in more general contexts.

lasagna (or **lasagne**).

La Scala. Celebrated opera house in Milan; its formal name is **Teatro alla Scala.**

LaSorda, Tom. (1954–) CEO of Chrysler Group. But **Tommy Lasorda** (1927–) is the former baseball player and manager.

Lassen Peak. Volcanic mountain in northern California.

lasso, pl. *lassos.*

last, latest. Various authorities have issued various strictures against using *last* when you mean *latest.* Clearly, *last* should not be used when it might be misinterpreted, as in "the last episode of the television series" when you mean the most recent but not the final one. However, it should also be noted that *last* in the sense of *latest* has a certain force of idiom behind it, and when ambiguity is unlikely (as in "He spoke about it often during the last presidential election campaign"), a reasonable measure of latitude should be granted.

Lateran Treaty (1929). Treaty between Italy and the Vatican by which the papacy recognized Italy as a state and Italy recognized the Vatican City as a sovereign papal state.

latitude.

Latour, Château. A wine from Bordeaux.

La Tour, Georges de. (1593–1652) French artist.

Latter-day Saints. The Mormons' name for themselves.

laudable, laudatory. Occasionally confused. *Laudable* means deserving praise. *Laudatory* means expressing praise.

Launcelot/Lancelot. Both spellings are used for the Arthurian knight, the first by Malory, the second by Tennyson.

laundromat is no longer a trademark.

law and order is singular.

lawful, legal. In many contexts the words can be used interchangeably, but not always. *Lawful* means "permissible under the law" (*lawful behavior, lawful protest*). *Legal* has that meaning plus the additional sense of "relating to the law," as in *legal system* or *legal profession.*

lay, lie. *Lay* and *lie*, in all their manifestations, are a constant source of errors. There are no simple rules for dealing with them. You must either commit their various forms to memory or avoid them altogether. The forms are as follows:

	lay	lie
present:	I lay the book on the table.	I lie down / I am lying down.
past:	Yesterday I laid the book on the table.	Last night I lay down to sleep.
present perfect:	I have already laid the book on the table.	I have lain in bed all day.

The most common type of error is to say, "If you're not feeling well, go upstairs and lay down." It should be "lie down."

Lazarus, Emma. (1849–1887) American poet, remembered chiefly for "The New Colossus," the poem inscribed on the Statue of Liberty.

L-dopa. Drug used for treatment of Parkinson disease.

leach, leech. The first describes the seepage of fluids, the second a bloodsucking invertebrate.

lead, led. The past tense of the verb to *lead* is *led*. When *lead* is pronounced *led* it applies only to the metallic element.

Leadbelly (or **Lead Belly**). (1888–1949) American blues musician; born Huddie William Ledbetter.

Leavitt, Henrietta Swan. (1868–1921) American astronomer.

lebensraum. (Ger.) "Living space"; imperialist notion pursued by Hitler that Germans were entitled to occupy neighboring lands.

Le Carré, John. (1931–) Pen name of David Cornwell, British novelist.

Le Corbusier. (1887–1965) Pseudonym of Charles Édouard Jeanneret, Swiss architect and town planner.

Lederberg, Joshua. (1925–) American biologist, awarded Nobel Prize in Physiology or Medicine in 1958.

lederhosen. Leather shorts.

Lee Kuan Yew. (1923–) Prime Minister of Singapore (1959–1990).

Leeuwarden, Netherlands; capital of Friesland.

Leeuwenhoek, Anton van. (1632–1723) Dutch naturalist associated with microscopes.

Leeward Islands. Former British colony in the Caribbean comprising Anguilla, Antigua, the British Virgin Islands, Montserrat, Nevis, and St. Kitts; the name now applies to all those plus Guadeloupe, the U.S. Virgin Islands, and other smaller islands in the Lesser Antilles north of the Windward Islands.

Le Fanu, Joseph. (1814–1873) Irish writer.

Lefschetz, Solomon. (1884–1972) Russian-born American mathematician.

Léger, Fernand. (1881–1955) French painter.

legerdemain. Not -*der*-.

Leghorn. English name, now seldom used, for Livorno, Italy.

legible, legibility.

Légion d'honneur. Supreme French order of merit.

Legionnaires' disease.

legitimize, not *legitimatize*.

Lehman Brothers. U.S. financial services firm; formally Lehman Brothers Holdings Inc.

Lehman College, City University of New York.

Lehmann, Rosamond. (1901–1990) English novelist.

Leibniz, (Gottfried Wilhelm) Baron von. (1646–1716) German philosopher and mathematician.

Leicestershire, England. Abbr. Leics.

Leiden, Leyden. The first is the usual spelling for the Dutch town; the second for the scientific instrument known as a Leyden jar.

Leinster. Province of the Republic of Ireland comprising the counties of Carlow, Dublin, Kildare, Kilkenny, Laois, Longford, Louth, Meath, Offaly, Westmeath, Wexford, and Wicklow.

Leipzig, Germany.

leitmotif (or **leitmotiv**). A recurring idea or dominant theme associated with a particular character or idea in a musical or literary work.

Leitrim. Irish county; pronounced *lee'-trim.*

Léman, Lac. French name for Lake Geneva.

Le Mesurier, John. (1912–1983) British actor.

Lemieux, Mario. (1965–) Canadian ice hockey player.

Lemmon, Jack. (1925–2001) American actor.

LeMond, Greg. (1961–) American cyclist.

lend, loan. *Loan* as a verb ("He loaned me some money") is now more or less standard, though one or two authorities continue to disdain it, favoring *lend* on grounds of tradition.

Lendl, Ivan. (1960–) Czech tennis player.

Leningrad. Russian city, now called St. Petersburg again.

lens, pl. *lenses.*

Leonardo da Vinci. (1452–1519) Renaissance genius. *The Da Vinci Code* notwithstanding, a work or object associated with him should be called a Leonardo, not a Da Vinci.

Léopoldville. Former name of Kinshasa, Democratic Republic of the Congo.

Le Pen, Jean-Marie. (1928–) French politician, founder of National Front.

leprechaun. Not *lepra-.*

lèse-majesté. (Fr.) "Wounded majesty"; treason or a similar offense or insolence toward anyone to whom deference is due. The spelling is sometimes anglicized to *lese-majesty.*

Lesotho. Small, landlocked African kingdom; formerly called Basutoland. Capital Maseru. The people of Lesotho are known as Basotho (sing. and pl.).

less, fewer. The simplest rule is to use *less* with singular nouns (*less money, less sugar*) and *fewer* with plural ones (*fewer houses, fewer cars*).

Lesseps, Ferdinand Marie, Vicomte de. (1805–1894) French engineer closely associated with the Suez Canal. On second reference, de Lesseps.

L'Étoile. Area around Arc de Triomphe, Paris.

Letzeburgesch. German dialect spoken in Luxembourg.

level, mark. These are often pointlessly employed. "Stock prices once again fell below the 12,000 level" says no more than ". . . fell below 12,000."

Leverrier, Urbain Jean Joseph. (1811–1877) French astronomer.

Lévesque, René. (1922–1988) Canadian politician, leader of Parti Québécois.

Levi's. Jeans produced by Levi Strauss.

Lévi-Strauss, Claude. (1908–) French anthropologist.

Leviticus. Book of the Old Testament.

Levittown, New York and Pennsylvania.

Lewis, Meriwether. (1774–1809) Not *-whether*. The coleader (with William Clark) of the Lewis and Clark expedition of 1804–1806.

Lewis, Wyndham. (1884–1957) English writer and artist.

Leyden jar, but the Dutch town is now usually spelled *Leiden*.

Lhasa for the capital of Tibet, **Lhasa apso** for the breed of dog.

liable, likely, apt, prone. All four indicate probability, but they carry distinctions worth noting. *Apt* is better reserved for general probabilities ("It is apt to snow in January") and *likely* for specific ones ("It is likely to snow today"). *Liable* and *prone* are better used to indicate a probability arising as a regrettable consequence: "People who drink too much are prone to heart disease"; "If you don't pay your taxes, you are liable to get caught." A separate but common problem with *likely* is seen in this sentence: "Cable experts say the agreement will likely strengthen the company's position." Used as an adverb, *likely* needs to be accompanied by one of four helping words: *very,* *quite, more,* or *most.* Thus the sentence should say "will very likely strengthen."

liaison.

libel, slander. Although nearly all dictionaries define *libel* merely as a statement that defames or damages a person's reputation, it is worth remembering that it must do so unreasonably or inaccurately. It is the wrongness of a contention that makes it libelous, not the harshness or hostility of it. Although a libel usually takes the form of a written utterance, drawings and other visual depictions may also be libelous. In all cases, a libel must be published (the word comes from the Latin *libellus,* meaning "little book"). When defamatory remarks are merely spoken, the term to describe the act is *slander.*

liberté, égalité, fraternité. (Fr.) "Liberty, equality, fraternity"; slogan of the French Revolution.

Liberty, Statue of, was emplaced in 1886. It is officially known as *Liberty Enlightening the World.* Its designer was Frédéric-Auguste Bartholdi. Liberty Island was formerly called Bedloes Island.

Libeskind, Daniel. (1946–) Polish-born American architect.

lichee (or **litchi** or **lychee**). Chinese tree and its fruit.

Lichfield for the town and cathedral in Staffordshire, England, and for the photographer **Patrick Lichfield** (1939–2005), who was formally the Earl of Lichfield, Viscount Anson, and Baron Soberton.

Lichtenstein, Roy. (1923–1997) American artist.

lickerish. Greedy, lascivious.

licorice.

Liebfraumilch. White Rhine wine; in German it is *Liebfrauenmilch.*

Liechtenstein. Diminutive Alpine principality; capital Vaduz.

lifelong. Though the term needn't be taken absolutely literally in most contexts, it should have some sense of at least approximately covering the whole of the subject's existence, so that one might be called a lifelong Yankees fan, but not, say, a lifelong drug addict.

lighted, lit. Either is correct. *Lighted*, however, is more usual when the word is being used as an adjective ("a lighted torch").

lightning, not *lightening*.

light-year. The distance that light travels through empty space in one year (about 5.88 trillion miles; 9.46 trillion kilometers).

likable.

like, as. Problems often arise in choosing between *like* and *as*. On the face of it, the rule is simple: *as* and *as if* are always followed by a verb; *like* never is. Therefore you would say, "He plays tennis like an expert" (no verb after *like*) but "He plays tennis as if his life depended on it" (verb *depended*). Except in the most formal writing, however, only a stickler would object to formations such as "She looks just like her mother used to" and "He can't dance like he used to." There is also one apparent inconsistency in the rule in that *like* may be used when it comes between "feel" and an "-ing" verb: "He felt like walking"; "I feel like going abroad this year."

likelihood.

Lilienthal, Otto. (1849–1896) German inventor.

Lilliput (cap.) for the fictional place, but **lilliputian** (no cap.) for something small.

Lilly, Eli. Not *-ey*. U.S. pharmaceuticals company.

Lilongwe. Capital of Malawi.

lily, pl. *lilies.*

Limassol, Cyprus.

Limbourg, Limburg. The first is a province of Belgium; the second a province of the Netherlands. The cheese is Limburg or Limburger.

limited means constrained, set within bounds. Unless there is the idea of a limit being imposed, the word is better avoided. It is reasonable enough to say that a special offer is available for a limited time, but to write that "there was a limited demand for tickets" is absurd when what is meant is that fewer customers than had been hoped showed up.

linage, lineage. The first refers to lines of text; the second to ancestry.

linchpin, but **lynch law, lynch gang.**

Linnaean for the system of naming plants and animals by genus and species names (e.g., *Homo sapiens*). Some dictionaries also accept *Linnean* as an alternative spelling. The term comes from the Swedish botanist Carl Linné (1707–1778), who chose to Latinize his name as Carolus Linnaeus. For the rules of application concerning the Linnaean system, see GENUS, SPECIES.

lion's share is a cliché. Why not say "most" or "the larger part" or whatever is appropriate?

Lipari Islands. Group of islands off Sicily, also known as the Aeolian Islands.

Lipchitz, Jacques. (1891–1973) French sculptor.

Lippmann, Walter. (1889–1974) American journalist.

liquefy, liquefaction.

liqueur.

lira. Currency of Turkey; pl. *liras*. It has not been the currency of Italy since 2002, but for historical purposes it may be worth noting that the Italian plural was *lire*.

lissome.

literally means actually, not figuratively. If you don't wish to be taken literally, don't use *literally*.

literati. Literary elite; learned people. But **littérateur** for a person of letters.

Livni, Tzipora. (1958–) Deputy prime minister of Israel (2006–).

Ljubicic, Ivan. (1979–) Croatian tennis player.

Ljubljana. Capital of Slovenia; pronounced *loob-lee-yah'-na*.

Llanfairpwllgwyngyllgogerychwyrndrobwll-llantysiliogogogoch. Village in Wales, on the island of Anglesey, famous for having the longest name in Britain.

Lloyd George, David. (1863–1945) (No hyphen.) British prime minister (1916–22); but **Earl Lloyd-George of Dwyfor** (hyphen) for his title as a peer.

Lloyd Webber, Andrew. (1948–) Now **Lord Lloyd-Webber** (hyphen), British composer of musicals; brother of **Julian Lloyd Webber** (1951–), cellist.

Lloyd's of London (apos.) for the venerable insurance exchange, but **Lloyds TSB** (no apos.) for the British bank.

Llullaillaco. Mountain on border of Argentina and Chile.

loath, loathe. The first is an adjective meaning reluctant; the second, a verb meaning to despise.

loathsome.

LoBiondo, Frank. (1946–) U.S. representative from New Jersey.

local residents. Residents generally are local, so in most contexts the first word can be deleted.

loc. cit., the abbreviation of *loco citato* (Lat.), means "in the place cited."

Locke, John. (1632–1704) English philosopher.

lodestar, lodestone. These are the preferred spellings, but **loadstar** and **loadstone** are also accepted.

Lódź, Poland; pronounced *woodj*.

logarithm.

Lomé. Capital of Togo.

Longchamp, not -*champs*, for the French racecourse.

Longfellow, Henry Wadsworth. (1807–1882) American poet.

Longleat House, Wiltshire, England.

longueur. Note -*ueu*-. Boring interval or section of an entertaining work.

Look Homeward, Angel. Note comma. Novel by Thomas Wolfe (1929).

Lord's Cricket Ground, London.

Lorenz, Konrad. (1903–1989) Austrian zoologist.

losable.

Los Alamitos Race Course, Los Angeles.

Louis Roederer champagne.

Louis Vuitton. French luxury goods company.

Lourenço Marques. Former name of Maputo, capital of Mozambique.

Louvain. French and English spelling of Belgian university town known as Leuven in Flemish.

louver. A type of slatted cover.

Love's Labour's Lost. Comedy by Shakespeare. There may also have been a companion play, now lost, called **Love's Labour's Won.**

LPG. Liquefied petroleum gas.

luau. Hawaiian feast.

lubricous is generally the preferred spelling for the word meaning slippery or lewd, but most dictionaries also accept *lubricious.*

Luddite. A worker opposed to technological change.

Ludwigshafen, Germany.

Lufthansa. German national airline.

Luftwaffe. German air force.

luge. Type of sled.

luminesce, luminescence.

lumpenproletariat. Bottom of the working class.

Luxembourg, Grand Duchy of. In French, Grand-Duché de Luxembourg; the capital is also Luxembourg (or Luxembourg City, for clarity).

Luxemburg, Rosa. (1871–1919) Political activist.

lux mundi. (Lat.) "Light of the world."

luxuriant, luxurious. The words are not interchangeable, though the meanings sometimes overlap. *Luxuriant* indicates profusion ("luxuriant hair"). *Luxurious* means sumptuous and expensive ("a luxurious house"). A luxuriant carpet is a shaggy one; a luxurious carpet is an expensive one.

Lyly, John. (c. 1555–1606) English playwright.

Lyonnaise, lyonnaise. The first is a region of France; the second is a style of cooking.

Lysistrata. Comedy by Aristophanes.

Mm

Maas. Dutch name for the European river known in English as the Meuse.

Ma'at. Egyptian goddess of truth.

Mac, Mc, M'. In British usage all such words are treated as if they were spelled *Mac* when determining alphabetical order. Thus *McGuire* would precede *Mason*. In the United States, the alphabetical order of the letters is followed literally, and *Mason* would precede *McGuire*.

macadam. A type of road surface, named after John McAdam (1756–1836), a Scottish engineer.

macaque. Monkey of the genus *Macaca*.

macaronic verse. A type of poetry in which two or more languages are mingled.

MacArthur, Charles. (1895–1956) American playwright and screenwriter, and father of **James MacArthur** (1937–), actor.

MacArthur, Douglas. (1880–1964) American general.

MacArthur Foundation, John D. and Catherine T. U.S. charity famous for generous awards.

Macaulay, Baron Thomas Babington. (1800–1859) British historian.

Maccabees. Jewish dynasty of second and first centuries BC.

Macdonald, Dwight. (1906–1982) American writer and critic.

Macdonald, Sir John Alexander. (1815–1891) Canadian prime minister (1867–1873, 1878–1891).

MacDonald, Ramsay. (1866–1938) British prime minister (1924, 1929–1935).

Macdonald, Ross. Pen name of Kenneth Millar (1915–1983), Canadian-American author of detective fiction.

Macdonnell Ranges, Northern Territory, Australia.

Macgillicuddy's Reeks. Mountain range in County Kerry, Ireland.

MacGraw, Ali. (1938–) American actress.

MacGregor. Scottish clan.

Machiavelli, Niccolò di Bernardo dei. (1469–1527) Florentine statesman and political theorist, best known for *Il Principe* (*The Prince*), 1513.

machicolation. Gallery at the top of a castle tower.

Mach number. (Cap. *M*.) The ratio of the speed of an object to the speed of sound in the medium (usually air) through which the object is traveling: e.g., an aircraft traveling at twice the speed of sound is said to be going at Mach 2. Named after **Ernst Mach** (1836–1916), an Austrian physicist.

Macintosh for the computer made by Apple, but **McIntosh** for the apple.

Mackenzie, river and mountains in western Canada, but **McKenzie** for the lake and bay in Ontario and the pass in Oregon.

Mackinac Island and **Straits of Mackinac,** in Lake Huron, but **Mackinaw City,** Michigan. The type of woolen coat is called a *mackinaw,* but *Mackinaw blanket* and *Mackinaw boat* are both capitalized. For all spellings, the pronunciation is *mack-in-aw.*

MacLaine, Shirley. (1934–) American actress; born Shirley MacLean Beaty.

MacLean, Alistair. (1922–1987) British writer of adventure novels.

Maclean's. Canadian weekly newsmagazine.

MacLehose & Sons. Scottish printers.

MacLeish, Archibald. (1892–1982) American poet.

Macleod, Lake, Western Australia.

MacMurray, Fred. (1907–1991) American actor.

MacNeice, (Frederick) Louis. (1907–1963) Irish-born British poet.

MacNelly, Jeff. (1947–2000) American cartoonist.

Macon, Georgia, but Mâcon for the French city and wine.

Macy's department stores. Formally R. H. Macy & Co.; now a subsidiary of Federated Department Stores.

Madagascar. Island republic off Southeast Africa, formerly Malagasy Republic; capital Antananarivo.

mademoiselle. (Fr.) Not *-dam-*. An unmarried female; pl. *mesdemoiselles.*

Madhya Pradash. Indian state.

Madison, Dolley. (1768–1849) Not *Dolly.* U.S. first lady, wife of James Madison. But note that some commercial products spell the name **Dolly Madison.**

Madras, India; now called Chennai; on first reference, it is probably best to use both names.

Madrileño. Citizen of Madrid.

maelstrom.

Maeterlinck, Count Maurice. (1862–1949) Belgian poet and dramatist; awarded Nobel Prize in Literature (1911).

Mafeking, Mafikeng. The first is the historical spelling for the site of a famous siege during the Boer War; the second is the current spelling of the South African town.

Mafioso. A member of the Mafia; pl. *Mafiosi.*

Magdalen College, Oxford, but **Magdalene College,** Cambridge. Both are pronounced *maudlin.* The New Testament figure is **Mary Magdalene.**

Magellan, Ferdinand. (1480–1521) Portuguese explorer; led first expedition that circumnavigated the globe, though he himself was killed en route; in Portuguese, Fernão de Magalhães.

Maggiore, Lake, Italy.

Maghreb. Collective name for Algeria, Morocco, and Tunisia.

Maginot Line. Line of defensive fortifications across northeastern France, breached by Germany in 1940.

Magna Carta (or **Charta**). Charter of rights signed by King John at Runnymede, England, in 1215.

magnum opus, opus magnum. (Lat.) The first is an author's principal work; the second is a great work.

Magritte, René. (1898–1967) Belgian surrealist painter.

Mahabhrata. Indian epic.

maharaja, maharanee. Indian prince and princess.

Mahatir bin Mohamad, Dr. (1925–) Prime minister of Malaysia (1981–2003).

Mahfouz, Naguib. (1912–2006) Egyptian novelist; awarded Nobel Prize for Literature in 1988.

mahjong. Chinese game played with tiles.

mahogany.

Maillol, Aristide. (1861–1944) French sculptor.

maître d'hôtel. (Fr.) Hotel manager or headwaiter; pl. *maîtres d'hôtel.*

Majlis. Parliament of Iran.

major, as in a "major initiative," "major embarrassment," "major undertaking," and so on, remains a severely overworked word, and thus brings a kind of tofu quality to much writing, giving it bulk but little additional flavor. Nearly always it is worth the effort of trying to think of a more precise or expressive term.

majority should be reserved for describing the larger of two clearly divisible things, as in "A majority of the members voted for the resolution." But even then a more specific description is usually better: "52 percent," "almost two-thirds," "more than 70 percent," etc. When there is no sense of a clear contrast with a minority (as in "The majority of his spare time was spent reading"), *majority* is always better avoided.

Makassar Strait. Between Borneo and Sulawesi, Indonesia.

Makhachkala. Formerly Petrovskoye, capital of Dagestan, Russia.

Maki, Fumihiko. (1928–) Japanese architect.

Malabo. Formerly Santa Isabel, capital of Equatorial Guinea.

Malagasy Republic. Former name of Madagascar; *Malagasy* (sing. and pl.) remains the term for a person or persons from the island, and for the language spoken there.

malarkey.

Malawi. Formerly Nyasaland. African republic; capital Lilongwe.

mal de mer. (Fr.) Seasickness.

Maldives. Island republic in the Indian Ocean; capital Malé.

maleficence, malfeasance. The first means a propensity to cause hurt or harm. The second is a legal term describing wrongdoing.

Mali. Formerly French Sudan. African republic; capital Bamako.

Maliki, Nouri. (1950–) Prime minister of Iraq (2006–); sometimes also known as Jawad Maliki.

Mallarmé, Stéphane. (1842–1898) French poet.

malleable.

Mallorca. Spanish spelling of *Majorca*.

malmsey. A sweet wine; pl. *malmseys*.

malodorous.

Malory, Sir Thomas. (d. 1471) Fifteenth-century English author and compiler of Arthurian legends (notably *Le Morte d'Arthur*). But **George Mallory** (two *l*'s) for the Everest explorer (1886–1924).

Malvinas, Islas. Argentinian name for the Falkland Islands.

Mamaroneck, New York.

Mammon. (Cap.) Wealth regarded as an object of worship.

manacle. Not *-icle*. Shackle.

manageable, manageability.

Manassas. Virginia town near the site of two battles in the Civil War, usually called the battle of Bull Run in the North and the battle of Manassas in the South.

manatee. Sea cow.

mandamus. Writ commanding that a particular thing be done or a public duty performed.

mandatory, mandatary. The first means compulsory; the second is a much rarer word, which applied to holding a mandate.

Mandlikova, Hana. (1962–) Czech tennis player.

Manet, Édouard. (1832–1883) French artist.

maneuver.

mangoes/mangos. Either is correct.

Manhattan, not -*en*, for the island borough at the heart of New York City; the cocktail is **manhattan** (lowercase).

manifesto, pl. *manifestos.*

Manila. Capital of the Philippines. The paper and envelopes, etc., are usually spelled lowercase: **manila.**

Manitoulin Island, Lake Huron, Canada.

mannequin, manikin. The words are broadly interchangeable, but the first is usually reserved for the types of dummies found in store windows and the second for anatomical models used for teaching. An alternative spelling of **manikin** is **mannikin.**

manner born, to the. Not *manor.* The line is from *Hamlet.*

mano a mano. (Sp.) "Hand to hand."

mantel, mantle. The first is the usual spelling for the frame around a fireplace; the second for all other senses. Note also the spellings of the associated words **mantelshelf** and **mantelpiece.**

Mao Zedong (formerly **Mao Tse-tung**). (1893–1976) Founder and chairman of the People's Republic of China (1949–1959), and chairman of the Chinese Communist Party (1935–1976).

Mapplethorpe, Robert. (1947–1989) American photographer.

Maputo. Formerly Lourenço Marques; capital of Mozambique.

Maquis. French resistance during World War II.

Maracaibo. City and lake in Venezuela.

maraschino cherry.

March, Fredric. (1897–1975) Not *Frederick.* American actor; born Frederick McIntyre Bickel.

marchioness. Wife or widow of a marquis, or a woman holding the title of marquess.

Marciano, Rocky. (1923–1969) American boxer, world heavyweight champion (1952–1956); born Rocco Marchegiano.

Marconi, Guglielmo. (1874–1937) Italian inventor of wireless telegraphy; awarded Nobel Prize for Physics (1909).

margarine. Not -*ger*-.

margarita. A cocktail.

Margaux, Château. French wine.

marginal is unobjectionable when used to describe something falling near a lower limit ("a marginal profit"). But it is a lame choice when all you mean is small or slight.

Margrethe II. (1940–) Queen of Denmark (1972–).

Marianas Trench. Site of greatest depth (36,220 feet; 11,040 meters) of the Pacific Ocean. The nearby island chain is called the **Mariana** (not -*s*) **Islands** or the **Marianas.**

Marianske Lazne. Czech spa more widely known by its German name of **Marienbad.**

Marie Antoinette. (1755–1793) Austrian-born queen of France (1774–1793) and wife of King Louis XVI.

marionette.

markka. Former unit of Finnish currency.

Marlboro cigarettes.

Marmara, Sea of.

marmoset. Monkey.

Maroochydore, Queensland, Australia.

marquee. Large tent used for entertaining; in the United States it signifies a projection over an entrance, especially at the front of a theater.

Marquesas Islands. Archipelago in South Pacific.

Marrakesh, Morocco.

Marriage-à-la-Mode. (Hyphens.) Play by John Dryden (1672).

Marriott. Hotels group.

Marsalis, Wynton. (1961–) U.S. musician.

Marseille (or **Marseilles**), France. The French national anthem is **"La Marseillaise."**

marshal. Not -*all.*

Marshall Islands. Island nation in the Pacific Ocean; capital Majuro.

Marshall Plan, officially the European Recovery Program, was an assistance program to help European nations rebuild after World War II. It was named for **George C. Marshall** (1880–1959), secretary of state.

Marshalsea Prison, London.

Martin Luther King Day is observed in the United States on the third Monday of January.

Marunouchi. Financial district of Tokyo.

Marylebone. Roads, district, and church in London.

Mary, Queen of Scots. (1542–1587) Scottish queen, executed for treason. Some sources write her name without the comma.

Masaccio. (1401–1428) Italian painter; real name Tommaso di Ser Giovanni di Mone Cassai.

Maserati. Italian sports car.

Mason-Dixon line. Boundary line between Maryland and Pennsylvania surveyed by **Charles Mason** and **Jeremiah Dixon** in 1763–1767, traditionally regarded as the dividing line between the North and the South in the United States.

Massapequa, Massapequa Park, East Massapequa, etc., New York.

masseur (masc.), **masseuse** (fem.).

MasterCard.

masterful, masterly. Most authorities continue to insist that we observe a distinction between these two—namely that *masterly* should apply to that which is adroit and expert and *masterful* to that which is imperious and domineering. Useful as the distinction might be, it has to be noted that no leading dictionary insists on it and most don't even indicate that such a distinction exists.

Matabeleland. Region of Zimbabwe.

Matagordo Bay, Texas.

Matamoros, Mexico, but **Matamoras,** Pennsylvania.

materialize is usually no more than a somewhat pompous synonym for *occur, develop,* or *happen.*

Mathewson, Christy. (1880–1925) American baseball pitcher.

Mato Grosso, Brazil.

Matthau, Walter. (1920–2000) American actor.

matzo. Type of unleavened bread; pl. *matzos* (or *matzoth* or *matzot*).

Maudsley Hospital, London. Not *Maude-.*

Maundy Thursday. Not *Maunday.* The day before Good Friday.

Maupassant, (Henri René Albert) Guy de. (1850–1893) French author.

Mauretania, Mauritania. The first is the spelling for the ancient African country and two famous Cunard ships. The second is the spelling of the modern-day African country formally known as the Islamic Republic of Mauritania.

mausoleum.

mauvaise honte. (Fr.) Dishonest or needless shame.

Mayne, Thom. (1944–) American architect.

mayonnaise.

Mazatlán, Mexico.

mazel tov. (Heb.) "Good luck."

mazurka. Polish dance.

Mazzini, Giuseppe. (1805–1872) Italian republican and revolutionary.

Mbabane. Capital of Swaziland.

Mbeki, Thabo (Mvuyelwa). (1942–) South African president (1999–).

McAfee Coliseum, Oakland.

McCarran International Airport, Las Vegas.

McCarthy, Cormac. (1933–) American novelist.

McCarthy, Eugene (Joseph). (1916–2005) American Democratic politician.

McCarthy, Joseph (Raymond). (1900–1957) U.S. senator notorious for a prolonged campaign against Communists during congressional hearings, known as the Army-McCarthy hearings, in the 1950s.

McClellan, George B(rinton). (1826–1865) American general and politician.

McCormick, Cyrus. (1809–1884) American manufacturer and inventor.

McCormick Place. Convention center in Chicago.

McCowen, Alec. (1925–) British actor.

McCrea, Joel. (1905–1990) American film actor.

McCullers, Carson. (1917–1967) American novelist and playwright.

McDonald's (note apos.) for the fast-food chain. The company is the McDonald's Corporation.

McDonnell Douglas Corporation. Now part of Boeing.

McDowall, Roddy. (1928–1998) British-born American actor.

McEnroe, John. (1959–) American tennis player.

McEwan, Geraldine. (1932–) British actress.

McEwan, Ian. (1948–) British novelist.

McGillis, Kelly. (1957–) American actress.

McGill University, Montreal.

McGoohan, Patrick. (1928–) American actor.

McGovern, George. (1922–) American Democratic politician.

McGraw-Hill Companies, The. U.S. media and financial services company.

McGregor, Ewan. (1971–) Scottish actor.

McGuffey Eclectic Reader (not *McGuffey's*) is the formal name for the schoolbook popularly known as *McGuffey's Reader;* named for the educator **W. H. McGuffey** (1800–1873).

McGwire, Mark. (1963–) American baseball player.

McIntosh apple (after the Canadian John McIntosh), but **Macintosh** computer.

McJob. (Cap. *M*, cap. *J*.) Slang term for a low-wage job, usually in the service sector.

McKinley, Mount. Alaskan mountain that is the highest peak in North America (20,320 feet; 6,194 meters), alternative name **Denali**. It stands within Denali National Park and Preserve. Mount McKinley was named for **William McKinley** (1843–1901), U.S. president (1897–1901).

McLean, Virginia, suburb of Washington, D.C.; pronounced *muk-lane'*.

McShane, Ian. (1942–) British actor.

ME. Short for *myalgic encephalomyelitis,* a type of chronic malaise; also, postal abbreviation of Maine.

mea culpa. (Lat.) "My fault."

mean, median. Each of these terms has a very specific meaning. *The American Heritage Dictionary* defines *mean* as a number that typifies a set of numbers, such as a geometric mean or an arithmetic mean, or the average value of a set of numbers. *Median* signifies the middle value in a distribution, above and below which lie an equal number of values. Both terms are at best vaguely understood by the general reader, and thus your most prudent course of action is to use them extremely sparingly in anything other than technical writing.

measurable.

Mecklenburg. Former state in Germany.

Medal of Honor. Not *Congressional Medal of Honor.* Highest U.S. military decoration.

Médecins Sans Frontières. Medical aid charity, known in the United States as Doctors Without Borders.

Medellín, Colombia.

media is a plural. The singular is *medium.* Television is a medium; newspapers and television are media. However, *mediums* is the correct plural for describing spiritualists.

Medici. Leading family of Renaissance Florence, whose more noted members were **Cosimo de' Medici** (1389–1464), called Cosimo the Elder; **Lorenzo de' Medici** (1449–1492), called Lorenzo the Magnificent; **Giovanni de' Medici** (1475–1521), later Pope Leo X; and **Giulio de' Medici** (1478–1534), later Pope Clement VII. The French spelling is normally used for **Catherine de Medicis** (1519–1589), wife of Henry II of France, and **Marie de Medicis** (1573–1642), wife of Henry IV of France.

medieval.

mediocre.

meerschaum. White claylike mineral traditionally used to make pipe bowls.

meet, mete. In the sense of justice or punishment, the first means suitable, and the second means to allot. Thus one metes out punishment, but a fitting punishment is meet.

mega. Prefix meaning one million. A megabyte in computing is a million bytes (or a thousand kilobytes).

megahertz (one word, no cap.), but the abbreviation is MHz.

megalomania.

Meigs Field. Chicago airport; formally Merril (not -*ll*) C. Meigs Field. It closed in 2003.

Meiji. Reign of Emperor Mutsuhito (1867–1912), marking Japan's emergence as a modern industrial state.

mein Herr, meine Dame. (Ger.) Sir, lady; pl. *meine Herren, meine Damen.*

Meir, Golda. (1898–1978) Israeli prime minister (1969–1974).

Meissen porcelain. Named for the German city in which it originated.

meitnerium. Chemical element.

melamine. A type of plastic. It is not capitalized.

Melanchthon, Philipp (or **Philip**). (1497–1560) German academic; colleague of Martin Luther and a leader of the Reformation.

melee. In French, *mêlée.*

mellifluous. Sounding sweet.

memento, pl. *mementoes.*

memorabilia. Note that the word is a plural.

memorandums.

Memorial Day. Day commemorating the war dead, held the last Monday in May; originally called Decoration Day.

ménage à trois. (Fr.) Sexual relationship among three people living together.

menagerie.

Mencken, H. L. (for Henry Louis). (1880–1956) American writer, critic, and editor.

Mendel, Gregor Johann. (1822–1884) Austrian botanist whose work became the basis of modern genetics.

Mendelssohn, Felix. (1809–1847) German composer; full name Jakob Ludwig Felix Mendelssohn-Bartholdy.

Mendes da Rocha, Paulo. (1928–) Brazilian architect.

Mendès-France, Pierre. (1907–1982) French prime minister (1954–1955).

meningitis. Inflammation of the **meninges,** or cranial membranes; note that *meninges* is plural; a single membrane is a *meninx.*

Menninger Clinic, the. Psychiatric hospital founded in 1925, moved to Houston, Texas, in 2003; the **Menninger Foundation** remains in Topeka.

menorah. Seven-branched candelabrum used in Jewish worship in ancient times; today's Hanukkah menorah has nine branches.

Menorca. Spanish name for Minorca.

Menotti, Gian Carlo. (1911–2007) Italian-born American composer.

men's, women's. However eagerly department stores and the like may strive to dispense with punctuation in their signs (writing "Mens Clothing" or "Womens Department"), the practice is subliterate and to be avoided in any serious writing. Equally incorrect, if slightly less common, is placing the apostrophe after the "s" (e.g., "mens' hats," "womens' facials"). However, note that the apostrophe *is* discarded in such compounds as *menswear* and *womenswear*. See also CHILDREN'S.

Menuhin, Yehudi. (1916–1999) American-born British violinist.

meow. The sound that cats make; in Britain and elsewhere it is usually spelled **miaow.**

Mephistophelean (or **Mephistophelian**). Evil; after *Mephistopheles,* the devil to whom Faust sold his soul.

Mercalli scale. A measure of earthquake intensity; named for the Italian volcanologist **Giuseppe Mercalli** (1850–1914).

Mercedes-Benz. (Hyphen.) The plural is *Mercedeses,* but is best avoided.

meretricious. Vulgar, insincere.

meringue. Confection made from egg whites and sugar.

merino. Type of sheep; pl. *merinos.*

meritocracy. System of government based on merit.

Merkel, Angela. (1954–) German chancellor (2005–).

Merrion Square, Dublin.

mesmerize.

Messaggero, Il. Italian newspaper.

Messerschmitt, not *-schmidt,* for the type of aircraft.

metal, mettle. *Metal* denotes chemical elements such as gold and copper; *mettle* is for contexts describing courage or spirit.

metamorphose (verb), **metamorphosis** (noun), pl. *metamorphoses.*

metaphor, simile. Both are figures of speech in which two things are compared. A *simile* likens one thing to another, dissimilar one: "He ran like the wind"; "She took to racing as a duck takes to water." A *metaphor,* on the other hand, acts as if the two compared things are identical and substitutes one for the other. Comparing the beginning of time to the beginning of a day, for instance, produces the metaphor "the dawn of time."

metathesis. The transposition of sounds or letters in a word or between words; the latter commonly are called spoonerisms.

mete, meet. The first means to allot; the second means suitable. One metes out punishment, but a fitting punishment is meet.

meteor, meteorite, meteoroid. *Meteoroids* are pieces of galactic debris floating through space. If they enter Earth's atmosphere as shooting stars, they are *meteors*. If they survive the fall to Earth, they are *meteorites*.

meter, but **metric** and **metrical;** one meter equals 39.37 inches.

meticulous. Several usage books, though fewer and fewer dictionaries, insist that the word does not mean merely very careful, but rather excessively so. Unless you mean to convey a negative quality, it is usually better to use *scrupulous, careful, painstaking*, or some other synonym.

metonymy. Figure of speech in which a thing is described in terms of one of its attributes, as in calling the monarch "the crown."

Metro-Goldwyn-Mayer. Hollywood film studio, abbreviated MGM.

metronome. Instrument for marking time.

mettle. Courage or spirit.

Meuse. River in northern Europe; in Dutch, Maas.

mezzanine.

Mezzogiorno. The southern, poorer half of Italy.

mezzotint. Method of engraving, and the engraving so produced.

MGM. Metro-Goldwyn-Mayer.

miaow. British spelling of *meow*.

Michaelmas. Feast of St. Michael, September 29.

Michelangelo. (1475–1564) Italian artist, architect, and engineer; full name **Michelangelo di Lodovico Buonarroti Simoni.**

micro. Prefix meaning one-millionth, or very small.

Micronesia, Federated States of. Comprises Korsae, Ponape, Truk, and Yap; capital Kolonia.

Middlesbrough. Not *-borough.* City in northern England.

Mid Glamorgan. (Two words, no hyphen.) County in Wales.

Midi-Pyrénées. Region of France.

Midwest (one word), **Middle West** (two words).

Mientkiewicz, Doug. (1974–) American baseball player.

Mies van der Rohe, Ludwig. (1886–1969) German-born U.S. architect.

mijnheer, mynheer. The first is the Dutch spelling, the second the English of the Dutch term for "sir." Either should be capitalized when placed before a name.

mileage.

miles gloriosus. Latin for "glorious soldier." A braggart, particularly a braggart soldier. Pronounced *meel-us glor-ee-oh-sus.*

milieu. Environment.

militate, mitigate. Often confused. To *militate* is to operate against or, much more rarely, for something: "The news of the scandal militated against his election promises." To *mitigate* means to assuage, soften, make more endurable: "His apology mitigated the insult." *Mitigate against* often appears and is always wrong.

Milius, John. (1944–) American film writer and director.

Milken, Michael. (1946–) American financier.

Millais, Sir John Everett. (1829–1896) British painter.

Millay, Edna St. Vincent. (1892–1950) American poet.

millennium. Note *-nn-*. The preferred plural is *millenniums*, but *millennia* is also accepted.

milli-. Prefix meaning one-thousandth.

milliard. British term now almost never used there or anywhere else, meaning 1,000 million or 1 trillion.

millipede.

Milošević, Slobodan. (1941–2006) President of Serbia (1989–1997). He died while on trial on charges of genocide and crimes against humanity in The Hague.

milquetoast, not *milk-*, for a timid person. The name comes from an old newspaper cartoon called *The Timid Soul* featuring a character named Caspar (not *-er*) Milquetoast.

Mindanao. Island in the Philippines.

Mindszenty, József, Cardinal. (1892–1975) Roman Catholic primate of Hungary, long opposed to Communist regime.

minimize, strictly speaking, does not mean merely to play down or soften. It means to reduce to an absolute minimum.

Minorca, Balearic Islands, Spain; in Spanish, Menorca.

Minos. In Greek mythology, a son of Zeus and Europa, and king of Crete.

Minotaur. In Greek mythology, a figure that is half man and half bull.

Minsk. Capital of Belarus.

minuscule. Frequently misspelled. Think of *minus,* not *mini.*

minute detail. The two words not only are tautological, but also have a kind of deadening effect on any passage in which they appear, as here: "Samples of the shards were brought back to the college, where they were studied in minute detail." Why not just say "Samples of the shards were brought back to the college for study"? One can normally assume that any objects being subjected to study will be examined closely.

minutia. A detail; pl. *minutiae.* Note that the latter is pronounced *min-oo-she,* not *min-oo-she-ay.*

mirabile dictu. (Lat.) Wonderful to relate.

Miricioiu, Nelly. (1952–) Romanian opera singer.

MIRV. Multiple independently targeted reentry vehicle; a type of ballistic missile.

miscellaneous.

mischievous.

mise-en-scène. Stage or film scenery, or the general setting of an event.

mishit.

misogamist, misogynist. The first hates marriage, the second hates women.

misshapen.

Mississauga. Suburb of Toronto.

Missolonghi, Greece.

misspell. If there is one word that you don't wish in print to misspell, it is this one. Note *-ss-*.

misspend.

misstate.

misstep.

mistime.

mistletoe.

mistral. Cold, unpleasant wind in France.

MIT. Massachusetts Institute of Technology.

mitigate, militate. The first means to soften or make more endurable; the second to act against.

mitochondrion. Type of cell organelle; pl. *mitochondria*.

Mitsukoshi. Japanese department store chain.

Mitterrand, François (Maurice Marie). (1916–1996) President of France (1981–1995).

Mitzi E. Newhouse Theater, Lincoln Center, New York.

Miyazawa, Kiichi. (1919–2007) Prime minister of Japan (1991–1993).

Mnemosyne. Greek goddess of memory and mother of the nine Muses by Zeus.

MO. Postal abbreviation of Missouri. The traditional abbreviation is **Mo.**, with period.

Möbius strip (or **band**). A piece of paper or other material twisted in such a way as to form a continuous surface; named after its discoverer, German mathematician **August Möbius** (1790–1868).

Mobutu Sese Seko. (1930–1997) President of Zaire (1965–1997); born Joseph-Desiré Mobuto.

Moby-Dick. (Note hyphen.) Novel by Herman Melville (1851). The full title on publication was *Moby-Dick; or, the Whale.*

moccasin.

modem is short for *modulator/demodulator.*

Modigliani, Amedeo. (1884–1920) Italian artist.

modus operandi. (Lat.) The way of doing something.

modus vivendi. (Lat.) Way of life, or a kind of truce pending the settlement of a dispute.

Mogadishu. Capital of Somalia.

Mohave, Mojave. The first is the spelling for the Native American tribe and mountains in Arizona; the second is the spelling of the desert.

Mohorovičić discontinuity. Boundary between Earth's crust and mantle, named for the Croatian geophysicist **Andrija Mohorovičić** (1857–1936).

Mojave Desert, but **Mohave** for the Native American tribe and mountains in Arizona.

Moldova. Not *Moldavia.* Eastern European republic, formerly called Bessarabia, formerly part of Soviet Union; capital Chişinău. The people and language are Moldovan.

Molière. (1622–1673) French playwright; born Jean-Baptiste Poquelin.

mollycoddle.

Molly Maguires. Secret society active in Pennsylvania in nineteenth century.

molt. Not *moult.*

molybdenum. Chemical element; symbol Mo.

Mombasa. Seaport and resort in Kenya.

Mona Lisa. Painting by Leonardo da Vinci, also called *La Gioconda.*

Mönchen-Gladbach, Germany.

Mondrian, Piet. (1872–1944) Dutch abstract painter; born Pieter Cornelis Mondriaan.

Monégasque for a person or thing from Monaco. Not *Mona-.*

moneyed, not *monied,* for someone with wealth.

mongooses is the plural of *mongoose.* (The word is of Indian origin and has no relation to the English *goose.*)

moniker (not *monicker*) for a name or nickname.

Monnet, Jean. (1888–1979) French statesman; but **Claude Monet** for the artist.

Monongahela. River in West Virginia and Pennsylvania.

mononucleosis is the American term for the illness known in Britain and elsewhere as glandular fever, a consideration that should be borne in mind if writing for an international audience.

Monserrat, Spain, but **Montserrat,** Leeward Islands.

monsieur, pl. *messieurs.*

Montagnard. French for "mountain dweller," it is the name given to the radical faction during the French Revolution because of the elevated position of their seats in the National Convention. The term is also applied to some Southeast Asian hill tribes.

Montaigne, Michel (Eyquem) de. (1533–1592) French philosopher and essayist.

Mont Blanc. Alpine mountain. But **Montblanc** for the pen.

Montenegro, Republic of. Formerly part of Yugoslavia; capital Podgorica.

Monterey for the city and bay in California and towns in Indiana, Massachusetts, Tennessee, and Virginia, but **Monterrey** for the city in Mexico and town in Colorado.

Montesquieu, Charles-Louis de Secondat, Baron de La Brède et de. (1689–1755) French philosopher and jurist.

Montessori. System of teaching developed by **Maria Montessori** (1870–1952), Italian doctor and educator.

Monteverdi, Claudio Giovanni Antonio. (1567–1643) Italian composer.

Montevideo. Capital of Uruguay.

Montparnasse, Paris.

Montpelier for the capital of Vermont, but **Montpellier,** France.

Mont-Saint-Michel, France (hyphens).

Montserrat, Leeward Islands, but **Monserrat,** Spain.

moose. Pl. same.

More, Sir Thomas (also **St. Thomas**). (1478–1535) English statesman and author.

morganatic marriage. One between a noble and a commoner in which the commoner and his or her descendants enjoy no privileges of inheritance.

Morgan le Fay. Sister of King Arthur.

Morgenthau, Henry, Jr. (1891–1967) American statesman, secretary of the treasury (1934–1945).

moribund does not mean sluggish or declining; it means dying, on the point of death. To be *moribund* is to be critically, indeed irreversibly, ill.

Morison, Samuel Eliot. (1887–1976) American historian.

Mormon Church. Officially the Church of Jesus Christ of Latter-day Saints.

Morocco, Morrocan.

Morris, Gouverneur. (1752–1816) American statesman, signatory of U.S. Constitution.

Morrison, Toni. (1931–) American novelist, awarded Nobel Prize in Literature in 1993.

mortar, in the context of weaponry, is the launching device, not the explosive projectiles. It is generally better, and sometimes necessary, to write that troops fired mortar rounds (or bombs or shells, etc.) rather than simply that they fired mortars.

Morte d'Arthur, Le. Not *La.* Fifteenth-century prose narrative by Thomas Malory relating the legend of King Arthur.

mortise lock.

Moselle for the river and wine; in German, Mosel.

Moser-Pröll, Annemarie. (1953–) Austrian skier.

Moskva. Russian for Moscow.

Moslem is an accepted variant, but **Muslim** is generally preferred.

mosquitoes.

Mossad. Israeli secret service.

most. Unless you are striving for an air of folksiness, *most* as an adverb should be confined to signifying the topmost degree ("the most delicious cake") or as a synonym for *very* ("Your offer is most welcome"). As an alternative for *almost* or *nearly* ("He would eat most anything") it is generally not welcome in serious writing.

Mother's Day.

mot juste. (Fr.) The right word.

motto, pl. *mottoes.*

mountebank. A charlatan.

Mourning Becomes Electra. Play by Eugene O'Neill (1931).

moussaka.

mousy (pref.), **mousey** (alt.).

Mozambique, but **Mozambican.**

mozzarella.

Mpumalanga. South African province, formerly Eastern Transvaal.

MRSA. Short for methicillin-resistant Staphylococcus aureus, a type of bacterial infection.

MS is the abbreviation for *manuscript;* pl. *MSS* (capitalized but without periods).

MT is the postal abbreviation of Montana; the traditional abbreviation is **Mont.,** with period.

Mubarak, (Muhammad) Hosni (Said). (1928–) Egyptian president (1981–).

mucous, mucus, mucosa. The first is the adjectival form, the second the noun form. Thus, *mucus* is the substance secreted by the *mucous* membranes. A more formal name for the latter is *mucosa.*

Mueller, Lisel. (1924–) German-born American poet.

Muenster/Munster. Either is correct for the cheese from Alsace. See also MUNSTER, MÜNSTER.

muezzin. In Islam, an official who calls the faithful to prayer.

mufti. Plain clothes worn by a person who usually wears a uniform.

Muhammad (or **Mohammed**). (c. 570–632) Founder of Islam.

Mühlhausen, Germany.

mujahideen is the most common spelling in English for Islamic guerrilla fighters, but there are many alternative spellings, including **mujahidin, mujahedin,** and **mujahedeen.**

Mukhabarat. Iraqi secret police.

mukluk, muktuk. The first is a kind of boot; the second is whale blubber as food.

mulatto, pl. *mulattos.*

mullah. Muslim teacher.

mulligatawny soup.

Mumbai. Indian city formerly known as Bombay.

Munch, Edvard. (1863–1944) Norwegian artist.

Munster, Münster. The first is a province of Ireland comprising six countries: Clare, Cork, Kerry, Limerick, Tipperary, and Waterford. The second is a city in North Rhine-Westphalia, Germany.

Murchison River, Australia; **Murchison Falls,** Uganda.

Murfreesboro, battle of. (1863) U.S. Civil War; sometimes called the battle of Stones River.

murmur.

Murphy's Law. If anything can go wrong, it will.

Muscovite for a person from Moscow. The name comes from the ancient principality of Muscovy.

Muses. The nine daughters of Zeus and Mnemosyne who presided over the arts: Calliope (eloquence and epic poetry), Clio (history), Erato (elegiac poetry), Euterpe (music), Melpomene (tragedy), Polyhymnia (lyric poetry), Terpsichore (dancing), Thalia (comedy), and Urania (astronomy).

Musharraf, Pervez. (1943–) President of Pakistan (1999–2008).

"Music hath charms to soothe a savage breast" is the correct quotation from the Congreve play *The Mourning Bride.* Not "*the* savage breast" or "a savage *beast.*"

musk-ox (hyphen), but **muskmelon, muskrat, muskroot.**

Muslim (pref.), **Moslem** (alt.).

Mussolini, Benito. (1883–1945) Italian prime minister (1922–1943) and dictator.

Mussorgsky/Moussorgsky, Modest Petrovich. (1839–1881) Russian composer.

mustache.

mutatis mutandis. (Lat.) "With the necessary changes."

mutual, common. Many authorities continue to insist, with varying degrees of conviction, that *mutual* should be reserved for describing reciprocal relationships between two or more things and not loosely applied to those things held in common. Thus, if you and I like each other, we have a mutual friendship. But if you and I both like Shakespeare, we have a common admiration. The use of *mutual* in the sense of *common* has been with us since the sixteenth century and was given a notable boost in the nineteenth with the appearance of the Dickens novel *Our Mutual Friend*. Most authorities accept it when *common* might be interpreted as a denigration, but even so in its looser sense the word is generally better avoided. It is, at all events, more often than not superfluous, as here: "They hope to arrange a mutual exchange of prisoners" (*Daily Telegraph*). An exchange of anything can hardly be other than mutual.

muumuu. Loose-fitting Hawaiian dress.

Muzak. (Cap.)

MW. Megawatt.

mW. Milliwatt.

myalgic encephalomyelitis. (Abbr. ME.) A type of chronic malaise.

Myanmar, Burma. *Burma* is the former official name of the Southeast Asian nation and the one preferred by most publications and other informed users outside Burma. *Myanmar* was for a time used by many publications, but now its use is mostly confined to the country's government and institutions under its influence.

Some authorities write "Burma/Myanmar." The United Nations uses just Myanmar.

Mycenae. Ancient Greek city and civilization; things from or of there are Mycenaean.

My Lai, Vietnam; site of notorious massacre of villagers by U.S. troops (1968).

myrrh.

myself. Except when it is used for emphasis ("I'll do it myself") or reflexively ("I cut myself while shaving") *myself* is almost always timorous and better avoided. In the following two examples, the better word is inserted in brackets: "Give it to John or myself [me]"; "My wife and myself [I] would just like to say . . ."

myxomatosis. Viral disease in rabbits.

Nn

NAACP. National Association for the Advancement of Colored People.

Nacogdoches, Texas.

NAFTA. North American Free Trade Agreement, a 1994 trade pact signed by Canada, Mexico, and the United States.

Nagorno-Karabakh. Armenian-dominated enclave in the former Soviet republic of Azerbaijan.

Nags Head, North Carolina.

Nagurski, Bronko. (1908–1990) Canadian-born American football player; real name Bronislau Nagurski.

Naipaul, V.S. (for **Vidiadhar Surajprasad**) (1932–) Trinidad-born British writer; awarded Nobel Prize for Literature in 2001.

naïve, naïvety.

namable. That which can be named.

namby-pamby.

Namen (Flemish)/**Namur** (French). Belgian city.

nano-. Prefix meaning one-billionth.

naphtha. Note *naph-tha,* not *nap-tha-.*

Napoleon I. (1769–1821) born Napoleon Bonaparte; emperor of the French (1804–1815).

narcissism.

narcissus. Bulbous flowering plant of the lily family; pl. *narcissuses/narcissi.*

Narragansett Bay, Rhode Island.

NASA. National Aeronautics and Space Administration.

nasal.

Nascar. National Association for Stock Car Auto Racing.

NASDAQ. National Association of Securities Dealers Automated Quotations; stock market specializing in technology stocks.

Nash (or **Nashe**), **Thomas.** (1567–1601) English dramatist.

National Governors' Association. (Apos.)

National Institutes of Health, Bethesda, Maryland. Note *Institutes* plural. It is part of the U.S. Department of Health and Human Services.

NATO. North Atlantic Treaty Organization. As of 2007, the member countries were Belgium, Bulgaria, Canada, Czech Republic, Denmark, Estonia, France, Germany, Greece, Hungary, Iceland, Italy, Latvia, Lithuania, Luxembourg, Netherlands, Norway, Poland, Portugal, Romania, Slovakia, Slovenia, Spain, Turkey, United Kingdom, United States.

Natty Bumppo. Main character in James Fenimore Cooper's *Leatherstocking Tales*.

Naugahyde is a trademark.

naught, nought. Although dictionaries increasingly treat the words as interchangeable, traditionally the first means *nothing* (as in "His efforts came to naught"), while the second is used to signify the figure zero. The game is *noughts and crosses* (known in the United States as tic-tac-toe).

nauseous is an adjective describing something that causes nausea ("a nauseous substance"). To feel sick is to be **nauseated.**

Navajo/Navaho. The first is generally preferred, the second accepted.

naval, navel. The first pertains to a navy and its possessions or operations; the second to belly buttons and like-shaped objects. The oranges are navel.

navigable.

Nazism. Not *-ii-*.

n.b. (or **NB**). Abbreviation of *nota bene* (Lat.), "note carefully." Note that n.b. is spelled with periods and NB without.

NCAA. National Collegiate Athletic Association.

Ndeti, Cosmas. (1971–) Kenyan distance runner.

Ndjamena (or **N'Djamena**). Capital of Chad.

'Ndrangheta. Organized crime group in Calabria, Italy.

Neandertal increasingly is the preferred spelling for the extinct species of human, though the formal scientific rendering *Homo neanderthalensis* still generally keeps the *-thal* spelling. *Neanderthal man* as a term for the species is both sexist and old-fashioned.

near disaster. "His quick thinking saved an RAF jet pilot from a near disaster." Not quite. The pilot was saved from a disaster. A near disaster is what he had.

neat's-foot oil. A substance used to treat leather.

Nebuchadnezzar. (c. 625–551 BC) King of Babylon (605–561 BC).

nebuchadnezzar, an exceptionally large bottle of champagne, twenty times the size of a normal bottle.

nebula. The plural can be either *nebulae* or *nebulas*.

necessarily, necessity.

needless to say is a harmless enough expression, but it often draws attention to the fact that you really didn't need to say it.

nefarious.

negligee.

negligible.

Negretti & Zambra. Maker of musical instruments.

Nehemiah. Jewish leader in fifth century BC after whom an Old Testament book is named.

Nehru, Jawaharlal. (1889–1964) Indian prime minister (1947–1964).

Neiman Marcus, the department store group, no longer hyphenates its name.

neither. In *neither . . . nor* constructions, the verb should always agree with the noun nearest it. Thus, "Neither De Niro nor his agent was available for comment." When the noun nearest the verb is plural, the verb should also be plural: "Neither the president nor his advisors were available for comment." When *neither* is used on its own without the *nor*, the verb should always be singular: "Neither of the men was ready"; "Neither of us is hungry." In short, more often than not a singular verb is called for—but that singularity is by no means invariable. Try to remember that *neither* emphasizes the separateness of items. It doesn't add them together, at least not grammatically.

nemesis. A nemesis (from Nemesis, the Greek goddess of vengeance) is not merely a rival or traditional enemy, but one who exacts retributive justice or is utterly unvanquishable.

neodymium. A chemical element.

neologism. A newly coined word.

nephritis. Inflammation of the kidneys.

Nephthys. Egyptian goddess, companion of the dead.

ne plus ultra. (Lat.) Perfection, the acme.

Neptune. Roman god of the sea, identified with the Greek god Poseidon, and the eighth planet from the sun.

nerve-racking. Not -*wracking*. See RACK, WRACK.

n'est-ce pas? (Fr.) "Is that not so?"; pronounced *ness-pah*.

Netanyahu, Benjamin. (1949–) Israeli politician, prime minister (1996–1999).

Netherlands, the. The capital is Amsterdam, but the seat of government is The Hague. (As with all place names, *the* is not capitalized with the country name, but is with the city name.)

netsuke. Japanese carved ornament.

Nettles, Graig. (1944–) American baseball player.

Netzahualcóyotl. Part of the Mexico City conurbation.

Neuchâtel. Swiss town and wine.

Neufchâtel. French town and cheese.

Neugebauer, Randy. (1949–) U.S. representative from Texas.

Neuilly-sur-Seine. Suburb of Paris.

neurasthenia. Chronic lethargy.

Neuwirth, Bebe. (1958–) American actress.

nevertheless. (One word.)

Newberry Library, Chicago.

Newbery Airport, Buenos Aires; officially Aeroparque Jorge Newbery.

Newbery Medal. Formally the **John Newbery Medal;** award for outstanding children's literature.

New England. Although it has no official standing, it comprises six states: Connecticut, Maine, Massachusetts, New Hampshire, Rhode Island, and Vermont.

New Hebrides. Former name of Vanuatu.

New Year's Day, New Year's Eve.

New York City comprises five boroughs, each coextensive with a state county (in parens.): the Bronx (Bronx County), Brooklyn (Kings County), Manhattan (New York County), Queens (Queens County), and Staten Island (Richmond County).

Niagara Falls.

Niamey. Capital of Niger.

Nibelungenlied. German epic poem written in the early thirteenth century.

niblick. Golf club used for getting the ball out of bad lies.

niceish is the spelling for something that is rather nice.

nickel. Not -*le.*

Nicklaus, Jack. (1940–) American golfer.

Nicosia, Cyprus; to the Greeks it is Levkosia.

nicotine.

Nielsen ratings. The company is ACNielsen (one word).

Nietzsche, Friedrich Wilhelm. (1884–1900) German philosopher; the adjective is *Nietzschean.*

Nightingale, Florence. (1820–1910) English nurse and hospital reformer.

Niigata, Honshu, Japan. Note -*ii-.*

Niihau. Hawaiian island. Note *-ii-*.

Nijinsky, Vaslav. (1890–1950) Russian dancer and choreographer.

Nijmegen, Netherlands.

Nikkei 225 Index. Principal Japanese stock market index; *Nikkei* is derived from *Nihon Keizai Shimbun*, a business newspaper.

Niña, Pinta, and **Santa María.** The ships in Columbus's fleet during the 1492 crossing of the Atlantic.

nincompoop. Not *nim-*.

Nisei. Literally "second generation." Term used in North America for native U.S. or Canadian citizens born to immigrant Japanese parents; often loosely used to describe all Japanese expatriates, particularly in the context of World War II internment.

nitty-gritty. (Hyphen.)

nitwit.

Nixon, Richard Milhous. (1913–1994) Not *-house*. U.S. president (1969–1974).

Nizhny Novgorod, Russia; called Gorky during Communist era.

Nobel Prizes are awarded in six categories: Chemistry, Literature, Peace, Physics, Physiology or Medicine, and Economics— though the last named is not strictly a Nobel Prize (its formal title is the Bank of Sweden Prize in Economic Sciences). Nobel Prizes are named for the Swedish inventor and industrialist **Alfred Nobel** (1833–1896).

noblesse oblige. (Fr.) "Nobility obligates"; applied to duties that come with rank.

nobody (one word), but **no one** (two words).

noisome has nothing to do with noise or noisiness. It is related to *annoy* and means offensive or objectionable and is most often used to describe unpleasant smells.

nolo contendere. (Lat.) "I do not wish to contend"; tantamount to a plea of guilty, but leaves the defendant with the option of denying the same or similar charges in other proceedings.

nom de guerre. (Fr.) An assumed name; in most contexts it is a cliché.

nom de plume. A writer's pseudonym.

nomenklatura. Secret list of names from which people in the USSR were chosen for advancement.

nonagenarian. Person from ninety to ninety-nine years old.

non-Christian, but **unchristian.**

non compos mentis. (Lat.) "Not of sound mind."

none. Although *none* can always take a singular verb, there is no rule recognized by any authority on English grammar that it cannot equally well take a plural one.

nonetheless. (One word.)

non sequitur. (Lat.) "It does not follow"; the combination of two or more statements that are jarringly unrelated, as in "He was born in Omaha and his shoes were brown."

no one (two words), but **nobody** (one word).

Nord-Pas-de-Calais. Region of France.

Nor'easter is a strong or stormy wind from the northeast.

Norge. The Norwegian name for Norway.

normalcy. Although most dictionaries accept it as standard, it is still derided as a casualism by many authorities, who suggest *normality* instead.

Northern Ireland. Part of the United Kingdom, comprising six counties: Antrim, Armagh, Down, Fermanagh, Londonderry, and Tyrone.

North Fork BanCorp. New York–based banking company.

nosy. Not *-ey.*

nota bene. (Lat.) "Note well"; abbreviated **n.b.** (with periods) or **NB** (without).

Notes from Underground. Not *the Underground.* Novel by Dostoyevsky.

not so much is often followed by *but* when the word should be *as*, as here: "He was not so much a comic actor, but a real comedian." Make it "He was not so much a comic actor as a real comedian."

notwithstanding. (One word.)

Nouakchott. Capital of Mauritania.

n'oubliez pas. (Fr.) "Don't forget."

noughts and crosses. British name for tic-tac-toe.

nouveau riche. (Fr.) Mildly disparaging description of someone whose wealth is recently acquired; pl. *nouveaux riches.*

Novocaine. (Cap.)

Novosibirsk, Russia.

NOW. National Organization for (not *of*) Women.

nowadays.

NTSB. National Transportation Safety Board.

NTT DoCoMo. Japanese telecommunications company.

Nuits-Saint-Georges. French wine.

Nuku'alofa/Nukualofa. Capital of Tonga.

Nullarbor Plain, Western Australia. Often misspelled *Nullabor.*

number. Used with the definite article, *number* always takes a singular verb ("The number of people in the world is rising"); used with an indefinite article it always takes a plural verb ("A number of people are unhappy").

numismatics. The study or collection of coins or medals.

numskull, not *numbskull,* is the preferred spelling for most, but not all, authorities.

Nunavut. Canadian territory created in 1999.

Nunivak. Second-largest Alaskan island (after Kodiak).

Nuremberg (in German, Nürnberg) for the Bavarian city. Not *-burg.*

Nureyev, Rudolf. (1938–1993) Russian ballet dancer.

Nuuk. Capital of Greenland; formerly Godthaab.

Nyasaland. Former name of Malawi.

Nyerere, Julius (Kambarage). (1922–1999) President of Tanganyika and (after its union with Zanzibar) of Tanzania (1961–1985).

Nymphenburg Palace, Munich; in German, Schloss Nymphenburg.

Oo

O, oh, oho. The first normally appears in literary or religious contexts; it is always capitalized and never followed by punctuation. The second is used in more general contexts to denote emotions ranging from a small sigh to an outcry; it is capitalized only at the start of sentences and normally followed by either a comma or exclamation mark. *Oho,* with or without an exclamation mark, denotes an expression of surprise.

OAS. Organization of American States.

OAU. Organization of African Unity.

Oaxaca. City and state in southern Mexico.

Obadiah. Old Testament prophet.

Obama, Barack. (1961–) Democratic politician, 44th president of the United States (2009–); full name **Barack Hussein Obama**.

Obasanjo, Olusegun. (1937–) President of Nigeria (1999–2007).

obbligato. In music, an indispensable part.

obeisance. A show of deference.

Oberammergau. Village in Bavaria, Germany, where celebrated passion play is performed every ten years.

obiter dictum. (Lat.) A remark made in passing; pl. *obiter dicta.*

objet d'art, pl. *objets d'art.*

objet trouvé. (Fr.) "A found object."

oblivious. Many authorities long maintained that *oblivious* can mean only forgetful. You cannot properly be oblivious of something that you were not in the first place aware of. But in its broader sense of merely being unaware or impervious, *oblivious* is now accepted universally.

oblique.

obloquy. Verbal abuses; pl. *obloquies.*

O'Brien, Flann. Pen name of Brian O'Nolan (1911–1966), Irish writer, who also wrote a column in the *Irish Times* under the pseudonym Myles na Gopaleen.

obscurum per obscurius. (Lat.) "The obscure by means of the more obscure."

obsidian. Glassy volcanic rock.

obsolete, obsolescent. Things that are no longer used or needed are obsolete. Things that are becoming obsolete are obsolescent.

obstetrics, obstetrician.

obstreperous. Noisy, vociferous.

obtuse angle. One between 90 and 180 degrees.

obviate does not mean reduce or make more acceptable, as is often thought: "A total redesign of the system should obviate complaints about its reliability" (*London Times*). It means to make unnecessary.

Occam's/Ockham's razor. Paring all presumptions to the minimum, a principle attributed to the English philosopher **William of Occam,** or **Ockham** (c. 1285–c. 1349).

occult.

occur, take place. *Take place* is better reserved for scheduled events. When what is being described is accidental, *occur* is the better word.

ocher.

ochlocracy. Government by mob rule.

octet.

octocentennial. Eight-hundredth anniversary.

octogenarian. Person from eighty to eighty-nine years old.

octopus, pl. *octopuses* (or, in technical writing, *octopodes*).

oculist.

Oder-Neisse Line. Boundary between Germany and Poland.

Odets, Clifford. (1906–1963) American playwright.

odometer. Device for measuring distance traveled.

odoriferous.

Od's bodkins. Archaic oath, probably a corruption of "by God's body."

Odysseus (Greek)**/Ulysses** (Lat.). In Greek mythology, the king of Ithaca.

OECD. Organization for (not *of*) Economic Cooperation and Development. The members are Australia, Austria, Belgium, Canada, Czech Republic, Denmark, Finland, France, Germany, Greece, Hungary, Iceland, Ireland, Italy, Japan, Luxembourg, Mexico, the Netherlands, New Zealand, Norway, Poland, Portugal, Slovakia, South Korea, Spain, Sweden, Switzerland, Turkey, United Kingdom, United States.

Oedipus complex. Term coined by Freud to describe a child's (usually a son's) feelings of love for the parent of the opposite sex mingled with dislike for the parent of the same sex.

oenology/enology. Study of wines. A connoisseur is an **oenophile**.

oeuvre. An artist's body of work.

O'Faoláin, Seán. (1900–1991) Irish novelist and short story writer.

Offaly. County in Republic of Ireland.

Offa's Dike/Dyke. Eighth-century earthwork between England and Wales.

Offenbach, Jacques. (1819–1880) German-born French composer; born Jakob Eberst.

off of is redundant. Write "Get off the table," not "Get off of the table."

Ogdon, John. (Andrew Howard) (1937–1989) British pianist.

ogre.

Oh, Oho. See O, OH, OHO.

O'Hare International Airport, Chicago.

O. Henry. Pen name of William Sydney Porter (1862–1910), American short story writer. The candy bar is **Oh Henry!**

Oireachtas for the Irish legislature, consisting of the president and the two assemblies, the Dáil Éireann and Seanad. It is pronounced *ur'-akh-tus.*

Ojos del Salado. Andean mountain on Chilean-Argentinian border; second-highest peak in the Western Hemisphere (22,600 feet; 6,910 meters).

Okeechobee. Lake and inland waterway, Florida.

O'Keeffe, Georgia. (1887–1986) American artist.

Okefenokee Swamp. Florida and Georgia.

Okhotsk, Sea of.

Olajuwon, Hakeem. (1963–) Nigerian-born American basketball player.

Olazábal, José María. (1966–) Spanish golfer.

Oldenburg, Claes. (1929–) Swedish-born American sculptor.

Old Peculier. An English beer.

Olduvai Gorge, Tanzania.

Olivetti. Formally Ing. C. Olivetti & Co. SpA, Italian industrial group, once famous for typewriters.

Olmert, Ehud. (1945–) Prime minister of Israel (2006–).

Olympic-size swimming pool. An official Olympics swimming pool is fifty meters long. Almost no one owns a private pool that large, so the description in respect to private pools is almost always a gross exaggeration.

Omar Khayyám is the correct spelling of the Persian poet and mathematician. Note *-yy-.*

omelet/omelette. Either is correct.

omit, omitted, omitting, omissible.

omnipotent, omniscient. The first means all-powerful, the second all-knowing.

on, upon. Although some journalists think there is, or ought to be, a distinction between these two, there isn't. The choice is sometimes dictated by idiom ("on no account," "upon my soul"), but in all other instances it is a matter of preference.

one can be a grammatically tricky word. It takes a singular verb in straightforward constructions like "one out of every seven men is bald." But when extra words are attached to it—*one or more, one of those*—it ceases to govern the verb and the sense of the sentence becomes plural. Thus the sentence "Inside each folder is one or more sheets of information" should be "are one or more" and "Nott is one of those rare politicians who doesn't mind what he says" should be "don't mind what they say." A helpful trick to determine whether a singular or plural verb is needed is to invert the word order of the sentence: "Of those politicians who do not mind what they say, Nott is one."

O'Neal, Shaquille. (1972–) American basketball player.

one or more is plural. For a discussion, see ONE.

only. In general, *only* ought to be attached to the word or phrase it is modifying and not set adrift, as here: "The A Class bus only ran on Sundays" (*Observer*). Taken literally, the sentence suggests that on other days of the week the bus did something else—perhaps flew? The writer would better have said that the bus "ran only on Sundays" or "on Sundays only."

Oftentimes, to be sure, clarity and idiom are better served by bringing *only* to a more forward position ("This will only take a minute," "The victory can only be called a miracle"). And increasingly, it must be said, authorities are inclined toward leniency with regard to where *only* is permitted. Certainly it is always better to avoid an air of fussiness. But when, as in the example above, a simple repositioning puts the word in the right place without creating a distraction, there is no reason not to do it.

onomatopoeia. The formation of words based on the sounds they denote, as with *buzz, bang,* and *vroom-vroom.*

on to, onto. Until the twentieth century *onto* as one word was almost unknown in both Britain and America, and its standing remains somewhat dubious in Britain. Today in the United States (and increasingly in Britain), *onto* is used where the two elements function as a compound preposition ("He jumped onto the horse") and *on to* is used where *on* is an adverb ("We moved on to the next subject").

oolong tea.

oozy.

op. cit. *Opere citato* (Lat.); "in the work cited." Note two periods.

openness. Note -*nn*-.

opéra bouffe, opera buffa. The first is a farcical French opera; the second a farcical Italian one.

Opéra-Comique, Paris theater.

ophthalmologist, oculist, optometrist, optician. *Ophthalmologist* is often misspelled and even more frequently mispronounced. Note that it begins *oph-* and not *opth-* and that the first syllable is pronounced *off*, not *op*. Thus, it is similar in pronunciation and spelling to *diphtheria, diphthong,* and *naphtha,* all of which are also frequently misspelled and misspoken.

    Ophthalmologist and *oculist* both describe doctors who specialize in diseases of the eye. An *optometrist* is one who is trained to test eyes but is not a medical doctor. An *optician* is one who makes or sells corrective lenses.

Oporto, Portugal; in Portuguese, Pôrto.

opossum (or **possum**). The plural can be either *opossum* or *opossums* (or *possum/possums*).

Oppenheimer, J(ulius) Robert. (1904–1967) American physicist.

oppressor.

optimistic, pessimistic. Strictly speaking, both words should be used to describe a general outlook rather than a specific view, particularly with regard to the inconsequential. "He was optimistic that he would find the missing book" would be better with "was hopeful" or "was confident."

optimum does not mean greatest or fastest or biggest, as is sometimes thought. It describes the point at which conflicting considerations are reconciled. The optimum flying speed of an aircraft is the speed at which all the many variables that must be taken into account in flying—safety, comfort, fuel consumption, and so on—are most nearly in harmony.

opus magnum, magnum opus. (Lat.) The first is a great work; the second is an author's principal work.

or. When *or* links two or more singular items in a sentence, the verb must always be singular. "It was not clear whether the president or vice president were within hearing range at the time" should be "was within hearing range."

oral, verbal. *Oral* can apply only to spoken words; *verbal* can describe both spoken and written words.

orange pekoe tea.

ordinal numbers. First, second, third, etc. See also CARDINAL NUMBERS.

ordinance, ordnance. The first is a command or decree; the second refers to military stores and materials.

ordonnance. The proper arrangement of parts in a literary, musical, artistic, or architectural work.

Ordzhonikidze, Russia; formerly Dzaudzhikau.

Oresteia. Trilogy by Aeschylus (c. 458 BC).

Orestes. In Greek mythology, the son of Clytemnestra and Agamemnon.

Öresund. Strait between Sweden and Denmark.

Oriel College, Oxford University.

originally is often needlessly inserted into sentences where it conveys no additional information, as here: "The plans were originally drawn up as long ago as 1972" (*Observer*).

Origin of Species, On the, the seminal book by Charles Darwin, whose full title is *On the Origin of Species by Means of Natural Selection, or the Preservation of Favoured Races in the Struggle for Life* (1859).

Orinoco. South American River, rising in Venezuela.

Orkney Islands, Scotland. Properly they can be called Orkney or the Orkney Islands, but not *the Orkneys*. A native or resident is an **Orcadian.**

Orly Airport, Paris.

orology. The study of mountains.

Ortega y Gasset, José. (1883–1955) Spanish philosopher.

orthoepy. The study of pronunciation. Curiously, there are two accepted pronunciations: *or'-tho-ep-ee* and *or-tho'-ip-ee*.

orthography. Correct or accepted spelling; the study of spelling.

orthopedics. The area of medicine concerned with bones and muscles.

Orwell, George. Pen name of the British writer Eric Blair (1903–1950).

oscillate.

oscilloscope.

OSHA. Occupational Safety and Health Administration.

Osiris. Egyptian god of the underworld.

Osservatore Romano, L'. Vatican newspaper.

Ostend. Belgian port; in Flemish, Oostende.

osteo-. Prefix meaning bone(s).

osteomyelitis. Infection in the bone or bone marrow.

Österreich. The name in German for Austria.

Oświęcim. The Polish name for Auschwitz, German concentration camp in Poland during World War II.

otolaryngology. The branch of medicine dealing with ear, nose, and throat disorders.

Ottawa, Ontario. Capital of Canada.

Otway, Thomas. (1652–1685) British playwright.

Ouachita (or **Washita**). River and mountains in Arkansas and Oklahoma.

Ouagadougou. Capital of Burkina Faso.

oubliette. Dungeon with access only through a trapdoor in the ceiling.

Oudenarde, Battle of. (1708.)

Ouija board. (Cap. *O.*)

"Ours is not to reason why, ours is but to do or die" is often heard, but is wrong. The lines from Tennyson's "Charge of the Light Brigade" are "Their's not to reason why,/Their's but to do and die." Note that the closing words "do and die" give the lines an entirely different sense from "do or die." Finally, it should be noted that Tennyson's punctuation of *theirs* is irregular (see POSSESSIVES).

outspokenness. Note -*nn*-.

ouzo. Greek drink.

over. The notion that *over* is incorrect for "more than" (as in "over 300 people were present at the rally") is a widely held superstition. The stricture has been traced to Ambrose Bierce's *Write It Right* (1909), a usage book teeming with quirky recommendations, many of which you will find repeated nowhere. There is no harm in preferring "more than," but also no basis for insisting on it.

Overbeck, Johann Friedrich. (1769–1869) German painter.

Overijssel. Province of the Netherlands.

Overlord. Code name given to the Normandy invasion by Allied forces on D-Day in 1944.

overly. Making *over* into *overly* is a little like turning *soon* into *soonly*. Adding -*ly* does nothing for *over* that it could not already do.

overripe, overrule, overrun, etc. Note -*rr*-.

overweening. Arrogant or presumptuous expectations are overweening ones. There is no word *overweaning*.

Ovid, properly **Publius Ovidius Naso.** (43 BC–AD 17) Roman poet.

ovum, pl. *ova*.

Oxford Movement. A movement in the Church of England, begun at Oxford in 1833, seeking a return to certain Roman Catholic doctrines and practices.

Oxford University colleges. All Souls, Balliol, Brasenose, Christ Church, Corpus Christi, Exeter, Green, Hertford, Jesus, Keble, Lady Margaret Hall, Linacre, Lincoln, Magdalen, Merton, New College, Nuffield, Oriel, Pembroke, (The) Queen's, St. Anne's, St. Antony's, St. Catherine's, St. Cross, St. Edmund Hall, St. Hilda's, St. Hugh's, St. John's, St. Peter's, Somerville, Trinity, University, Wadham, Wolfson, Worcester.

Oxon. *Oxonia* (Lat.), Oxford or Oxfordshire; *Oxoniensis* (Lat.), of Oxford.

oxymoron. The intentional mingling of contradictory ideas or expressions for rhetorical effect, as in "getting nowhere fast."

Ozawa, Seiji. (1935–) Japanese conductor.

"Ozymandias" for the sonnet by Shelley (1818). Not *Oxy-*.

Pp

pablum (or **pabulum**). Food; in figurative sense it is used to convey the idea of being weak or nutritiously insipid. When capitalized it is a trademark for a brand of baby food.

pachyderm. Thick-skinned animal such as an elephant or rhinoceros.

paddywhack. A tantrum.

Paderewski, Ignace Jan. (1860–1941) Polish concert pianist, composer, and prime minister (1919–1920).

Padova. The Italian name for Padua.

paean, paeon, peon. A *paean* (alternative spelling *pean*) is a hymn or song of praise. A *paeon* is a metrical foot in classical poetry. A *peon* is a servant or peasant.

paella. Spanish dish of rice and chicken or seafood.

Paganini, Niccolò. (1782–1840) Italian violin virtuoso and composer.

Paget's disease. Bone disorder.

Pago Pago. Capital of American Samoa; pronounced *pango pango*.

Pahlavi, Mohammed Reza. (1919–1980) Shah of Iran (1941–1979).

Paige, Satchel. (1906–1982) Legendary baseball pitcher, born Leroy Robert Paige. Name often shortened to "Satch."

pail, pale. The first is a small bucket; the second means lacking color. The expression is *beyond the pale*. Historically the Pale signified the areas of Ireland controlled by the English; lands beyond were therefore beyond English control.

paillasse. A thin and very basic mattress.

Paine, Thomas. (1737–1809) British-born American political philosopher and pamphleteer.

Paiute. Native American people.

palate, palette, pallet. *Palate* has to do with the mouth and taste. *Palette* is the board used by artists. *Pallet* is a mattress, a machine part, or the wooden platform on which freight is stood.

palaver. Fuss.

Palazzo Vecchio, Florence.

Paleocene. Geological epoch.

paleology. Study of antiquities.

paleontology. Study of fossils.

Palikir. Capital of Micronesia.

palindrome. A word or passage that reads the same forward and backward, as in "A man, a plan, a canal: Panama."

palisade.

Palladian architecture. The style of architecture of **Andrea Palladio** (1508–1580).

pall-mall, pell-mell. The first was a game popular in the eighteenth century. A favored site for playing it later became the London street Pall Mall. For the act of moving crazily or in haste, the word is *pell-mell*. All versions of the word, including Pall Mall, are pronounced *pell mell*.

Palme, Olof. (1927–1986) Swedish politician.

Palmers Green, London (no apos.).

PalmPilot (one word) for the handheld organizer.

palomino. Type of horse; pl. *palominos*.

palsy.

Pamuk, Orhan. (1952–) Turkish novelist, awarded Nobel Prize for Literature in 2006.

panacea is a universal remedy, a cure for all woes, and is not properly applied to a single shortcoming.

pandemonium.

panegyric. A formal speech of praise.

Pangloss. An excessively optimistic character in Voltaire's *Candide*; hence any optimistic person.

panjandrum. Self-important person, pompous official.

Pankhurst, Emmeline. (1858–1928) English activist for women's rights. Her daughters, **Dame Christabel Pankhurst** (1880–1958), **Sylvia Pankhurst** (1882–1960), and **Adela Pankhurst** (1885–1961), were similarly dedicated to women's causes.

Pão de Açucar. Portuguese for Sugarloaf Mountain, Rio de Janeiro.

Paolozzi, Eduardo. (1924–) Scottish sculptor.

Papal Nuncio. A prelate acting as an ambassador of the pope.

paparazzi is plural; a single roving photographer who stalks celebrities is a *paparazzo*.

papier mâché.

Pap test. A test for cervical cancer and other disorders devised by Dr. **George Papanicolaou** (1883–1962), a Greek-American doctor.

papyrus. Writing material; pl. *papyruses* or *papyri*.

Paracelsus. (1493–1541) Swiss physician and alchemist; real name Theophrastus Philippus Aureolus Bombastus von Hoheneim.

paradisaical. Not *-iacal*. Having the nature of paradise.

paraffin.

paragon. Model of excellence.

parakeet.

parallel, paralleled, paralleling.

paralysis, paralyze.

Paraná. South American river.

paranoia, paranoiac.

paraphernalia.

paraphrase.

paraquat. Lethal herbicide.

parasite.

parasol.

parbleu! (Fr.) Exclamation of surprise.

Parcheesi. (Cap.)

pardonnez-moi. (Fr.) "Pardon me."

par excellence. (Fr.) The best of its type.

pariah. Person of low standing; a social outcast.

Paribas. Short for Compagnie Financière de Paris et des Pays-Bas; French bank.

pari passu. (Lat.) With the same speed, at an equal rate.

parka. Type of coat.

Parkinson's disease is the traditional name, but increasingly the non-possessive **Parkinson disease** is displacing it, particularly in medical texts.

Parkinson's Law. "Work expands to fill the time available for its completion." Stated by **C. Northcote Parkinson** (1909–1993), British writer.

parlay, parley. The first is to use one gain to make another ("He parlayed his winnings into a small fortune"). The second is a conference.

Parmesan cheese. (Cap. *P.*) In Italian, *parmigiano* (no cap.).

Parmigianino, Il. (1504–1540) Italian painter; real name Girolamo Francesco Maria Mazzola.

Parnassus, Mt. Former name of Líakoura, a Greek mountain.

paroxysm.

parquet flooring.

Parr, Catherine. (1512–1548) Sixth wife of Henry VIII.

parricide. The murder of a parent or close relative.

Parry, Sir William Edward. (1790–1855) British admiral and explorer.

Parsifal. Opera by Wagner (1879).

Parsiism. Indian religion, related to Zoroastrianism.

Parsons Green, London (no apos.).

Parthian shot. A remark or blow made while retreating.

parti pris. (Fr.) A prejudice.

Parti Québécois. Canadian political party.

partly, partially. Although they are often interchangeable, their meanings are slightly different. *Partially* means incompletely and *partly* means in part. "The house was made partially of brick and partially of stone" would be better as "partly of brick and partly of stone."

parturition. Birth.

parvenu (masc.)/**parvenue** (fem.). An upstart; a person who has risen above his original social class; pl. *parvenus* (masc.)/*parvenues* (fem.).

Pasadena, California, home of the Rose Bowl, or Tournament of Roses.

paso doble. (Sp.) A type of dance.

Pasolini, Pier Paolo. (1922–1975) Italian writer, actor, and film director.

passable, passible. The first means capable of being passed ("The road was passable") or barely satisfactory ("The food was passable"); the second means capable of feeling or suffering.

Passchendaele. Not -*dale.* Belgian village, scene of bloody battle in World War I.

passe-partout. A passkey; adhesive tape used in picture framing.

passersby.

past. Often a space waster, as in this example: "Davis said the dry conditions had been a recurrent problem for the past thirty years." In this sentence, and in countless others like it, "the past" could be deleted without any loss of sense. Equally tautological and to be avoided are such expressions as *past records, past history, past experience, past achievements,* and *past precedents.* See also LAST, LATEST.

Pasteur, Louis. (1822–1895) French chemist.

pastiche. A work inspired by a variety of sources.

pastille.

pastrami.

pâté de foie gras.

Patek Philippe. Swiss watch manufacturer.

paterfamilias. (One word.) Male head of house.

Paterson, New Jersey.

pâtisserie

Pattenmakers' Company. London livery company; not *Pattern-*. (A patten is a type of shoe or clog.)

Pauli, Wolfgang. (1900–1958) Austrian-born physicist, awarded Nobel Prize for Physics (1945).

Pavarotti, Luciano. (1935–2007) Italian tenor.

pavilion. Not *-ll-*.

pax vobiscum. (Lat.) "Peace be with you."

Pays-Bas. French name for the Netherlands.

Pb is the chemical symbol for lead; short for *plumbum*.

PCBs. Polychlorinated biphenyls, organic substance used in hydraulics and electrical systems; banned in most Western countries.

peaceable, peaceful. *Peaceful* means tranquil and serene. *Peaceable* is a disposition toward the state of peacefulness.

peak, peek. The first is a point or summit; the second means to steal a look.

Pearse, Padraic. (1879–1916) Irish writer and nationalist.

Peary, Robert Edwin. (1856–1920) American admiral and explorer, first to reach the North Pole (1909).

pease pudding.

peccadillo. A minor fault; pl. *peccadilloes*.

pedal, peddle. The first applies to devices or actions involving foot power—the pedal on a piano, to pedal a bicycle. The second is a verb only, meaning to sell goods in an informal or itinerant manner. The person who sells such goods is a **peddler.**

pedant, pedagogue. The two are synonyms. They describe someone who makes an ostentatious show of his learning or is dogmatically fussy about rules. Some dictionaries still give *pedagogue* as a synonym for *teacher* or *educator*, but its pejorative sense has effectively driven out the neutral one.

pederasty. Sexual relations between an adult male and boy.

Peeblesshire. Former Scottish county. Note *-ss-*.

peek, peak. The first means to steal a look; the second is a point or summit.

peekaboo. (No hyphens.)

Peekskill, New York.

Peel, Sir Robert. (1788–1850) British prime minister (1834–1835, 1841–1846).

Pei, I. M. (for **Ieoh Ming**). (1917–) Chinese-born American architect.

Peirce, Charles Sanders. (1839–1914) American philosopher; pronounced *purse*.

Pekingese dog.

pekoe. A tea.

Pelagianism. (Cap.) A heresy.

pelargonium. Flowering plant popularly known as the geranium.

Pelé. Nickname of Edson Arantes do Nascimento (1940–), celebrated Brazilian soccer player.

pell-mell. In a state of confusion. See also PALL MALL.

Peloponnesus. Southern peninsula of Greece; in Greek it is Pelopónnisos.

pelota. Another name for the game of jai alai.

pemmican. Dried meat.

penance.

PEN. Short for Poets, Playwrights, Editors, Essayists, and Novelists; an international association.

pendant (noun), **pendent** (adj.).

Penetanguishene, Ontario.

penicillin.

Peninsular and Oriental Steamship Company. British shipping company commonly known as P&O.

Penney, J.C. U.S. department store group, is now **JCPenney** (one word).

penniless.

penn'orth (British, mostly historical.) A penny's worth.

Pensacola, Florida.

Pentateuch. The first five books of the Old Testament: Genesis, Exodus, Leviticus, Numbers, and Deuteronomy.

pentathlon, modern. The five events are swimming, fencing, pistol shooting, cross-country running, and cross-country horseback riding.

Pentecost. The Christian Whit Sunday, the seventh Sunday after Easter; the Jewish Shavuot, the sixth and seventh days of Sivan.

peon, paean, paeon. A *peon* is a servant or peasant; a *paean* is a hymn or song of praise; a *paeon* is a metrical foot in ancient Greek and Latin poetry.

peony. A flowering plant.

PepsiCo Inc. U.S. company that owns Pepsi-Cola.

Pepys, Samuel. (1633–1703) English Admiralty official, remembered for his diary; pronounced *peeps*.

per. Many usage guides suggest, and a few insist, that Latinisms like *per* should be avoided when English phrases are available—that it is better to write "ten tons a year" than "ten tons per year." That is certainly reasonable enough in general, but I would suggest that when avoidance of the Latin would result in clumsy constructions such as "output a man a year," you shouldn't hesitate to use *per*.

per ardua ad astra. (Lat.) "To the stars through adversities."

P/E ratio. Short for *price-to-earnings ratio;* a stock market measure in which a value of a stock is determined by dividing the stock's price by the company's earnings per share.

percent, percentage point. If interest rates are 10 percent and are raised to 11 percent, they have gone up by one percentage point, but by 10 percent in value (i.e., borrowers must now pay 10 percent more than previously). In everyday contexts the distinction is not always vital, but in contexts in which the percentage rise is large and confusion is likely, the distinction is crucial.

perceptible.

Perceval, Spencer. (1762–1812) British prime minister (1809–12); only British prime minister to be assassinated.

perchance. Possibly.

Perelman, S. J. (for **Sidney Joseph**). (1904–1979) American humorist.

perestroika. (Russ.) Restructuring.

Pérez de Cuéllar, Javier. (1920–) Peruvian diplomat; secretary-general of the United Nations (1982–92).

perfectible, perfectibility.

perforce. Without choice.

perigee. The lowest or nearest point in an orbit; opposite of *apogee.*

Pérignon, Dom. Champagne.

perinatal. Pertaining to the period immediately before and after birth.

peripatetic. Wandering.

periphrasis. Using more words than necessary, circumlocution; pl. *periphrases.*

perishable.

periwinkle.

Perlman, Itzhak. (1945–) Israeli violinist.

permissible.

pernickety.

Perón, (María) Eva (Duarte de). (1919–1952) Nickname Evita; second wife of **Juan Perón** (1895–1974), president of Argentina (1946–1955, 1973–1974).

perpetrate, perpetuate. Occasionally confused. To *perpetrate* is to commit or perform. To *perpetuate* is to prolong or, literally, to make perpetual. The Boston Strangler perpetrated a series of murders. Those who write about him perpetuate his notoriety.

Persephone. In Greek mythology, queen of the underworld; identified with the Roman goddess Proserpina

Perseus. In Greek mythology, son of Zeus who murdered Medusa.

persevere, perseverance.

persiflage. Idle banter.

persimmon.

personal, personally. When it is necessary to emphasize that a person is acting on his own rather than on behalf of a group or that he is addressing people individually rather than collectively, *personal* and *personally* are unexceptionable. But usually the context makes that clear and the word is used without purpose, as here: "Dr. Leonard has decided to visit personally the Oklahoma parish which is the center of the dispute." If he visits, Dr. Leonard can hardly do it otherwise than personally. Many other common terms—*personal friend, personal opinion, personal favorite*—are nearly always equally redundant.

personnel.

perspicacity, perspicuity. The first means shrewdness, the second lucidity.

pertinacious. Persistent.

peruse. It is a losing battle no doubt, but perhaps worth pointing out that *peruse* does not mean to look over casually. It means to read or examine carefully.

pesos.

Pétain, Henri Philippe. (1856–1951) French general and politician, head of the Vichy government (1940–1944).

PETCO Park. San Diego baseball stadium, home of the Padres.

Peter Principle. The idea that people are promoted until they reach a level at which they are incompetent.

Petri dish. (Cap. *P.*)

Petrograd. Originally St. Petersburg, then Leningrad; reverted to St. Petersburg in 1991.

Petrovskoye. Former name of Makhachkala, Russia.

Pettenkofer, Max Joseph von. (1818–1901) German chemist.

Pettersen, Suzann. (1981–) Norwegian professional golfer.

pettifog. Quibble over petty matters; legal trickery.

petty bourgeois. A small businessman; member of the lower-middle class. In French, *petit bourgeois.*

peu à peu. (Fr.) "Little by little."

Peugeot. French automobile.

peut-être. (Fr.) Perhaps.

Pevsner, Sir Nikolaus. (1902–1983) German-born British art historian.

pfennig. Former German coin worth one one-hundredth of a mark.

PFLP. Popular Front for the Liberation of Palestine.

PGA. (No apos.) Professional Golfers Association.

pH. Potential of hydrogen, a measure of acidity in a solution.

Phalange. Political party in Lebanon.

phalanx, pl. *phalanxes/phalanges.*

pharaoh. Not *-oah.*

pharmacopoeia. A book containing descriptions of medicines and drugs.

phenomenon, pl. *phenomena.*

Phidias. (c. 498–c. 432 BC) Greek sculptor, responsible for all or part of the Parthenon.

philanderer. An unfaithful person.

Philip Morris. U.S. tobacco and diversified products company.

Philippi. Ancient city in Macedonia.

Philippians. Book of the New Testament.

philippic. A verbal denunciation.

Philippine Sea.

Philippines, Republic of the. Note *-l-, -pp-.* Island state in the Pacific Ocean; capital Manila. A person from the Philippines is a **Filipino**

if male, a **Filipina** if female. **Filipino** or **Pilipino** is also the name of the national language.

Philips. Dutch electrical company; formally, NV Philips Gloeilampenfabrieken.

Philips Arena, Atlanta.

philistine. Person who is indifferent or hostile to matters of culture.

Phillips screws and screwdrivers. Named for their originator, **Henry F. Phillips.**

Phillips Academy, Andover, Massachusetts. Private high school; also called Phillips Andover or just Andover. Not to be confused with PHILLIPS EXETER ACADEMY.

Phillips Collection, Washington, D.C.

Phillips curve. In economics, a measure showing the relationship between inflation and unemployment.

Phillips Exeter Academy, Exeter, New Hampshire. Private high school; commonly called just Exeter. Not to be confused with PHILLIPS ACADEMY of Andover, Massachusetts.

Phillips Petroleum. U.S. oil group.

Phillips Son & Neale. (No comma.) London Auction house.

Philomel/Philomela. Poetic name for the nightingale.

phlebitis. Inflammation of the veins.

Phnom Penh. Capital of Cambodia.

phony.

Phyfe, Duncan. (1786–1854) Scottish-born American furniture maker; born Duncan Fife.

phyllo (or **filo**). Pastry.

phylum. Taxonomic division of plants and animals; pl. *phyla.*

Physic, Regius Professor of. Cambridge University. Not *Physics.*

physiognomy. Facial characteristics.

physique.

pi. Ratio of circumference to diameter of a circle, equivalent to 3.14159 . . . ; also the sixteenth letter of the Greek alphabet.

pianissimo, pianississimo. In music, the first means very soft, and the second means as softly as possible.

Picard, Jean. (1620–1682) French astronomer.

Picasso, Pablo. (1881–1973) Spanish artist.

picayune. A trifling matter.

Piccadilly.

piccalilli. A kind of relish.

Piccard, Auguste. (1884–1962) Swiss physicist.

piccolo. A small flute pitched an octave higher than a normal flute; pl. *piccolos.*

picnicked, picnicking, picnicker.

pico-. Prefix meaning one-trillionth.

Pico della Mirandola, Count Giovanni. (1463–1494) Italian philosopher.

pidgin, creole. Pidgin is a language spontaneously devised by two or more peoples who have no common language. Pidgins are generally very rudimentary. If contact between the different peoples is prolonged and generations are born for whom the pidgin is their first tongue, the language will usually evolve into a more formalized system of speech called a creole. Most languages that are commonly called pidgins are in fact creoles.

pièce de résistance. (Fr.) Most outstanding item, particularly applied to the finest dish in a meal.

piecemeal.

pied-à-terre. (Fr.) (Hyphens.) A secondary residence; pl. *pieds-à-terre.*

Piedmont. Region of Italy; in Italian, Piemonte.

Pied Piper of Hamelin.

Piero della Francesca. (c. 1418–1492) Italian artist.

pierogi (or **pirogi**). Polish dumpling; pl. same.

Pierre, South Dakota. The state capital; pronounced *peer.*

Piers Plowman, The Vision of William Concerning. Epic poem by William Langland (c. 1360–1399).

Pietermaritzburg, South Africa Capital of Natal.

pigeonhole. (One word.)

piggyback.

Pikes Peak. (No apos.) Summit (14,100 ft.; 4,341 m.) in Rocky Mountains, Colorado; named after Zebulon Montgomery Pike, its discoverer.

Pilates. (Cap.) Trademarked exercise system.

Pilipino. Language of the **Philippines.**

Pilsener (or **Pilsner**). Beer.

Pilsudski, Józef. (1867–1935) Polish statesman.

pimento, pl. *pimentos. Pimiento* and *pimientos* are accepted alternatives.

Pincay, Laffit, Jr. (1946–) Panamanian-born American jockey.

pineal gland.

Pinero, Sir Arthur Wing. (1855–1934) English comedic playwright.

Ping-Pong. (Caps.)

Pinocchio. Note *-cc-*.

Pinochet, Augusto. (1915–2006) President of Chile (1973–1990).

pinscher, Doberman. Breed of dog.

pint. A liquid measure equal to sixteen ounces in the United States, twenty ounces in Britain.

Pinturicchio. Nickname of Bernardino di Betto Vagio (1454–1513), Italian painter.

Pinyin. System for romanizing Chinese names. Pinyin was devised in 1953 but has been in widespread international use only since about 1977. See also CHINESE NAMES.

piquant. Pungent, alluring.

pique. Resentment. "Fit of pique" is a cliché.

Piraeus. Port of Athens.

Pirandello, Luigi. (1867–1936) Italian author and playwright; awarded Nobel Prize for Literature in 1934.

Piranesi, Giovanni Battista (or **Giambattista**). (1720–1778) Italian artist and architect.

piranha. Species of fish.

Pirelli. Italian tire manufacturer.

pirouette. Graceful turn on one foot.

Piscataway, New Jersey.

Pissaro, Camille. (1830–1903) French painter.

pistachio. Nut-bearing tree; pl. *pistachios.*

pistil. Part of a flower.

pitiable, pitiful, pitiless, but **piteous.**

Pitti Palace, Florence. In Italian, Palazzo Pitti.

Pittsburgh, Pennsylvania. Not *-burg.*

pixels. Picture elements, the little squares from which computer graphics are composed.

pixie. Not *pixy.* A sprite.

Pizarro, Francisco. (c. 1475–1541) Spanish conquistador, conquered Peru, founded Lima.

pizzeria. Not *pizza-.* Restaurant where pizzas are made.

Plaid Cymru. Welsh nationalist political party; pronounced *plide kum'-ree.*

plan ahead. Always tautological. Would you plan behind?

Planck, Max. (1858–1947) German physicist, awarded Nobel Prize for Physics in 1918.

planetarium, pl. *planetariums/planetaria.*

planetesimal. Orbiting body with planetlike qualities, but too small to qualify as such.

Plantagenets. Dynasty of English monarchs from Henry II to Richard III (1154–1485).

plaster of paris. (No cap.)

plat du jour. (Fr.) "Dish of the day."

plateau. pl. *plateaus* (or *plateaux*).

platen. The roller on a typewriter.

plate tectonics. Not *tech-.* The science of Earth's crust and its movements.

Platt-Deutsch/Plattdeutsch. German dialect, also called Low German.

platypus, pl. *platypuses.*

plausible, plausibility.

"Play it, Sam" is the correct line from the movie *Casablanca*; Humphrey Bogart never actually said, "Play it again, Sam."

playwright. Not *-write.*

PLC. (U.K.) Public limited company, one whose shares are sold publicly and quoted on the stock market; equivalent to the American *Inc.* or German *AG.* Many companies write "plc" or "Plc," but there is no logical reason for so doing.

plead innocent is wrong, at least in the English-speaking world. Under the British and American judicial systems, one pleads guilty or not guilty.

plebeian. Common, vulgar, of the lower classes.

plebiscite. Vote of the people.

Pleiades. In Greek mythology, the seven daughters of Atlas and Pleione; a cluster of stars in the constellation Taurus.

Pleistocene. Geological period.

plenary. Full, complete. A plenary session of a council is one attended by all the members.

plenitude. Not *plenti-.* An abundance.

plenteous.

Plessy v. Ferguson. 1896 Supreme Court case that upheld the view that children of different races could be educated separately as long as the quality of education was equal.

plethora is not merely a lot; it is an excessive amount, a superabundance. For a word that is often similarly misused, see SPATE.

pleurisy. Inflammation of the membrane covering the lungs.

Plexiglas. (Cap.) Not *-ss.*

Plimsoll line/mark. Point down to which a ship may be loaded.

PLO. Palestine Liberation Organization.

plum, plumb. If it is edible or vegetative the word is *plum* (*plum pud-*

ding, sugerplum, plum tree), but in all other senses the word is *plumb* (*plumb line, plumb the depths, plumb tired out*).

plumage.

plummy. An affected rich, full voice.

plus is a preposition, not a conjunction, and therefore does not influence the number of the verb. Two and two are four, but two plus two *is* four.

Plutarch. Properly Ploutarchos (c. 46–c. 120). Greek historian, biographer, and philosopher.

plutocrat. Person who has influence or power because of wealth.

p.m./PM. *Post meridiem* (not *-ien*), (Lat.) after noon.

PNC Park. Pittsburgh baseball stadium, home of the Pirates.

Pocahontas. (c. 1595–1617) North American Indian princess, known for saving the life of John Smith.

Pocatello, Idaho.

pocket borough. A British parliamentary borough controlled by one person or group; common before parliamentary reforms of 1832.

Podhoretz, Norman. (1930–) American journalist and writer.

Poe, Edgar Allan. (1809–1849) American poet and short story writer.

poet laureate. For the plural, *poets laureate* or *poet laureates* are both generally accepted.

pogrom. Methodical massacre of a minority group.

poinsettia. Winter-flowering plant.

pokey, poky. The first is slang for jail; the second means small, cramped, or slow.

Poliakoff, Stephen. (1954–) British dramatist.

poliomyelitis. Commonly shortened to *polio*. Once called (somewhat misleadingly) infantile paralysis.

politburo/Politburo. The chief committee of a Communist Party.

Polizei. (Ger.) Police.

Pollaiuolo, Antonio. (1429–1498) Italian painter, sculptor, and goldsmith.

Pollock, Jackson. (1912–1956) American artist.

Pollyanna. An optimistic person, particularly one who is foolishly so; after the heroine of a 1913 novel by Eleanor Porter.

polonaise. A slow Polish dance, or the music for it.

poltergeist.

Poltoratsk. Former name of Ashgabat, capital of Turkmenistan.

polyandry. State or practice of a woman having more than one husband at the same time.

polygamy. State or practice of a man having more than one wife at the same time.

polypropylene. Type of plastic.

pomegranate. Round fruit with many seeds.

Pomeranian. A toy breed of dog.

Pompeian. Of Pompeii, the Roman city destroyed by the eruption of Mt. Vesuvius in AD 79.

Pompey. (106–48 BC) Properly **Gnaeus Pompeius Magnus**; Roman soldier and statesman.

Pompidou Center, Paris. Formally Le Centre National d'Art et de Culture Georges Pompidou; also called Centre Beaubourg.

pompon. Not -*pom*. A ball or tuft of material.

Ponce de León, Juan. (1460–1521) Spanish explorer, discovered Florida.

Pontchartrain, Lake, Louisiana.

Ponte Vecchio. Famous bridge over the Arno, Florence, Italy.

Pont l'Évêque. French town and type of cheese named after it.

pooh-bah. Person who holds many offices at once, from the character Pooh-Bah in Gilbert and Sullivan's *The Mikado*.

pooh-pooh. To dismiss or make light of.

Popescu-Tăriceanu, Călin. (1952–) Prime minister of Romania (2004–).

poppadam (or **poppadom**). Indian thin, crisp, fried bread.

populace, populous. The first describes a general population. The second means heavily populated.

porcupine.

pore, pour. Occasionally *pour* appears where *pore* is intended. As a verb, *pore* means to examine carefully ("He pored over the documents") or, more rarely, to meditate. *Pour* indicates a flow, either literally ("He poured the water down the drain") or figuratively ("The rioters poured through the streets").

port, starboard. When facing forward on a ship, port is to the left, starboard to the right.

Port-au-Prince. (Hyphens.) Capital of Haiti.

portentous. Not *-ious*.

portico. A porch supported by pillars; pl. *porticoes/porticos*.

portland cement. (Not cap.)

portmanteau word. A word blending two others, e.g., *smog = smoke + fog*.

Portmeirion, Wales. Fanciful Italianate village built by Sir Clough Williams-Ellis, and a brand of pottery that originated there.

Port Moresby. Capital of Papua New Guinea.

Porto-Novo. (Hyphen.) Capital of Benin.

Portuguese.

Port-Vila. (Hyphen.) Capital of Vanuatu.

Portzamparc, Christian de. (1944–) Moroccan-born French architect; on second reference he is Mr. (or Monsieur) Portzamparc, not de Portzamparc.

Poseidon. Greek god of the sea; identified with the Roman god Neptune.

position. Often a pointer to verbosity. "They now find themselves in a position where they have to make a choice" would be immeasurably better as "They now have to make a choice."

possessives. Problems with possessives are discussed in some detail in the Appendix under APOSTROPHE, but three especially common faults are worth mentioning here.

1. Failure to put an apostrophe in the right place. This is par-

ticularly frequent with words like *men's, women's,* and *children's,* which all too often appear as *mens', womons',* and *childrens'*.

2. Failure to put an apostrophe in at all. This practice—spelling the words *mens, womens,* and *childrens* and so on—is particularly rife among retailers. It is painful enough to behold there, inexcusable elsewhere.

3. Putting an apostrophe where none is needed. Possessive pronouns—*his, hers, ours, theirs,* and so on—do not take an apostrophe. But sometimes one is wrongly inserted, as here: "I don't think much of your's" (*Independent* headline).

(See also "OURS IS NOT TO REASON WHY . . .")

possible is wrongly followed by *may* in constructions such as the following: "It is possible that she may decide to go after all" (*Daily Telegraph*). Make it either "It is possible that she will decide to go after all" or "She may decide to go after all." Together the two words are wrong and unnecessary.

posthaste. (One word.) With speed.

posthumous. After death.

postilion.

postmeridian, post meridiem. The first means related to or happening in the afternoon. The second, also pertaining to the period after noon, is the Latin term better known to most of us as the abbreviation p.m. Note the different terminal spellings.

postpartum. After birth.

postprandial. After dinner.

potage. Soup.

potpourri, pl. *potpourris.*

Poughkeepsie, New York.

Poulenc, Francis. (1899–1963) French composer.

Poulters' Company. London livery company; not *Poulterers'.*

pour, pore. The first means to flow or rain heavily; the second means to examine carefully.

pourboire. (Fr.) A gratuity.

pour encourager les autres. (Fr.) "To encourage the others."

Poussin, Nicolas. (1594–1665) French painter.

Powell, Anthony. (1905–2000) British novelist; pronounced *pole.*

powwow. A conference.

Powys, John Cowper. (1872–1963) English poet and novelist; the names are pronounced *cooper* and *po-iss.*

PPI. Abbreviation of *producer price index;* in economics, a measure of changes in commodity prices.

practical, practicable. Anything that can be done and is worth doing is practical. Anything that can be done, whether or not it is worth doing, is practicable.

practice, practiced, practicing.

praemonitus praemunitis. (Lat.) "Forewarned is forearmed."

praeseodymium. Chemical element.

Praetorian Guard. Elite Roman army unit.

Praha. Czech spelling of Prague.

Praia. Capital of Cape Verde.

precautionary measure is a common phrase, but it can nearly always be shortened simply to *precaution.*

precipitant, precipitate, precipitous. All three come from the same root, the Latin *praecipitare* ("to throw headlong"). *Precipitous* means very steep: cliff faces are precipitous. *Precipitant* and *precipitate* both indicate a headlong rush and are almost indistinguishable in meaning, but *precipitant* tends to emphasize the abruptness of the rush and *precipitate* the rashness of it. The most common error is to use *precipitous* to describe actions ("his precipitous departure from the cabinet"). *Precipitous* can describe only physical characteristics.

precondition, preplanning, prerecorded, etc. Almost always redundant:

"A lot of headaches can be avoided with a little careful preplanning" (*Chicago Tribune*). All planning must be done in advance. *Pre-* adds nothing to its meaning and should be deleted, as it should have been in these examples: "There are, however, three preconditions to be met before negotiations can begin" (*Guardian*); "The company's music performance reflected both the volatility and opportunities for growth in the worldwide market for prerecorded music" (advertisement in the *Economist*).

precursor. Not *-er*.

predilection.

prehensile. Able to grasp.

premier, premiere. The first means first in position or importance. The second is a debut.

Preminger, Otto. (1906–1986) Austrian-born American film director.

premises is always plural when referring to property. There is no such thing as a business premise.

prepositions. The lingering belief that sentences should not end with prepositions is entirely without foundation.

prerogative. An exclusive right.

Prescelly Mountains, Wales.

prescribe, proscribe. *Prescribe* means to set down as a rule or guide. *Proscribe* means to denounce or prohibit. If you get bronchitis, your doctor may prescribe antibiotics and proscribe smoking.

present, presently. Like *current* and *currently,* these two often appear needlessly in sentences, as here: "A new factory, which is presently under construction in Manchester, will add to capacity." The sentence says as much without *presently* as with it.

Presidents' Day. Note apos. Third Monday of February.

presumptive, presumptuous. The first is sometimes used when the second is intended. *Presumptuous* means impudent and inclined to take liberties, or to act in a manner that is excessively bold and forthright. *Presumptive* means giving grounds to presume and is primarily a technical term. The wrong use is seen here: "She considered the question with the equanimity of someone who has long been immune to presumptive prying" (*Sunday Telegraph*).

pretension, but pretentious.

prevalent, prevalence.

prevaricate, procrastinate. Occasionally confused. *Prevaricate* means to speak or act evasively, to stray from the truth. *Procrastinate* means to put off doing.

prevent often appears incorrectly in sentences such as this: "They tried to prevent him leaving." It should be either "They tried to prevent his leaving" or "They tried to prevent him from leaving." See GERUNDS (2).

preventive, preventative. "One way to ease their difficulties, they decided, was to practice preventative medicine" (*Economist*). *Preventative* is not incorrect, but *preventive* is shorter.

Pribilof islands, Alaska.

PricewaterhouseCoopers. Accountancy company.

"Pride goes before a fall" is wrong. The quotation, from Proverbs, is "Pride goeth before destruction, and an haughty spirit before a fall."

prima facie. "At first sight," on the face of it.

primeval. Not -*evil*.

primogeniture. The practice by which an entire inheritance passes to the firstborn male child.

primus inter pares. (Lat.) "First among equals."

Princes Street, Edinburgh, Scotland.

Princes Town, Trinidad.

principal, principle. *Principle* means fundamental and is usually applied to fundamental beliefs or truths ("It's not the money, it's the principle") or to fundamental understandings ("They have signed an agreement in principle"). It is always a noun. *Principal* can be a noun meaning chief or of first importance ("He is the school's principal") or an adjective with the same meaning ("The principal reason for my going . . .").

pristine does not mean spotless. It means original or primeval or in a state virtually unchanged from the original.

privilege.

prix fixe. (Fr.) Fixed price; pl. *prix fixes.*

Prix Goncourt. Preeminent French literary award.

p.r.n. Short for *pro re nata* (Lat.), "as necessary." Used by doctors on prescriptions to indicate that a drug should be administered as necessary and not on a fixed schedule.

proboscis. An animal's trunk, long snout, or feeding tube; pl. *proboscises.*

proceed, but **procedure.**

procrastinate, prevaricate. The first means to postpone doing; the second means to be untruthful.

Procrustean. Producing or striving to produce absolute conformity, usually through severe or absolute means; from Procrustes, a mythological Greek robber who made his victims fit a bed by stretching them or cutting off their limbs.

Procter & Gamble for the household products company. Often misspelled *Proctor.*

prodigal does not mean wandering or given to running away, a sense sometimes wrongly inferred from the biblical story of the Prodigal Son. It means recklessly wasteful or extravagant.

progenitor. Ancestor.

prognosis, pl. *prognoses.*

Prohibition (cap.) lasted from 1920 to 1933; it was brought in by the Eighteenth Amendment to the Constitution and the Volstead Act, and repealed by the Twenty-first Amendment.

Prokofiev, Sergei. (1891–1953) Russian composer.

Promised Land, the. (Caps.)

promissory note.

prone, prostrate, recumbent, supine. *Supine* means lying faceup (it may help to remember that a supine person is on his spine). *Prone* and *prostrate* are regarded by most dictionaries and usage authorities—but by no means all—as meaning lying facedown. (A few say that they can also apply to a person or thing lying faceup.) *Prostrate* should, in any case, suggest throwing oneself down, either in submission or for protection; someone who is merely asleep should not be called prostrate. *Recumbent* means lying flat in any position, but, like *repose*, it should indicate a position of ease and comfort. For the other sense of *prone*, see LIABLE, LIKELY, APT, PRONE.

pronunciation. Not *pronoun-*.

propaganda.

propagate.

propellant is the usual spelling, but *propellent* is also accepted.

proper nouns. Many writers stumble when confronted with finding a plural form for a proper noun, as in the two following examples, both from *The Times* of London and both wrong: "The Cox's were said by neighbors to . . . happily married"; "This is the first of a new series about the Rush's." The rule for making plurals of proper nouns is precisely the same as for any other nouns. If you have no trouble turning "one fox" into "two foxes" or "one church" into "two churches," you should have no trouble making "the Rush family" into "the Rushes" and "the Cox couple" into "the Coxes." In short, for names ending in *s, sh, ch,* or *x*, add *es: Lewises, Lennoxes, Clemenses.* For all others, simply add *s: Smiths, Browns, Greens, the two Koreas.* The rule is invariable for Anglo-Saxon names. For others, there are a few exceptions, among them *Rockies, Ptolemies, Alleghenies, Mercuries,* and (in some publications) *Germanies.* At all events, the addition of an apostrophe to make any noun plural is always wrong.

prophecy, prophesy. The first is the noun; the second the verb. Thus: "I prophesy war; that is my prophecy."

propinquity. Nearness or similarity.

proprietor, but **proprietary.**

pro re nata. See P.R.N.

prosciutto. Italian ham; pl. *prosciutti* (or *prosciuttos*).

prosthesis, pl. *prostheses.*

prostrate should be used only with the sense of throwing oneself down in submission or for protection.

protagonist. Literally the word means "first actor" (from the Greek *protos* and *agonistes*) and by extension may be applied to the person who most drives the action in any affair. The word is not the opposite of *antagonist;* it does not necessarily have anything to do with heroic or admirable behavior or bear any relationship to the Latin *pro-,* meaning for or on behalf of. A protagonist may champion a cause, and in practice often does, but that isn't implicit in the word.

protégé (masc.), **protégée** (fem.). One under the protection or tutelage of an experienced person.

pro tem is the abbreviation of *pro tempore* (Lat.), "for the time being."

protester.

protocol.

prototype is the word for an original that serves as a model for later products of its type. Thus *first prototype, experimental prototype, model prototype,* and most other qualifying descriptions are generally redundant.

proved, proven. In general *proved* is the preferred past tense form ("the accused was proved innocent") and *proven* the preferred form for adjectival uses ("a proven formula").

provenance. Place of origin.

Provence-Alpes-Côte d'Azur. French region.

proverbial. Unless there is some connection to an actual proverb, the word is wrongly used and better avoided.

provided, providing. Most authorities consider the first preferable to the second in constructions such as "He agreed to come provided he could get the day off work," but either would be correct. "If" is often better still.

Pryor, Richard. (1940–2005) American comedian and actor.

Przewalski's horse, Przewalski's gazelle. Two rare species, both named for **Nikolai Przewalski** (or **Przhevalsky**), Russian explorer (1839–1888).

pseudonym. Pen name.

psittacosis. Sometimes called parrot fever; a disease of birds that can be passed to people.

ptarmigan.

pterodactyl.

publicly. Not *-ally*.

Publishers Weekly. (No apos.) American trade magazine.

Puccini, Giacomo. (1858–1924) Italian composer of operas.

Pudd'nhead Wilson, The Tragedy of. Novel by Mark Twain (1894).

puerile. Childish.

puerperal. Pertaining to childbirth, as in *puerperal psychosis.*

Puerto Rico. Formerly a U.S. territory, now a self-governing commonwealth.

Puget Sound, Washington.

Pulitzer Prize. Named for **Joseph Pulitzer** (1847–1911).

pumice. Volcanic rock.

pumpernickel. Coarse wholemeal rye bread.

punctilious.

Punxsutawney, Pennsylvania; town noted for its Groundhog Day ceremonies.

Purim. Jewish holiday; pronounced *poo-rim*, not *pyur-im*.

purlieu, purlieus. The first denotes bounds or limits; the second denotes outlying areas or environs.

purposely, purposefully. The first means intentionally. The second means with an objective in mind. "She purposely nudged me" means it was no accident. "She purposefully nudged me" means she did it to make a point or draw my attention to something.

Pushkin, Alexander. (1799–1837) Russian poet.

pusillanimous. Cowardly.

putrid, but **putrefy, putrefaction.**

Puttnam, David. (1941–) British film producer; now formally Lord Puttnam.

pygmy, pl. *pygmies.*

Pyle, Ernie. (1900–1945) American journalist.

Pynchon, Thomas. (1937–) American novelist.

Pyongyang. Capital of North Korea.

pyorrhea. Infection of the gums, more formally called periodontal disease.

Pyrenees, Pyrenean.

Pyrrhic victory is not a hollow triumph. It is one won at huge cost to the victor.

Pythagoras. (582–507 BC) Greek philosopher and mathematician; the adjectival form is *Pythagorean.*

Qq

Qaddafi/Gaddafi, Muammar al-. (1942–) Libyan head of state (1969–). Either spelling is acceptable, but *Gaddafi* is more commonly used than *Qaddafi*. He has no official title or position.

Qaeda, Al (from the Arabic *al-qā'ida*), is the most common spelling in American English for the terrorist group, but there are many variants, including commonly *Al Qaida, al-Qaeda,* and *al-Qaida*.

Qahira, El. Arabic for Cairo.

Qantas. Although the full name is no longer used, for historical purposes it may be worth noting that Qantas is short for Queensland and Northern Territory Aerial Service. Not *Air* and not *Services*.

Qatar. Persian Gulf emirate; capital Doha. The airline is **Qatar Airways.**

QED (no periods) is the abbreviation of *quod est demonstrandum* (Lat.), "which was to be demonstrated."

Qom. Alternative spelling for **Qum,** Iranian holy city.

Q-tip is a trademark.

quadrennium. A period of four years. Nearly everyone will understand you better if you just say "a period of four years."

quadriplegia. Not *quadra-*. Paralysis of all four limbs.

quadruped. Not *quadra-, quadri-*. A four-legged animal. The adjectival form is *quadrupedal*.

Quai d'Orsay. The French Foreign Ministry, so called because it is on a street of that name in Paris.

Quakers are formally known as the Society of Friends.

Qualcomm. Wireless technology company.

quandary Not *quandry* or *quandery*.

quand même. (Fr.) "All the same."

quantum leap has become a cliché and is better avoided. A separate objection is that its general sense of a revolutionary step forward is at variance with its strict scientific sense of a movement or advance that is discrete and measurable, but not necessarily, or even usually, dramatic.

Qu'Appelle. Canadian river.

quark. Hypothetical subatomic particle.

quasar is derived from, and means, "quasi-stellar object."

quaternary. Of or pertaining to groups of four. When capitalized, it describes the geological period, part of the Cenozoic era, when humans first appeared.

quatrefoil. In architecture, a four-pointed tracery.

quattrocento. Abbreviation of Italian *millequattrocento*, the fifteenth century, used especially in reference to Italian art and culture.

quaver. To tremble.

queasy.

Québécois (or **Quebecer**) for someone from **Quebec.** The Canadian political party is always Parti Québécois.

Queen Elizabeth II. (1926–) Her formal title, though seldom used, is Elizabeth the Second, by the Grace of God, of the United Kingdom of Great Britain and Northern Ireland and of Her Other Realms and Territories, Queen Head of the Commonwealth, Defender of the Faith. She became queen in 1952; her coronation was in 1953.

Queens. (No apos.) Borough of New York.

Queensberry rules. Not -*bury*. Code of conduct for boxing; formally they are the Marquess of Queensberry Rules.

Queensboro Bridge, New York, but **Queensborough Community College.**

Queens College, City University of New York, **Queen's College,** Oxford, **Queens' College,** Cambridge.

quelque chose. (Fr.) Something, a trifle.

¿qué pasa? (Sp.) "What's up?"

querulous. Fretful, peevish.

query, inquiry, enquiry. A *query* is a single question. An *inquiry* or *enquiry* may be a single question or an extensive investigation. Either spelling is correct, but *inquiry* is preferred by most dictionaries.

que será, será. (Sp.) "Whatever will be, will be." The same expression in Italian is *che sarà, sarà.*

qu'est-ce que c'est? (Fr.) "What is this?"

question, leading. A leading question is not a challenging or hostile one, as is sometimes thought, but the opposite. It is a question designed to encourage the person being questioned to make the desired response. A lawyer who says to a witness, "So you didn't see the murder, did you?" has asked a leading question.

question mark has become an overworked embellishment of the expression "a question hanging over," which is itself wearyingly overused. Consider: "The case . . . has raised a question mark over the competence of British security" (*The Times*). Would you say of a happy event that it had raised an exclamation mark over the proceedings or that a pause in negotiations had a comma hanging over them?

questionnaire. Note *-nn-*.

Quetzalcoatl. Aztec god.

queue, queuing.

Quezon City. Former capital of the Philippines (1948–1976).

quid pro quo. (Lat.) Tit for tat, a fair trade-off.

quiescent.

qu'importe? (Fr.) "What does it matter?"

quincentennial. Five-hundredth anniversary.

Quinnipiac University, Connecticut.

Quinquagesima. The fiftieth day before Easter, the Sunday before Ash Wednesday.

quinquennial can mean either to last for five years or to occur once every five years. Because of the inherent ambiguity, the word is almost always better replaced with a more specific phrase.

quinsy. Historic name for tonsillitis.

quintessence, quintessential.

quisling. One who collaborates with a foreign enemy; after **Vidkun Quisling** (1887–1945), pro-Nazi Norwegian prime minister appointed by Germany.

Quito. Capital of Ecuador.

qui vive, on the. In a state of watchfulness.

Qum (or **Qom**). Holy city in Iran.

quod est demonstrandum. (Abbr. QED.) (Lat.) "Which was to be demonstrated."

quod vide. (Abbr. q.v.) (Lat.) "Which see"; used for cross-references.

Quonochontaug, Rhode Island.

Quonset hut. Prefabricated metal shelter.

quorum, pl. *quorums.*

Quran. Alternative spelling of *Koran.*

q.v. *Quod vide* (Lat.), "which see." Used for cross-references.

qwerty keyboard. Standard English keyboard, so called because the first six letters of the first row of letters spell *qwerty.*

Rr

rabbet. Type of groove used in carpentry.

rabbi, rabbinical.

Rabelais, François. (c. 1494–c. 1553) French satirist.

Rabin, Yitzhak. (1922–1995) Israeli prime minister (1974–1977, 1992–1995).

raccoon.

Rachmaninoff (or **Rachmaninov**), **Sergei.** (1873–1943) Russian composer and pianist.

rack, wrack. *Wrack* is an archaic variant of *wreck* and now almost never appears except in the expression *wrack and ruin. Rack* means to put under strain. The expressions are *nerve-racking* and *to rack one's brain.*

racket (pref.)**/racquet** (alt.).

racy.

radiator. Not *-er.*

radius. The plural can be either *radii* or *radiuses.*

raffia. Fiber used for mats.

Rafsanjani, Ali Akbar (Hashemi). (1934–) President of Iran (1989–1997).

ragamuffin.

ragout. In French, *ragoût.*

raise Cain, to.

raison d'être. (Fr.) "Reason for being."

Rajasthan, India. Not *-stan.*

raki. Alcoholic drink of Eastern Europe and the Middle East.

Ralegh, Sir Walter. (1552–1618) English courtier, explorer, and author. *Raleigh* was once the conventional spelling, but *Ralegh* is now generally preferred in serious and academic writings. However, for the city in North Carolina, the bicycles, and the cigarettes, use **Raleigh.**

Ramadan. Ninth month of the Muslim year, and the fast that takes place in that month.

Ramses (sometimes **Rameses**). Name of twelve pharaohs of ancient Egypt.

rand. South African currency; the plural is also *rand*.

Rangers Ballpark in Arlington is the formal name of the home of the Texas Rangers baseball team.

ranges of figures. Sentences such as the following are common: "Profits in the division were expected to rise by between $35 and $45 million." Although most people will see at once that the writer meant to indicate a range of $10 million, literally she was saying that profits could be as little as $35 or as much as $45 million. If you mean "between $35 million and $45 million," it is always better to say so.

Ransom, John Crowe. (1888–1974) American poet and critic.

Ransome, Arthur. (1884–1967) British author of children's stories.

Raphael. (1483–1520) Italian painter; real name Raffaello Santi (or Sanzio).

"Rappaccini's Daughter." Story by Nathaniel Hawthorne (1844).

Rappahannock River, Virginia.

rappel, rappelled, rappelling.

rapprochement. (Fr.) Reconciliation.

rapt, wrapped. One is rapt in thought, not wrapped. *Rapt* means engrossed, absorbed, enraptured.

rara avis. (Lat.) "A rare bird"; an unusual or wonderful person or thing; pl. *rarae aves.*

rarefy, rarefaction, but **rarity.**

Rasselas, Prince of Abyssinia, The History of. Novel by Samuel Johnson (1759).

Rastafarianism. Religious sect.

ratatouille. Vegetable stew.

rational, rationale. The first means sensible or sound ("a rational decision"); the second describes a justification ("the rationale for his actions").

rattan. Type of cane.

ravage, ravish. The first means to lay waste. The second means to rape or carry off—or, a touch confusingly, to enrapture. Clearly, in all senses, for both words, care needs to be exercised to avoid confusion.

Ravenna, Italy.

Rawalpindi, Pakistan.

Ray, Satyajit. (1921–1992) Indian film director.

razed to the ground is a common but mistaken expression. The ground is the only place to which a structure can be razed. It is enough to say that a building has been razed.

razzmatazz.

re- words. Somewhat mystifyingly, many publications show a formidable resistance to putting hyphens into any word beginning with *re-*. Yet often the presence or absence of a hyphen can usefully and immediately denote a difference in meaning, as between *recollect* (remember) and *re-collect* (collect again), or between *recede* (withdraw) and *re-cede* (give back again, as with territory). My advice, for what it is worth, is always to insert a hyphen if you think it might reduce the chance of even momentary misunderstanding.

react is better reserved for spontaneous responses ("He reacted to the news by fainting"). It should not be used to indicate responses marked by reflection.

real. Brazilian currency; the plural is *reais*.

realpolitik. Politics based on the achievable.

reason . . . is because is a common construction that almost always points to an overwritten sentence. Consider an example: "The reason she spends less and less time in England these days is because her business interests keep her constantly on the move." Remove "the reason" and its attendant verb "is," and a crisper, more focused sentence emerges: "She spends less and less time in England these days because her business interests keep her constantly on the move."

reason why, like *reason . . . is because* (see above), is generally redundant. Consider two examples: "Grover said her contract had been terminated, but no one at the company would tell her the reason why"; "His book argues that the main reason why inner-city blacks are in such a sorry state is not because whites are prejudiced but that low-skilled jobs near their homes are disappearing." An improvement can nearly always be effected by removing one word or the other—e.g., "the reason" from the first example, "why" from the second.

receptacle.

recherché. Farfetched.

reciprocal, reciprocity.

reckless. Not *wreckless*, unless you are describing a setting in which there are no wrecks.

reconnaissance.

reconnoiter.

reducible.

reductio ad absurdum. (Lat.) To deflate an argument by proving it absurd.

reebok. Type of antelope.

Reekie, Auld. (Scot.) "Old Smoky"; nickname for Edinburgh.

reflector.

refute means to show conclusively that an allegation is wrong. It does not mean simply to dispute or deny a contention.

regalia is plural.

Regent's Park, London (apos.).

reggae. West Indian music.

regretfully, regrettably. The first means with feelings of regret ("Regretfully they said their farewells"); the second means unfortunately ("Regrettably I did not have enough money to buy it").

rehabilitate.

Reims, France, is the usual spelling, though *Rheims* is sometimes used. It is pronounced *reemz* in English but *ranz* in French.

relatively, like *comparatively*, should not be used unless there is some sense of a comparison or relationship. Often it can be removed without loss from sentences like "The group has taken the relatively bold decision to expand its interests in Nigeria."

religieuse. (Fr.) A nun; pl. *religieuses.*

religieux. (Fr.) A monk; pl. *religieux.*

Remarque, Erich Maria. (1898–1970) German-born American novelist.

Rembrandt Harmensz (or **Harmenszoon**) **van Rijn** is the full name for the Dutch painter (1606–1669).

remembrance. Not *-berance.*

remissible.

remittance, remitted.

remittent.

remunerate. Not *renum-.*

Renaissance, the. In European art, roughly the period 1300–1500.

rendezvous is the spelling for both the singular and plural.

renegade.

renege, reneged, reneging.

Renoir, Pierre-Auguste. (1841–1919) French painter; father of **Jean Renoir** (1894–1979), film director.

renown. Not *reknown.*

Rensselaer Polytechnic Institute.

Rentokil. Pest control company; not *-kill.*

repartee.

repellent.

repetition, repetitive.

replete is not merely full but overfull, stuffed.

replica. An exact copy. A scale model is not a replica. Only something built to the same scale as the original and using the same materials is a replica. It therefore follows that "exact replica" is always redundant.

repository.

reprehensible.

reproducible.

Repubblica, La. Italian newspaper. Note -bb-.

Resnais, Alain. (1922–) French film director.

respirator. Not -er.

respite, temporary or **brief.** It is in the nature of respites to be both. It is enough to say that somebody or something enjoyed a respite.

restaurateur. Not -rant-.

restive properly means balky or obstinate, refusing to move or budge. A crowd of protesters may grow restive upon the arrival of mounted police, but a person sitting uncomfortably on a hard bench is better described as restless.

résumé.

resuscitate, resuscitator.

retraceable.

retroussé (masc.)/**retroussée** (fem). Turned up, particularly applied to noses.

retsina. Greek white wine flavored with resin.

Reuters. (No apos.) News agency.

reveille.

Revelation, Book of. Not -ions.

reversible.

revert back is always redundant. Delete *back*.

revertible.

Reykjavik. Capital of Iceland.

Rhadamanthus. In Greek mythology, a judge of the dead.

Rhein. German spelling of Rhine.

Rhineland-Palatinate. German state; in German, Rheinland-Pfalz.

rhinestone. Artificial diamond.

rhinoceros, pl. *rhinoceroses.*

rhododendron.

Rhône. French river.

Rhône-Alpes, French region.

rhumb line.

rhythm, rhythmic.

RIBA. Royal Institute (not *Institution*) of British Architects.

Ribbentrop, Joachim von. (1893–1946) German politician.

ribonucleic acid. RNA.

Ricardo, David. (1772–1823) English political economist and politician.

Rice, Condoleezza. (1954–) American political adviser, secretary of state (2005–).

Richelieu, Armand Jean du Plessis, Cardinal, Duc de. (1585–1642) French prime minister (1624–42).

Richter scale for the standard measure of earthquake magnitudes. It is named for **Charles Richter** (1900–1985) of the California Institute of Technology, who invented it in the 1930s. The scale increases at a rate that is exponential rather than linear, making each level of increment vastly greater than most people appreciate. According to Charles Office and Jake Page in *Tales of the Earth,* a magnitude 8.3 earthquake is 50 times larger than a magnitude 7.3 quake and 2,500 times larger than a magnitude 6.3 quake. In practical terms, this means that Richter magnitudes are largely meaningless to most readers and comparisons involving two or more Richter measurements are totally meaningless. It is considerate to the reader to provide, wherever possible, some basis of comparison beyond the bare Richter numbers. It is also worth bearing in mind that the Richter scale measures only the magnitude of an earthquake at its point of origin and says little or nothing about the degree of devastation at ground level.

rickettsia. Microorganism that can transmit various diseases to humans.

RICO. Common abbreviation for Racketeer Influenced and Corrupt Organizations Act, law designed to attack organized crime.

ricochet, ricocheted, ricocheting.

RICS stands for Royal Institution of Chartered Surveyors, London.

Riefenstahl, Leni. (1902–2003) German actress and film director.

Riesling. (Cap.) German white wine.

Rievaulx Abbey, North Yorkshire, England; pronounced *ree-vo*.

riffraff.

Rigoletto. Opera by Verdi (1851).

rigor mortis.

Rijksmuseum, Amsterdam, the Netherlands.

Rikers Island, New York. (No apos.)

Riksdag. Swedish parliament.

Riley, the life of.

Rilke, Rainer Maria. (1875–1926) Austrian poet.

"Rime of the Ancient Mariner, The." Not *Rhyme*. Poem by Samuel Taylor Coleridge.

Rimsky-Korsakov, Nikolai (or **Nicholas**). (1844–1908) Russian composer.

Ringling Brothers and Barnum & Bailey Circus.

Rio de Janeiro, Brazil.

Rio Grande. Not *Rio Grande River*.

Rio Tinto-Zinc. British mining company. Note position of hyphen.

"Rip Van Winkle." Story by Washington Irving (1819).

risotto. Italian rice dish.

rissole. Deep-fried mincemeat or fish in the form of a ball or patty.

Rive Gauche. (Fr.) The Left Bank, most commonly used of the Seine in Paris.

Riyadh. Capital of Saudi Arabia; in Arabic, Ar Riyad.

RNA. Ribonucleic acid.

Roanoke, Virginia.

Robbins, Jerome. (1918–1998) American choreographer; born Jerome Rabinowitz.

Robespierre, Maximilien François Marie Isidore de. (1758–1794) French revolutionary.

Robins, A. H. U.S. pharmaceuticals company.

Rochefoucauld, François, Duc de La. (1613–1680) French writer known for his maxims.

Rockefeller, John D(avison). (1839–1937) American business tycoon. Note middle name was *Davison,* not *Davidson.*

rock 'n' roll.

Rockville Centre, New York. Not *Center.*

rococo.

Rodgers, Jimmie. (1897–1933) U.S. country music singer.

Rodgers, Richard. (1902–1979) American composer, collaborated often with Lorenz Hart and Oscar Hammerstein II.

Rodin, Auguste. (1840–1917) French sculptor.

Roebling, John Augustus. (1806–1869) American engineer, designer of Brooklyn Bridge.

Roedean School, Brighton, England.

Roederer, Louis, champagne.

Roeg, Nicolas. (1928–) British film director. Note unusual spelling of first name.

Rogers Centre. Not *-er.* Toronto sporting arena; formerly SkyDome.

Rogers, Ginger. (1911–1995) Actress and dancer; real name Virginia Katherine McMath.

Rogers, Richard. (Baron Rogers of Riverside) (1933–) British architect.

Rohrabacher, Dana. (1947–) Republican U.S. representative from California.

Roissy. Informal name of Charles de Gaulle Airport, Paris.

Rolls-Royce. (Hyphen.)

roly-poly.

ROM. Read-only memory, a type of computer memory.

roman-à-clef. (Fr.) A novel about real people but using fictitious names; pl. *romans-à-clef.*

roman-fleuve. (Fr.) A long novel, or series of novels, chronicling several generations of a family; pl. *romans-fleuves.*

Romania. Not *Ru-*.

Roman numerals. See Appendix.

Romanov. Dynasty that ruled Russia from 1613–1917.

Romansch/Romansh. Language spoken in parts of Switzerland.

Romberg, Sigmund. (1887–1951) Hungarian-born American composer of operettas.

Rommel, Erwin. (1891–1944) German field marshal, commander of the Afrika Korps in World War II.

Roppongi. Nightclub district of Tokyo.

Roquefort. A French cheese, from the village of Roquefort-sur-Soulzon.

Rorschach test. Psychological test involving ink blots devised by Swiss pyschiatrist and neurologist Hermann Rorschach (1884–1922).

Roseau. Capital of Dominica.

Rosebery, Lord. (1847–1929) Not *-berry.* British prime minister (1894–1895). His full name was Archibald Philip Primrose, Earl of Rosebery.

Rosenberg, Julius (1918–1953) and **Ethel** (1915–1953). Americans executed as Russian spies.

Rosenborg Castle, Copenhagen, Denmark.

Rosenkavalier, Der. Opera by Richard Strauss (1911).

Rosetta stone.

Rosh Hashanah (or **Hashana, Hoshana, Hoshanah**). Jewish New Year, usually late September or early October.

Ros-Lehtinen, Ileana. (1952–) Republican U.S. representative from Florida.

Rosmersholm. Play by Henrik Ibsen (1886).

Rossetti, Dante Gabriel. (1828–1882) English poet and painter, one of the founders of the Pre-Raphaelite Brotherhood; brother of **Christina Rossetti** (1830–1894), poet.

Rossini, Gioacchino Antonio. (1792–1868) Italian composer.

Rostand, Edmond. (1868–1918) Not -*mund.* French playwright and poet.

Rostenkowski, Dan. (1928–) American politician.

Rostropovich, Mstislav. (1927–2007) Russian cellist.

rosy. Not *rosey.*

Rothko, Mark. (1903–1970) Russian-born American painter.

Rothschilds, a family of European financiers. Among the more distinguished members are **Nathaniel Mayer Victor, Baron Rothschild** (1910–1990), English scientist and public servant; **Edmund Leopold de Rothschild** (1916–2007), British banker; and **Baron Élie Robert de Rothschild** (1917–).

rottweiler for the breed of dog. Note two *t*'s, one *l.*

Rouault, Georges Henri. (1871–1958) French expressionist painter.

Roubiliac, Louis François. (1695–1762) French sculptor.

Rousseau, Henri. (1844–1910) French painter. Nicknamed "Douanier," French for "customs clerk."

Rousseau, Jean-Jacques. (1712–1778) Swiss-born French political theorist.

Rowlandson, Thomas. (1756–1827) English caricaturist.

Royal and Ancient Golf Club, the. Formal name of the famous golf course at St. Andrews, Scotland.

Royal Dutch/Shell Group. Anglo-Dutch oil company.

Royal Institution of Chartered Surveyors, London; not *Institute.*

Royal Welch Fusiliers, Royal Welch Regiment. Not *Welsh.* British military regiments.

Royal, Ségolène. (1953–) French Socialist politician.

RSVP. *Répondez, s'il vous plaît* (Fr), "please reply." The term is not used in France.

RTE. Radio Telefís Éireann, Irish broadcasting corporation.

Rubáiyát of Omar Khayyám, The. Persian verses.

rubella, rubeola. Both are names for measles.

Rubens, Peter Paul. (1577–1640) Flemish painter.

Rubinstein, Artur. (1886–1982) Polish-born American pianist.

ruble. Russian unit of currency.

Rüdesheimer. German wine.

Rukeyser, Louis. (1933–2006) American economic commentator.

"Rule, Britannia." Note comma. British patriotic song.

rumba. A lively dance of Cuban origin.

rumbustious.

Rumpelstiltskin.

Runnymede. Meadow in Surrey, England, where King John signed the Magna Carta in 1215.

Ruppersberger, Dutch. (1946–) U.S. representative from Maryland; real name Charles Albert Ruppersberger III.

Ruritania. Fictional country in *The Prisoner of Zenda*, a novel by Anthony Hope (1894); and by extension a romantic, unreal country.

Ruy Lopez. A type of opening move in chess.

Ruysdael/Ruïsdael, Jacob van. (1628–1682) Dutch artist; pronounced *royz-dale.*

Ruzyně Airport, Prague.

Rwanda. Central African republic; capital Kigali.

Ryukyu Islands, Japan.

Ryun, Jim. (1947–) American distance runner and Republican politician.

Ss

Saarbrücken, Germany.

Saarinen, Eero. (1910–1961) Finnish-born American architect, and son of **Gottlieb Eliel Saarinen** (1873–1950), also a noted architect.

Saarland. German state.

sabotage, saboteur.

saccharin, saccharine. The first is an artificial sweetener; the second means sugary.

Sackville-West, Vita. (1892–1962) English writer.

sacrilegious. Sometimes misspelled *sacreligious* on the mistaken assumption that *religious* is part of the word. It isn't.

Saddam Hussein. (1937–2006) President of Iraq (1979–2003). His name in full was Saddam Hussein Abd al-Majid al-Tikrit.

Sadler's Wells. London theater.

safflower.

Sagittarius. A sign of the Zodiac.

sago, pl. *sagos.*

Sahara means desert, so the common expression "Sahara Desert" is redundant.

Saigon. Former name of Ho Chi Minh City, Vietnam.

Saint-Exupéry, Antoine (Marie Roger) de. (1900–1944) French aviator and author.

sake. Japanese rice wine.

Sakharov, Andrei. (1921–1989) Russian physicist and dissident; awarded Nobel Peace Prize (1975).

Saki. Pen name of H. H. Munro (1870–1916), English writer.

salable. Something that can be sold.

Sallie Mae. Nickname for Student Loan Marketing Board.

salmonella. Poisonous bacteria, named for its discoverer, American Dr. D. J. Salmon (1850–1914).

Salonika, Greece; not Thessaloniki.

salsify. Edible root; pl. *salsifies.*

SALT. Strategic arms limitation talks. The expression "SALT talks," though redundant, is sometimes unavoidable.

saluki. Breed of dog.

salutary. Not *-tory.* For a discussion of its usage, see HEALTHY, HEALTHFUL, SALUTARY.

Salvadoran. Not *-ean,* for a person or thing from El Salvador.

salvos/salvoes.

Sam Browne, not *Brown,* for the type of belt worn diagonally across the chest.

samizdat. Underground publication of banned texts in the former Soviet Union.

Samson. Not *Sampson.* Legendary figure of great strength.

samurai (sing. and pl.).

Sanaa (or **Sana'a**). Capital of Yemen.

sanatorium, pl. *sanatoriums/sanatoria.*

Sánchez-Vicario, Arantxa. (1971–) Spanish tennis player.

sanctimonious.

Sand, George. Pen name of Amandine Aurore Lucile Dupin, Baronne Dudevant (1804–1876), French writer.

sandal for the type of shoe. Not *sandle.*

sandalwood.

Sandburg, Carl. (1878–1967) American poet.

Sanders, Deion. (1967–) American football and baseball player.

Sandinistas/Sandinists. Revolutionary party in Nicaragua; named after General Augusto César Sandino (1895–1934), a Nicaraguan revolutionary.

sangfroid. Unflappability.

Sangre de Cristo Mountains, Colorado and New Mexico.

sangria. Spanish drink.

sanitary. Not -*tory.*

San Joaquin Valley, California.

San Luis Obispo, California; not *Louis.*

San Salvador. Capital of El Salvador.

sansculotte. (In French, *sans-culotte.*) "Without breeches"; an extreme revolutionary or republican. French revolutionaries were so called because they wore pantaloons rather than breeches.

sans serif. A typeface without serifs.

Santa Ana. Wind; it is also the name of a town in California.

Santa Isabel. Former name of Malabo, capital of Equitorial Guinea.

Santayana, George. (1863–1952) Spanish-born American poet, novelist, and philosopher.

Santo Domingo. Formerly Ciudad Trujillo; capital of the Dominican Republic.

Saône. French river.

São Paulo. Largest city in Brazil.

São Tomé and Príncipe. West African republic; capital São Tomé. Natives are known as São Toméans.

sapphire. Note -*pp-*. Precious stone.

Sappho. (c. 620 BC–c. 565 BC) Greek poetess.

Sara Lee, not *Sarah,* for the U.S. food company.

sarcoma. A malignant tumor in connective tissue, bone, or muscle; pl. *sarcomas/sarcomata.*

sarcophagus. Stone coffin; pl. *sarcophagi.*

Sardegna. Italian for Sardinia.

Sargasso Sea. Area of Atlantic Ocean where masses of floating seaweed are found.

Sargent, John Singer. (1856–1925) American painter.

Sarkozy, Nicolas. (1955–) French politician, president of France (2007–).

SARS. Severe Acute Respiratory Syndrome, a viral disorder.

sarsaparilla.

Sartre, Jean-Paul. (1905–1980) French philosopher, dramatist, and novelist.

SAS. Scandinavian Airlines System.

Saskatchewan. Canadian river and province.

Saskatoon. City in Saskatchewan.

sasquatch. North American abominable snowman.

sassafras. North American tree, source of flavoring.

Sassoon, Siegfried (Lorraine). (1886–1967) British poet.

satellite.

saucisse. (Fr.) Pork sausage.

saucy. Not -*ey*.

sauerbraten.

sauerkraut.

Saugatuck. River in Connecticut and town in Michigan.

Sauk Centre, Minnesota; birthplace of Sinclair Lewis. Note irregular spelling of *Centre*.

Sault Sainte Marie. Towns in Michigan and Ontario, and canal linking Lake Huron and Lake Superior.

Sausalito, California.

Sauternes. A sweet French wine and the village in Gironde from which it comes. The name of the wine is sometimes lowercased and, in the United States, spelled *sauterne*.

sauve qui peut. (Fr.) Literally "save who can." To flee wildly; every man for himself.

savanna (or **savannah**). Tropical and subtropical grassland.

Savannah, Georgia, but **Savana Island,** U.S. Virgin Islands, and **Savanna** for towns in Illinois and Oklahoma. The river is also **Savannah.**

Savile Row. Not -*ll*-. Sartorially famous street, London.

savoir-faire, savoir-vivre. Both are French, of course. The first indicates social grace; the second, good breeding.

Savonarola, Girolamo. (1452–1498) Italian religious and political reformer.

Saxony-Anhalt. German state; in German, Sachsen-Anhalt.

saxophone. Musical instrument invented by Adolphe Sax (1814–1894), a Belgian.

Scafell Pike. The highest hill in England at 3,206 feet. There is a separate neighboring eminence called Sca Fell (two words).

Scala, La. Opera house in Milan. Formally, Teatro alla Scala.

scalawag. A rascal.

scalene triangle. One with no equal sides.

scaloppine. Italian dish.

Scandinavia. Not *Scanda-*.

Scapigliatura, La. Nineteenth-century Italian literary movement. Literally, "the dishevelled ones."

scarce, scarcely.

scared, scarred. The first means frightened; the second, disfigured.

Scarlatti, Alessandro (1659–1725) and **Domenico** (1683–1757), father and son composers from Italy.

scarves, scarfs. Either is correct for the plural of *scarf*.

scary. Not *-ey*.

schadenfreude. (Ger.) Deriving pleasure from the misfortunes of others; pronounced *shah-den-froy-duh*.

Schaffner, Franklin. (1920–1989) American film director.

Schakowsky, Jan. (1944–) Democratic U.S. representative from Illinois.

Scheherazade. Fictional sultan's wife, narrator of *The Arabian Nights*; title of composition by Rimsky-Korsakov.

Schenectady, New York; pronounced *skuh-nek'-tuh-dee*.

Scheuer, James H. (1920–2005) New York congressman (1964–1992).

Scheveningen. Suburb of The Hague, the Netherlands.

Schiaparelli, Elsa. (1890–1973) Italian-born French fashion designer.

Schiller, (Johann Christoph) Friedrich von. (1759–1805) German poet, playwright, and historian.

schilling. Former Austrian unit of currency.

Schiphol Airport, Amsterdam.

Schirra, Wally. (1923–2007) American astronaut; formally he was Walter M. Schirra Jr.

schistosomiasis. Parasitic disease of tropical regions; also known as bilharziasis.

Schleiermacher, Friedrich Daniel Ernst. (1768–1834) German philosopher.

schlemiel. (Yid.) A fool.

Schlesinger, Arthur M(eier). (1888–1965) American historian, and father of **Arthur M(eier) Schlesinger Jr.** (1917–2007), American historian.

Schleswig-Holstein. German state.

Schlieffen, Alfred, Count von. (1833–1913) Prussian field marshal and military strategist.

Schliemann, Heinrich. (1822–1890) German archaeologist who excavated Mycenae and Troy.

schmaltz. Maudlin sentimentality.

Schmeling, Max. (1905–2005) German heavyweight boxer.

Schnabel, Artur. (1882–1951) Austrian-born American pianist.

Schnabel, Julian. (1951–) American painter.

schnapps. A strong alcoholic drink.

schnauzer. Breed of dog.

schnitzel. Veal cutlet.

Schnitzler, Arthur. (1862–1931) Austrian playwright and novelist.

Schoenberg (or **Schönberg**), **Arnold.** (1874–1951) Austrian composer.

Schoendienst, Red. (1923–) American baseball player and manager; real name Albert.

Schollander, Don. (1946–) American swimmer.

Schomburg Center for Research in Black Culture, New York City.

Schönbrunn Palace, Vienna, Austria.

Schopenhauer, Arthur. (1788–1860) German philosopher.

Schröder, Gerhard. (1944–) Chancellor of Germany (1998–2005).

Schubert, Franz. (1797–1828) Austrian composer.

Schulberg, Budd. (1914–) American screenwriter. Note unusual spelling of *Budd.*

Schulz, Charles M. (for Monroe). (1922–2000) American comic strip cartoonist, creator of *Peanuts.*

Schuman, Robert. (1886–1963) Luxembourg-born French statesman who devised the Schuman Plan, which led to the setting-up of the European Coal and Steel Community.

Schumann, Robert. (1810–1856) German composer.

schuss. Downhill run in skiing.

Schuylkill River. Pennsylvania; pronounced *skoo'-kill.*

schwa. Not *schwah*, for the phonetic symbol ə representing an indeterminate unstressed sound akin to "uh," as with the second and fourth vowel sounds of *memorandum* (i.e., *me-mə-ran-dəm*).

Schwabing. District of Munich.

Schwarzenegger, Arnold. (1947–) Austrian-born American bodybuilder, actor, and Republican politician; governor of California (2003–).

Schwarzkopf, Dame Elisabeth. (1915–2006) Austrian-British soprano.

Schwarzkopf, H. Norman. (1934–) American general, commander of Operation Desert Storm in the first Gulf War. The initial H. in his name stands for nothing.

Schwarzwald. (Ger.) The Black Forest.

Schwechat Airport, Vienna, Austria.

Schweitzer, Albert. (1875–1965) German theologian, medical missionary, philosopher, and musician. Established Lambaréné mission, French Equatorial Africa; awarded Nobel Peace Prize (1952).

Schweiz, die. German name for Switzerland.

Schygulla, Hanna. (1943–) German actress.

Scilly, Isles of. Group of islands off Cornwall; adj. *Scillonian*. Pronounced *silly*.

scintilla. A tiny amount.

Scofield, Paul. (1922–) British actor.

Scorsese, Martin. (1942–) American film director.

Scotch, Scottish, Scots. Except for Scotch whisky and well-established expressions such as Scotch broth and Scotch mist, *Scottish* and *Scots* are preferred. In particular, a person from Scotland is Scottish, *not* Scotch. The British army unit is the Scots Guards. The dog is a Scottish terrier.

Scotch tape. (Cap.)

scot-free. To escape without penalty.

Scott, Dred. A Missouri slave who unsuccessfully sued for his freedom on the grounds that his owner had taken him into free territory. The Supreme Court case of 1857 that resulted is called *Dred Scott v. Sanford*.

Scribners. U.S. publisher; formally Charles Scribner's Sons.

scrutiny, scrutinize. To *scrutinize* something means to look at it with particular attentiveness. Thus, qualifying words like *close* or *careful* are nearly always superfluous.

SCSI. Small computer system interface, a type of port on small computers.

scurrilous does not mean merely angry or insulting. It means grossly obscene or abusive. An attack must be exceedingly harsh to be scurrilous.

Scylla and Charybdis. In Greek mythology, Scylla (pronounced *silla*) was a six-headed monster who lived beside a treacherous whirlpool called Charybdis (pronounced *kuh-rib-dis*) off the coast of Sicily, so Scylla and Charybdis signify a highly unattractive dilemma.

SDI. Strategic Defense Initiative, commonly called "star wars." Plan propounded by President Reagan in 1983 to erect a shield of weapons in space over the United States to keep out incoming missiles.

Seaborg, Glenn. (1912–) American nuclear chemist and physicist; awarded Nobel Prize for Chemistry (1951).

Seanad Éireann. Upper house of Irish parliament pronounced *shin-add' air-ann'*.

Sears, Roebuck. Note the comma.

SEATO. Southeast Asia Treaty Organization.

Sebastopol/Sevastopol. The first is the historical spelling; the second the modern spelling for the Crimean city and Black Sea port, now part of Ukraine.

secede.

second-largest and other similar comparisons often lead writers astray as in "Japan is the second-largest drugs market in the world after the United States" when in fact what is meant is that Japan is the largest drugs market in the world after the United States or the second-largest drugs market in the world.

Securities and Exchange Commission. Note *and*. The regulatory body for U.S. stock markets; but note that it is the Securities Exchange Act.

sedentary.

Sedgemoor, Battle of. British battle at which forces of James II defeated the Duke of Monmouth, 1685.

Segovia, Andrés. (1894–1987) Spanish guitarist.

se habla español. (Sp.) "Spanish spoken here."

seigneur. Lord of a manor, feudal lord.

seismograph, seismometer, seismogram. Occasionally, and perhaps understandably, confused. A *seismometer* is a sensor placed in the ground to record earthquakes and other vibrations. A *seismograph* is the instrument that records the seismometer's readings. A *seismogram* is the printout or chart that provides a visual record of seismic activity.

seize.

Sejm. Parliament of Poland.

Selassie, Haile. See HAILE SELASSIE.

self-confessed, as in "a self-confessed murderer," is usually tautological. In most cases, *confessed* alone is enough.

Selfridges. (No apos.) London department store.

Selznick, David O. (for Oliver) (1902–1965) American film producer.

semblance.

Sendero Luminoso. (Sp.) Shining Path, Peruvian revolutionary group.

Senegal. West African republic; capital Dakar.

senhor, senhora, senhorita. (Port.) Mr., Mrs., Miss; first syllable pronounced *sun.*

Senna, Ayrton. (1960–) Brazilian Formula One racing car driver.

"Sennacherib, The Destruction of." Poem by Byron (1815).

Sennett, Mack. (1884–1960) Canadian-born American film producer and director; born Michael Sinnott.

señor, señora, señorita. (Sp.) Mr., Mrs., Miss.

sensual, sensuous. The words are only broadly synonymous. *Sensual* applies to a person's baser instincts as distinguished from reason. It should always hold connotations of sexual allure or lust. *Sensuous* was coined by Milton to avoid those connotations and to suggest instead the idea of being alive to sensations. It should be used when no suggestion of sexual arousal is intended.

Seoul. Capital of South Korea. An alternative name in Korea is Kyongsong.

Sephardi. A Jew of Spanish or Portuguese origin; pl. *Sephardim.* See also ASHKENAZI.

seppuku. Ritual suicide in Japan; hara-kiri.

septicemia. Blood poisoning.

septuagenarian. Not *septa-*. Person seventy to seventy-nine years old.

Septuagesima. Third Sunday before Lent, seventieth day before Easter.

sepulcher. Not *-re*.

seraglio. A harem.

Serengeti National Park, Serengeti Plain, Tanzania. Not *-getti*.

sergeant.

seriatim. Not *-tum*. In a series, one after another.

serving, servicing. *Servicing* is better reserved for the idea of installation and maintenance. *Serve* is the better word for describing things that are of general and continuing benefit.

sesquipedalian. A long word.

Session, Court of. Supreme court of Scotland. Not *Sessions*.

Seurat, Georges Pierre. (1859–1891) French painter.

Seuss, Dr. (1904–1991) Children's writer and illustrator, real name Theodore Seuss Geisel.

seven deadly sins. They are avarice, envy, gluttony, lust, pride, sloth, and wrath.

7-Eleven is the trademark name for the convenience stores chain.

7UP is the trademark name for the soft drink.

Seven Wonders of the World. They were the Hanging Gardens of Babylon, the Great Pyramids of Egypt, the Colossus of Rhodes, the Mausoleum at Halicarnassus, the Temple of Artemis at Ephesus, the statue of Zeus at Olympia, and the Pharos at Alexandria.

Sèvres porcelain.

Sexagesima. Second Sunday before Lent, sixtieth day before Easter.

Seychelles. Island republic in the Indian Ocean; capital Victoria. Adj. *Seychellois.*

sforzando. In music, an abrupt stress on a note or chord.

's Gravenhage. Formal name for The Hague, Netherlands; pronounced *skrah-ven-hah'-guh.*

Shake 'N Bake. American grocery product.

Shakespearean, Shakespearian. The first is the usual spelling in America and the second is the usual spelling in Britain, but, interestingly, don't look to *The Oxford English Dictionary* for guidance on any spellings concerning England's greatest poet. Perversely and charmingly, but entirely unhelpfully, the *OED* insists on spelling the name *Shakspere*, a decision it based on one of the six spellings Shakespeare himself used. It does, however, acknowledge that *Shakespeare* is "perhaps" the commonest spelling now used.

shaky (not *-ey*), **shakiness.**

shallot. A plant related to the onion.

"Shalott, The Lady of." Not *Shallot*. 1832 poem by Tennyson.

Shamir, Yitzhak. (1915–) Prime minister of Israel (1983–1984, 1988–1992); born Yitzhak Jazernicki.

Shandong. Chinese province; capital Jinan. Formerly spelled *Shantung*.

Shangri-La, not *-la*, for the Himalayan paradise created by James Hilton in the 1933 novel *Lost Horizon*.

Shankill Road, Belfast, Northern Ireland. Not *-hill*.

shank's mare or **pony.** To travel on foot.

Shanxi. Chinese province; capital Taiyuan.

SHAPE. Abbreviation of Supreme Headquarters, Allied Powers, Europe.

Sharapova, Maria. (1987–) Russian tennis player.

Shariah (or **Shari'ah**). Koranic law.

shar-pei. Breed of dog.

Sharpeville Massacre. Fatal shooting of sixty-seven black South African demonstrators by police at black township of Sharpeville, near Johannesburg, on March 21, 1960.

Shatt al-Arab. River that forms section of border between Iran and Iraq.

Shays' Rebellion. Not *Shay's*. Uprising by American farmers in 1786–1787 led by Daniel Shays of Massachusetts.

Shea Stadium, New York, home of the New York Mets baseball team.

Shedd Aquarium, Chicago.

Sheetrock, for a type of plasterboard, is a trademark.

shekel. Israeli unit of currency.

Shelley, Mary Wollstonecraft. (1797–1851) English writer, and second wife of **Percy Bysshe Shelley** (1792–1822), English poet.

shenanigans.

Shepard, Sam. (1943–) American actor and playwright; born Samuel Shepard Rogers.

Shepherd, Cybill. (1949–) American actress.

Shepherd Market, but **Shepherd's Bush,** London.

Sheremetyevo Airport, Moscow.

sheriff.

Sherpa (cap.), a Himalayan people living in Tibet and Nepal.

's-Hertogenbosch. City in the Netherlands, commonly called Den Bosch.

Shetland or **the Shetland Islands** are the accepted designations for the Scottish islands. *The Shetlands* is frowned on by some and thus better avoided. See also ORKNEY ISLANDS.

Shevardnadze, Eduard. (1928–) President of Georgia (the country, not the U.S. state), 1995–2003.

shibboleth. A word, phrase, or linguistic quirk common to all members of a particular group and by which they can be distinguished from others.

Shiite (or **Shi'ite**). Member of the Shia branch of Islam.

Shikoku. Japanese island.

shiksa. (Yid.) Disparaging term for a non-Jewish girl.

shillelagh. Irish cudgel; pronounced *shi-lay'-lee*.

Shinawatra, Thaksin. (1949–) Former prime minister of Thailand, deposed in coup in 2006.

Sholokov, Mikhail. (1905–1984) Russian novelist; awarded Nobel Prize for Literature in 1965.

Shostakovich, Dmitri. (1906–1975) Russian composer.

shriek.

shriveled, shriveling.

shrove. Past tense of *shrive,* to give confession.

Shrove Tuesday. The day before Ash Wednesday. **Shrovetide** is the three days before Ash Wednesday.

Shubert Theatre, New York City.

Shultz, George. (1920–) American statesman.

Shute, Nevil. Pen name of Nevil Shute Norway (1899–1960), British novelist.

Sibelius, Johan Julius Christian. (1865–1957) Finnish composer.

sibilant. Hissing.

Sibylline.

sic. (Lat.) Thus. Used, usually in square brackets, to show that a word or passage is being quoted exactly despite any errors or infelicities it may contain.

Sichuan. Chinese province formerly known as **Szechwan** or **Szechuan;** capital Chengdu.

sic transit gloria mundi. (Lat.) "So passes the glory of the world."

Sidgwick & Jackson. British publisher.

Sidney, Sir Philip. (1554–1586) English poet.

Sidney Sussex College, Cambridge University.

SIDS. Sudden infant death syndrome.

siege.

Siegfried Line. Defensive fortification built by Germany along its western border before World War II.

Siena, Italy.

Sierra Leone. Republic in West Africa; capital Freetown.

Sierra Nevada. Not *Sierra Nevada Mountains;* "mountains" is already present in the term.

sieve.

signatory.

Sign of Four, The, not *the Four,* for the Sherlock Holmes story.

signor, signora, signorina. Italian for Mr., Mrs., and Miss.

Sikkim. Former Himalayan kingdom annexed by India in 1975.

Sikorsky helicopters.

silhouette.

silicon chip. Not -*cone.*

sillabub. Variant spelling of **syllabub.**

Sillitoe, Alan. (1928–) English novelist.

silvan (pref.)/**sylvan** (alt.).

s'il vous plaît. (Fr.) "Please."

simile, metaphor. Both are figures of speech in which two things are compared. A *simile* likens one thing to another, dissimilar one: "He ran like the wind." A *metaphor* acts as if the two compared things are identical and substitutes one for the other; thus comparing the beginning of time to the beginning of a day produces the metaphor "the dawn of time."

Simon & Schuster. Publisher.

simpatico (It.)/***simpático*** (Sp.). Friendly, congenial.

simulacrum. A likeness or copy; a deceptive substitute.

Sinai. Not *the.*

since. A common error is seen here: "Since April the company stopped giving discounts to students." *Since* indicates action starting at a specified time in the past and continuing to the present. The verbs in sentences in which it appears must also indicate action that is continuing. Make it either "In April the company stopped" or "Since April the company has stopped."

sinecure. A profitable or advantageous position requiring little or no work.

Sinepuxent Bay, Maryland.

sine qua non. (Lat.) "A necessary condition."

sinfonietta. A small orchestra.

singe, singed, singeing.

Singin' in the Rain. Not *Singing*. Classic MGM musical (1952).

Sinhalese. Main population group of Sri Lanka.

Sinn Fein. (Gaelic) Literally "we ourselves"; Irish nationalist movement and political party. Pronounced *shinn fane*.

siphon is the usual spelling, but **syphon** is also acceptable.

sirocco. Type of hot wind originating in the Sahara and blowing over southern Europe.

Sistani, Grand Ayatollah Ali al-. (1930–) Senior Shia Muslim cleric in Iraq.

Sisyphus. Not -*ss*-. In Greek mythology, Sisyphus was a king of Corinth who was condemned for eternity to push a heavy stone up a hill, only to have it roll down again. Hence *Sisyphean* describes some endless task.

Sithole, Rev. Ndabaningi. (1920–2000) Zimbabwean clergyman and politician.

sitz bath. A chairlike tub in which the thighs and hips are immersed in water.

Sixth Avenue, New York; former, but still widely used, name for the Avenue of the Americas.

sizable.

Skagerrak. Note -*rr*-. Channel of the North Sea lying between Norway and Denmark.

skedaddle.

skein. Flock of geese in flight or bundle of thread or yarn; pronounced *skane*.

skeptic, skepticism.

ski, skied, skiing.

skiddoo. To depart hastily.

Skidmore, Owings and Merrill. American architectural firm.

skilless. Note -*ll*-. This clumsy word, meaning to be without skills, is better avoided.

skillful.

skirmish.

skulduggery. Not *skull-*.

sleight of hand. Not *slight*.

sloe. A bluish-black wild plum. Hence, **sloe-eyed, sloe gin.**

slough. Pronounced to rhyme with *cow,* it means a swamp or bog; pronounced to rhyme with *rough,* it means to shed skin.

smart alec (or **aleck**).

smidgen (or **smidgin** or **smidgeon**).

Smithsonian Institution, Washington, D.C.

smoky.

Smollett, Tobias. (1721–1771) British novelist.

Smuts, Jan Christian. (1870–1950) Prime minister of South Africa (1919–1924, 1939–1948).

Smyrna. Former name of Izmir, Turkish city on Aegean Sea.

SNCF. Société Nationale des Chemins de Fer, French national railway company.

sneaked, snuck. The day may come well when *snuck* supersedes *sneaked*—it probably already has done so in speech—but it is worth bearing in mind that many authorities continue to regard it as nonstandard. Use *sneaked* instead.

snippet.

Soane's Museum, Sir John, London. Note apos.

so as to. The first two words can generally be deleted without loss, as they might have been here: "The rest of the crowd stuffed hot dogs into their faces so as to avoid being drawn into the discussion."

sobriquet. A nickname; pronounced *so-bri-kay'*.

Society of Friends. Formal name of the Quakers.

Sofia. Capital of Bulgaria; in Bulgarian, Sofiya.

SoHo. Manhattan district; short for South of Houston Street.

soi-disant. (Fr.) Self-styled.

soigné (Fr. masc.)/**soignée** (Fr. fem.). Well groomed.

sojourn.

soliloquy, soliloquies.

Solomon R. Guggenheim Museum, New York City.

solos.

soluble, solvable. The first is something that can be dissolved; the second is something that can be solved.

Solzhenitsyn, Alexander. (1918–) Russian novelist.

somersault.

sometime, some time. Most often it is one word: "They will arrive sometime tomorrow." But when *some* is used as an adjective equivalent to *a short* or *a long* or *an indefinite*, it should be two words: "The announcement was made some time ago."

Three considerations may help you to make the distinction:

1. *Some time* as two words is usually preceded by a preposition ("for some time," "at some time") or followed by a helping word ("some time ago").

2. *Some time* can always be replaced with an equivalent expression ("a short time ago," "a long time ago," etc.); *sometime* cannot.

3. When spoken, greater stress is placed on *time* when *some time* is two words.

Sommet Center, Nashville; pronounced *so-may.*

Somoza, Anastasio. (1925–1980) President of Nicaragua (1967–1972, 1974–1979).

Sondheim, Stephen. (1930–) American composer and lyricist.

son et lumière. (Fr.) Nighttime sound and light show.

Sophocles. (495–406 BC) Greek playwright.

sophomore, sophomoric.

Sorbonne, Paris; formally Académie Universitaire de Paris.

Sorenstam, Annika. (1970–) Swedish professional golfer.

sortie. A quick attack, especially by the besieged on their besiegers; also, one mission by a single military aircraft.

Sotheby's. Auctioneers; formerly Sotheby Parke Bernet & Co., now Sotheby's Holdings Inc.

Sotomayor, Javier. (1967–) Cuban high jumper.

souchong. Chinese tea.

soufflé. Light, puffy dish made with egg whites.

souk. Market in Arab countries.

soupçon. A very small amount.

sou'wester. Rain hat with a broad brim at the back or a southwest wind.

Sovereign Bancorp Inc. Pennsylvania-based bank.

Soviet Union, the, formally ceased to exist in 1991. It comprised fifteen Union Republics: Armenia, Azerbaijan, Byelorussia, Estonia, Georgia, Kazakhstan, Kirghizstan, Latvia, Lithuania, Moldavia, Russia, Tajikistan, Turkmenistan, Ukraine, and Uzbekistan.

Soyinka, Wole. (1934–) Nigerian writer; awarded Nobel Prize for Literature 1986. Full name: Akinwande Oluwole Soyinka.

spate properly describes a torrent, not a flurry.

special, especial. The first means for a particular purpose, the second to a high degree. A special meal may be especially delicious.

specie. Coins, as opposed to paper money.

species, genus. The first is a subgroup of the second. The convention is to capitalize the genus but not the species. Thus, *Homo, sapiens.* The plurals are *species* and *genera.*

Spenser, Edmund. (1552–1599) English poet.

Spetsai, Greece.

spicy. Not *-ey.*

Spielberg, Steven. (1946–) American film director and producer.

spigot.

spiky. Not *-ey.*

spinnaker. Type of sail.

spinney. Small woodland.

Spinoza, Baruch de. (1632–1677) Dutch philosopher.

Spitsbergen. Norwegian island in the Svalvard archipelago in the Arctic Ocean.

spittoon.

split infinitives. The belief that it is a serious breach of grammar to split an infinitive (that is, to put an adverb between "to" and a verb as in "to boldly go") is without foundation. It is certainly not a grammatical error. If it is an error at all, it is a rhetorical fault—a question of style—and not a grammatical one. It is practically impossible to find a recognized authority who condemns the split infinitive.

spoliation, not *spoil-*, for the state of being spoiled.

spontaneous, spontaneity.

spoonfuls. Not *spoonsful* or *spoons full.*

Spratly Islands. South China Sea.

springbok. An antelope.

squeegee. Device for cleaning windows.

Srebrenica, Bosnia and Herzegovina; site of infamous massacre of 8,000 citizens by Serbian forces in 1995.

Sri Lanka. Island state off India, formerly called Ceylon; capital Colombo. Note the airline is **SriLankan** (one word) **Airlines.**

SS. Abbreviation of Schutzstaffel, infamous Nazi enforcement agency.

staccato.

Stakhanovite. In the former Soviet Union, a worker held up to the nation as a paragon.

stalactite, stalagmite. Stalactites point downward, stalagmites upward.

stalemate is a permanent deadlock—one so intractable that no further action is possible. A chess match that reaches stalemate is not awaiting a more decisive outcome; the stalemate *is* the outcome. *Standoff, deadlock,* or *impasse* are all better words if remedial action is still possible.

Stamford, Stanford. Occasionally confused. *Stamford* is the name of notable communities in Connecticut and the English county of Lincolnshire. *Stanford* is the university in Palo Alto, California. The intelligence test is the **Stanford-Binet** test.

stanch, staunch. Although *staunch* is given as an acceptable variant by most dictionaries, *stanch* is still generally the preferred spelling for the verb meaning to arrest the flow. As an adjective, *staunch* is the only spelling ("a staunch supporter").

stanchion.

St. Andrews, (no apos.) Scotland, site of St. Andrews University and golf's most revered course, the Royal and Ancient Golf Club.

St. Andrew's Day. (Apos.) November 30.

Stanislavsky system. Method of acting named for Konstantin Stanislavsky, a Russian teacher.

Stansted Airport, England.

St. Antony's College, Oxford University.

staphylococcus, a type of bacteria; pl. *staphylococci.*

starboard. The right-hand side of a ship when looking forward.

Stasi. Short for Staatssicherheitsdienst, Ministry for State Security in East Germany before unification.

stationary, stationery. The first means standing still, the second is writing paper and envelopes.

St. Barthélemy, French West Indies.

St. Benet's Hall, Oxford University.

St. Catharine's College, Cambridge University, but **St. Catherine's College,** Oxford University.

St. Catherines, Ontario.

St. Christopher and Nevis, Federation of. Formal name of Caribbean state commonly known as St. Kitts-Nevis.

St. Croix, U.S. Virgin Islands, formerly Santa Cruz; pronounced *kroy.*

Steffens, Lincoln. (1866–1936) Campaigning American journalist.

Stendhal. (1783–1842) Not *-dahl* Pen name of Marie Henri Beyle, French writer.

Sterne, Laurence. (1713–1768) English clergyman and writer.

stethoscope.

stevedore.

Stevens, Wallace. (1879–1955) American poet.

Stevenson, Adlai. (1900–1965) American Democratic politician, ran unsuccessfully for president in 1952 and 1956.

Stevenson, Robert Louis. (1850–1894) Scottish writer.

St.-Germain-des-Prés, Paris.

St. Helens, Mt. Volcano in Washington State, which famously erupted on May 18, 1980.

sticky.

Stieglitz, Alfred. (1864–1946) American photographer.

stiletto, pl. *stilettos.*

still lifes for the plural.

stilton for the cheese, but **Stilton** for the English village where it originated.

St. James Garlickhythe, London church.

St. James's, not *James'*, for the London palace, park, and square. Diplomats likewise are posted to the **Court of St. James's.**

St. Katharine's Dock, London. Not *Kather-*.

St. Kitts and Nevis is the common name for the Caribbean state formally known as the Federation of St. Christopher and Nevis; capital Basseterre. Residents are known as Kittians or Nevisians.

St. Maarten/St. Martin. Caribbean island divided into Dutch and French sides, respectively.

St. Martin-in-the-Fields, London.

St. Mary-le-Bow (hyphens), but **St. Mary le Strand;** London churches.

Stockhausen, Karlheinz. (1928–) German composer.

Stolichnaya. Brand of vodka.

stony.

Storey, David. (1933–) English novelist and playwright.

Storting. Norwegian parliament.

St. Pierre and Miquelon. French islands off east coast of Canada; formally they are a territorial collectivity.

Stradivarius. A violin or other stringed instrument made by **Antonio Stradivari** (c. 1645–1737).

straitjacket.

straitlaced.

Strasbourg, France.

strata, stratum. The first is sometimes used when the second is intended, as in "They dug into another strata and at last found what they were looking for." A single level is a stratum. *Strata* signifies more than one.

Strategic Defense Initiative (SDI). Commonly called "star wars"; plan propounded by President Ronald Reagan to erect a shield of space weapons over the United States to stop incoming missiles.

Stratford-on-Avon, Stratford-upon-Avon. Most gazetteers and other reference sources give Stratford-upon-Avon as the correct name for the birthplace of William Shakespeare, but it is worth noting that the local authority calls itself Stratford-on-Avon District Council.

Strauss, Johann, the Younger. (1825–1899) Austrian composer known for waltzes, polkas, marches, and operettas. His father, **Johann Strauss the Elder** (1804–1849), brothers **Eduard** (1835–1916) and **Josef** (1827–1870), and son **Johann Strauss III** (1866–1939) were also composers. None of them should be confused with the next entry.

Strauss, Richard. (1864–1949) German composer of operas and other musical works.

Stravinsky, Igor. (1882–1971) Russian-born American composer.

Streep, Meryl. (1951–) American actress.

Streisand, Barbra. (1942–) American singer and actress; not *Barbara*.

Strindberg, August. (1849–1912) Swedish playwright and writer.

strived, strove. Either is acceptable

Stroessner, Alfredo. (1912–2006) President of Paraguay (1954–1989).

Stroganoff. (Cap.) Strips of meat cooked in a sour-cream sauce.

strychnine.

St. Swithin's (or **Swithun's**) **Day.** July 15. According to legend, rain on that day will be followed by forty more days of rain.

Stuka. (Cap.) German dive bomber in World War II.

stupefy, stupefied, stupefaction. Don't confuse the spelling with *stupid*.

Sturm und Drang. (Ger.) "Storm and stress."

Stuttgart, Germany.

Stuyvesant, Peter. (1592–1672) Dutch governor of New Netherlands (1646–64), which later became New York.

St. Vincent and the Grenadines. Caribbean state; capital Kingstown.

stylus, pl. *styluses/styli.*

stymie. Thwart or immobilize.

Styrofoam is a trademark.

Styx. The river flowing around Hades.

submersible.

suborn does not mean undermine, as is sometimes thought; it is to induce someone into committing a wrongful act.

subpoena. A writ ordering a person to appear in court.

sub rosa. (Lat.) "Under the rose"; in secret.

sub silentio. (Lat.) In silence.

substitute should be followed only by *for*. You substitute one thing for another. If you find yourself following the word with *by* or *with* or any other preposition, you should choose another verb.

subterranean.

succès d'estime. (Fr.) An undertaking that makes little or no profit but wins critical acclaim.

succès fou. (Fr.) A huge success, a smash hit.

succubus. A female evil spirit that has sexual relations with a man.

A spirit that has intercourse with a sleeping female is an incubus.

Sucre. Official capital of Bolivia, although the seat of government is La Paz.

Sudetenland. German-speaking area of Czechoslovakia annexed by Hitler in 1938.

sudoku. Japanese number game. It is an abbreviation of *suuji wa dokushin ni kagiru,* "the numbers must be single."

Suetonius (Gaius Suetonius Tranquillus). (c. 70–c. 160) Roman historian and biographer.

suggestible.

sui generis. (Lat.) In a class of its own.

suing.

sukiyaki. Japanese dish.

Suleiman I. (c. 1490–1566) Sultan of the Ottoman Empire (1520–1566); called "the Magnificent."

sulfur.

Sullavan, Margaret. (1911–1960) Not *Sulli-.* Hollywood actress.

Sully Prudhomme. Pen name of René François Armand Prudhomme (1839–1907), French poet; awarded Nobel Prize for Literature in 1901.

Sulzberger, Arthur Ochs. (1926–) American newspaper publisher.

Sunni. Branch of Islam.

SunTrust Banks. U.S. banking group. Note *SunTrust* one word.

Sununu, John H(enry). (1939–) American Republican politician from New Hampshire.

Sun Yat-sen. (1866–1925) Chinese statesman and revolutionary.

Suomen Tasavalta. Finnish for "Republic of Finland."

supersede is one of the most frequently misspelled of words. Note the final syllable is *-sede,* not *-cede.*

Surayud Chulanont, General. (1943–) Former prime minister of Thailand (2006–2008). On second reference he is **General Surayud.**

Suriname, Surinam. Confusion still sometimes arises concerning the name of this small South American country. The spelling *Surinam* can now safely be regarded as historic and *Suriname* as the preferred modern spelling. The Suriname River and Suriname toad also take the modern spellings. Suriname was formerly Dutch Guiana.

surreptitious.

surrounded means completely encircled. To say that something is "surrounded on three sides" is a poor use of the word.

surveillance.

survivor. Not -*er.*

susceptible.

Susquehanna River, eastern United States.

sustenance.

susurrate. Whisper.

suttee. Hindu practice of a widow throwing herself on her husband's funeral pyre.

Suu Kyi, Aung San. (1945–) Burmese political activist, awarded Nobel Peace Prize in 1991.

Suva. Capital of Fiji.

Suvarnabhumi Airport, Bangkok.

Suwannee River, southern United States; immortalized in songs as "the Swanee."

Sverige. Swedish for Sweden.

Swayze, Patrick. (1952–) American actor.

Sweet 'N Low. Sugar substitute.

Swinburne, Algernon Charles. (1837–1909) English poet.

Swissair. (One word.) Former Swiss airline.

Swithin's (or **Swithun's**) **Day, St.** July 15. According to legend, rain on that day will be followed by forty days of the same.

sycamore. Tree.

Sydney, New South Wales, Australia.

syllabub (or **sillabub**). Type of dessert.

symbiosis. A relationship that benefits both parties.

Synge, J. M. (for John Millington). (1871–1909) Irish playwright.

synonym.

syphilis. Not -*ll*-.

syphon is acceptable, but **siphon** is generally preferred.

Szczecin, Poland; formerly Stettin.

Szechwan/Szechuan. Former spellings for the Chinese province that is now spelled *Sichuan;* the cuisine of the region, however, remains known in English by either of the earlier spellings.

Szilard, Leo. (1898–1964) Hungarian-born American physicist.

Szymborska, Wislawa. (1923–) Polish author; awarded Nobel Prize for Literature (1996).

tableau, pl. *tableaux.*

table d'hôte. Set meal at a fixed price.

tablespoonfuls.

tabula rasa. (Lat.) A blank slate, the mind at birth.

tachycardia. Abnormally fast heartbeat.

taffeta. Fabric.

tagliatelle. Type of pasta.

Taipei. Capital of Taiwan.

Taittinger champagne.

Taiwan. Formerly Formosa; officially the Republic of China, though that title is seldom used outside Taiwan itself.

Tajik for the language, **Tajikistani** for something that is from or of Tajikistan.

Taj Mahal. Celebrated mausoleum at Agra, India.

Takashimaya Company Limited. Leading Japanese retail group.

Takeshita, Noboru. (1924–2000) Japanese prime minister (1987–1989).

Taklimakan. Chinese desert.

Tale of a Tub, A. (Not *The.*) Satire by Jonathan Swift (1704).

Tales of Hoffmann, The. Opera by Jacques Offenbach (1881).

Taliban (or **Taleban**). Sunni Muslim insurgent force in Afghanistan.

Tallahassee. Capital of Florida.

Tallahatchie. River in Mississippi.

Tallinn. Capital of Estonia.

Talmud. Sacred Hebrew writings, the main body of laws for Judaism, comprising two parts: the Mishna, containing the laws themselves, and the Gemara, containing later commentaries and elaborations.

Tamaulipas, Mexico.

tambourine. Percussion instrument.

Tamburlaine the Great. Play by Christopher Marlowe; the Mongol conqueror himself is now usually spelled *Tamerlane* (1336–1405).

tameable.

Tammany Hall. Fraternal society of the Democratic Party in New York.

tam-o'-shanter. Scottish cap, named after the hero in the Burns poem "Tam o'Shanter."

T'ang (or **Tang**). Chinese dynasty, ruled 618–907.

Tanguy, Yves. (1900–1955) French-born American painter.

Tantalus. In Greek mythology, a son of Zeus for whom food and drink forever move out of reach whenever he tries to attain them.

Tanzania. African nation formed by the merger of Tanganyika and Zanzibar in 1964; capital Dodoma.

Taoiseach. The prime minister of Ireland; pronounced "tea-sock."

taradiddle (or **tarradiddle**). Nonsense.

tarantella. Type of Neapolitan dance. Not to be confused with **tarantula,** the type of spider.

Tar Heels (two words) for people and things associated with North Carolina, and for the sporting teams of the University of North Carolina.

tariff.

tarpaulin.

tartar. A sauce; dental plaque.

Tartar. Intractable, violent person; member of a Turkic-speaking people in central Asia.

Tartuffe. Play by Molière (1664).

Tashkent. Capital of Uzbekistan.

TASS. Short for Telegrafnoye Agenstvo Sovyetskovo Soyuza, Soviet news agency; now called ITAR-TASS News Agency.

Tate Gallery, the London art museum, now consists of four separate branches: Tate Britain and Tate Modern in London, and Tate Liverpool and Tate St. Ives in the provinces.

tattoo.

Taufa'ahau Tupou IV. (1918–2006) King of Tonga (1965–2006).

tautology, redundancy, pleonasm, solecism. Although various authorities describe various shades of distinction between the first three words, those distinctions are generally slight and frequently contradictory. Essentially all three mean using more words than necessary to convey an idea. Not all repetition is inexcusable. It may be used for effect, as in poetry, or for clarity, or in deference to idiom. "OPEC countries," "SALT talks," and "HIV virus" are all technically redundant because the second word is already contained in the preceding abbreviation, but only the ultra-finicky would deplore them. Similarly, in "wipe that smile off your face," the last two words are tautological—there is no other place a smile could be—but the sentence would not stand without them. Finally, *solecism* describes any violation of idiom or grammar. Redundancies, tautologies, and pleonasms are all solecisms.

taxiing for the act of moving a plane into position.

taxonomy. The science of classification of organisms.

Tay-Sachs disease. Genetic disorder that affects the nervous system.

Tbilisi. Formerly Tiflis; capital of Georgia.

Tchaikovsky, Peter Illich. (1840–1893) Russian composer.

Teamsters, International Brotherhood of. Trade union.

Teatro alla Scala. Formal name of the Milan opera house commonly called La Scala.

Technicolor. (Cap.)

tectonics. Not *tech-;* study of the structure and movement of Earth's crust.

Te Deum. Latin hymn.

tee-hee. The sound of laughter.

teetotaler.

Tegucigalpa. Capital of Honduras.

Tehachapi Mountains, California.

Tehran. Capital of Iran.

Tehuntepec, Isthmus of. Narrowest part of Mexico.

Teilhard de Chardin, Pierre. (1881–1955) French scientist, priest, and philosopher.

Telefónica. Spanish telecommunications company.

Telemachus. In Greek mythology, the son of Odysseus and Penelope.

Telstar. Communications satellite.

temblor, not *trem-,* for an earthquake.

temporary respite is redundant; all respites are temporary.

tempus fugit. (Lat.) "Time flies."

tendentious. Biased.

Tenerife, Canary Islands.

Tennyson, Alfred, Baron. (1809–1892) English poet; poet laureate (1850–92); known as Alfred, Lord Tennyson.

Tenochtitlán. Aztec capital on site of modern Mexico City.

Teotihuacán. Site of ancient Mexican city.

tepee. Not *tee-;* North American Indian tent.

tequila.

tera-. Prefix meaning 1 trillion.

Terence. Properly **Publius Terentius Afer** (c. 190–159 BC); Roman comedy writer.

teriyaki. Japanese marinated meat dish.

terminus, pl. *termini/terminuses.*

terracotta.

terra firma. Dry land.

terra incognita. (Lat.) Unknown territory

terrazzo. Stone flooring material.

terrine. An earthenware bowl, and the food prepared in it.

Tesla, Nikola. (1857–1943) Croatian-American scientist and inventor.

Tess of the D'Urbervilles. Novel by Thomas Hardy (1891).

tetchy. Touchy, ill-tempered.

tête-à-tête.

Tevere. Italian name for the Tiber River.

Tewkesbury, Gloucestershire, England; but **Tewksbury,** Massachusetts.

TGV. Train à Grande Vitesse, high-speed French train.

Thackeray, William Makepeace. (1811–1863) English novelist.

thalassic. Pertaining to the sea.

thalassocracy. Dominance of the seas.

than. Three small but common problems need noting.

1. In comparative constructions *than* is often wrongly used, as here: "Nearly twice as many people die under 20 in France than in Great Britain" (cited by Gowers). Make it "as in Great Britain."

2. It is wrongly used after *hardly* in sentences such as this: "Hardly had I landed at Liverpool than the Mikado's death recalled me to Japan" (cited by Fowler). Make it "No sooner had I landed than" or "Hardly had I landed when."

3. It is often a source of ambiguity in sentences of the following type: "She likes tennis more than me." Does this mean that she likes tennis more than I do or that she likes tennis more than she likes me? In such cases, it is better to supply a second verb if it avoids ambiguity, e.g., "She likes tennis more than she likes me" or "She likes tennis more than I do."

Thanksgiving Day. Fourth Thursday in November in the United States, second Monday in October in Canada.

that (as a conjunction). Whether you say "I think you are wrong" or "I think that you are wrong" is partly a matter of idiom but mostly a matter of preference. Some words usually require *that* (*assert, contend, maintain*) and some usually do not (*say, think*), but there are no hard rules. On the whole, it is better to dispense with *that* when it isn't necessary.

that, which. To understand the distinctions between *that* and *which* it is necessary to understand restrictive and nonrestrictive clauses. A nonrestrictive, or nondefining, clause is one that can be regarded as parenthetical: "The tree, *which had no leaves*, was a birch." The italicized words are effectively an aside and could be deleted. The real point of the sentence is that the tree was a birch; its leaflessness is incidental. A restrictive, defining clause is one that is essential to the sense of the sentence. "The tree *that had no leaves* was a birch." Here the leaflessness is a defining characteristic; it helps us to distinguish that tree from other trees. In correct usage *that* is always used to indicate restrictive clauses and *which* to indicate nonrestrictive ones. Restrictive clauses should never be set off with commas and nonrestrictive clauses always should.

"Their's not to reason why,/Their's but to do and die" are the correct lines and original (but incorrect then too) punctuation from Tennyson's "Charge of the Light Brigade."

Theophrastus. (c. 372–286 BC) Greek philosopher.

therapeutic.

Thermopylae. A pass in Greece between the mountains and the sea, used throughout history as an invasion route.

Thermos. (Cap.)

Theron, Charlize. (1975–) South African–born actress.

thesaurus, pl. *thesauri/thesauruses.*

thesis, pl. *theses.*

Thimphu. Capital of Bhutan.

thingamabob, thingamajig.

thinking to oneself, as in "I thought to myself: 'We're lost,' " is always tautological; there is no one else to whom one can think. Delete "to myself." Similarly vacuous is "in my mind" in constructions like "I could picture in my mind where the offices had been."

thinness, thinnest.

Third World. (Caps.)

Thirty Years/Years' War. (1618–1648) War between Catholic and Protestant factions fought principally in Germany.

Thomas, Dylan. (1914–1953) Welsh poet.

Thomson, Bobby. (1923–) Not *Thomp-*. Scottish-born American baseball player who hit a celebrated home run to give the New York Giants the National League pennant in 1951.

thorax, pl. *thoraces/thoraxes.*

Thoreau, Henry David. (1817–1862) American naturalist, poet, and writer.

Thornburgh, Dick. (1932–) Republican U.S. politician, governor of Pennsylvania (1979–87), and U.S. attorney general (1988–1991).

Thorndike, Dame Sybil. (1882–1976) English actress.

thorny. Not *-ey.*

though, although. The two are interchangeable except as an adverb placed after the verb, where only *though* is correct, and with the expressions *as though* and *even though*, where idiom precludes *although.*

Threadneedle Street, Old Lady of. Nickname for the Bank of England.

Three Mile Island. Nuclear power station, Harrisburg, Pennsylvania.

threshold.

thrived/throve. Either is acceptable, but most authorities prefer the latter.

Through the Looking-Glass and What Alice Found There is the full, formal title of the 1871 Lewis Carroll classic. Note the hyphen in *Looking-Glass.*

Thruway is the correct official spelling in many highway contexts (New York State Thruway Authority, Governor Thomas E. Dewey Thruway).

Thucydides. (c. 460–c. 400 BC) Greek historian of the Peloponnesian War.

Tiananmen Square, Beijing.

Tibullus, Albius. (c. 54–19 BC) Roman elegiac poet.

tic douloureux. Disorder of the facial nerves. Its formal medical designation is trigeminal neuralgia.

tickety-boo.

tic-tac-toe.

tiddly-winks.

Tiepolo, Giovanni Battista. (1696–1770) Italian artist.

Tierra del Fuego. South American archipelago.

Tiffany, Charles Lewis. (1812–1902) American jeweler and founder of the famous New York jewelry store; father of **Louis Comfort Tiffany** (1848–1933), American designer, known for design and production of Tiffany glass and Tiffany lamps.

Tigonankweine Range. Mountains in western Canada.

tilde. The mark (~) used in Spanish to denote the sound *ny,* as is *señor* or *cañón*; word pronounced *till'-duh.*

Tilden, Bill. (1893–1933) American tennis player, three-time world champion.

timber, timbre. The first is wood; the second refers to sound.

Timbuktu. Small city in Mali. The name is used to signify any very remote place.

time often has a curious magnetic effect, attracting extra words to sentences, as in: "The property was occupied for a short length of time." Make it "for a short time." Occasionally, *time* itself is superfluous, as in constructions of this sort: "The report will be available in two weeks' time." *Time* adds nothing to the sentence but wordiness.

time, at this moment in. Unless you are striving for an air of linguistic ineptitude, never use this expression. Say "now."

Timor Leste. Asian republic; capital Dili.

tin lizzie. A Model T Ford, not any old car.

tinnitus. Persistent ringing in the ears.

Tin Pan Alley. District of Manhattan where music publishers once congregated.

tinsel.

tintinnabulation. Ringing sound of bells.

Tintoretto. (1518–1594) Italian artist; real name Jacopo Robusti.

Tipperary. Town and county in the Republic of Ireland.

tipsy. Not *-ey*. Mildly intoxicated.

tiramisu. Italian dessert.

Tirol. German for Tyrol, region of Austria.

'Tis Pity She's a Whore. Not *a Pity*. Play by John Ford (1633).

Titian. (c. 1490–1576) Italian painter; in Italian, **Tiziano Vecellio.**

titillate.

titivate.

Tito, Marshal. (1892–1980) Prime minister of Yugoslavia (1945–1953), president (1953–1980); born Josip Broz.

tmesis. Interposing a word between the syllables of another, as in *abso-bloody-lutely.*

TNT. A well-known explosive. The initials are short for *trinitrotoluene.*

to all intents and purposes is unnecessarily wordy. "To all intents" is enough.

toboggan.

toby jug. (No caps.)

Tocqueville, Alexis (Charles Henri Maurice Clérel) de. (1805–1859) French politician and historian.

together with, along with. *With* in both expressions is a preposition, not a conjunction, and therefore does not govern the verb.

This sentence is wrong: "They said the man, a motor mechanic, together with a 22-year-old arrested a day earlier, were being questioned" (*London Times*). Make it "was being questioned."

Togolese. Of or from Togo.

Tojo, Hideki. (1884–1948) Japanese prime minister (1941–1944), executed as war criminal.

Tolkien, J.R.R. (1892–1973) English philologist and author of fantasies; the initials stood for John Ronald Reuel.

Tolstoy, Count Leo. (1828–1910) Russian novelist.

tomato, pl. *tomatoes.*

tomorrow.

Toms River, New Jersey.

ton, tonne. There are two kinds of *ton*: a long ton (used principally in the United Kingdom), weighing 2,240 lbs./1,016 kg., and a short ton (used in the United States and Canada), weighing 2,000 lbs./907 kg. A *tonne* is the British term for what in America is normally called a metric ton; it weighs 2,204 lbs./1,000 kg.

tonnages of ships. *Deadweight tonnage* is the amount of cargo a ship can carry. *Displacement tonnage* is the weight of the ship itself. *Gross tonnage* measures the theoretical capacity of a ship based on its dimensions. When using any of these terms, it is only fair to give the reader some idea of what each signifies.

tonsillitis.

Tontons Macoute. Civilian militia in Haiti; supporters of the Duvalier regimes.

Tony Awards. Theatrical awards named for the actress and producer Antoinette Perry. They have been awarded since 1947. Pl. *Tonys.*

topsy-turvy.

Torino. Italian for Turin.

tormentor. Not *-er.*

tornadoes.

Torquemada, Tomás de. (1420–1498) Spanish monk who organized the Inquisition.

torsos.

tortuous, torturous. *Tortuous* means winding and circuitous ("The road wound tortuously through the mountains"). When used figuratively it usually suggests deviousness ("a tortuous tax avoidance scheme"). The word is thus better avoided if all you mean is complicated or convoluted. *Torturous* is the adjectival form of *torture* and describes the infliction of extreme pain.

Toscanini, Arturo. (1867–1957) Italian conductor.

total. Three points to note:

1. *Total* is redundant and should be deleted when what it is qualifying already contains the idea of a totality, as here: "[They] risk total annihilation at the hands of the massive Israeli forces now poised to strike at the gates of the city" (*Washington Post*).

2. The expression *a total of*, though common, is also generally superfluous: "County officials said a total of 84 prisoners were housed in six cells" (*New York Times*). Make it "officials said 84 prisoners." An exception is at the start of sentences when it is desirable to avoid spelling out a large number, as in "A total of 2,112 sailors were aboard" instead of "Two thousand one hundred and twelve sailors were aboard."

3. "A total of 45 weeks was spent on the study" (*London Times*) is wrong. As with "a number of" and "the number of," the rule is to make it "the total of . . . was," but "a total of . . . were."

totaled, totaling.

to the tune of. A hackneyed circumlocution. "The company is being subsidized to the tune of $500 million a year" would be more succinct as "The company receives a subsidy of $500 million a year."

Toulouse-Lautrec, Henri de. (1864–1901) French painter; full name Henri Marie Raymond de Toulouse-Lautrec-Monfa.

toupee. (No accent.)

Tourette syndrome (pref.), **Tourette's syndrome** (alt.). Neurological disorder named for the French physician **Georges Gilles de la Tourette** (1859–1904).

Tournai, Belgium, but **Tournay,** France.

tournedos. (Sing. and pl.) Choice cut or cuts of beef.

tout à l'heure. (Fr.) Soon, just now, a moment ago.

tout de suite. (Fr.) Immediately.

tout le monde. (Fr.) Everybody.

tovarich/tovarish. Either is acceptable for the Russian word for *comrade;* in Russian, *tovarishch.*

toward, towards. The first is the preferred form in America, the second in Britain, but either is correct. *Untoward,* however, is the only accepted form in both.

toxemia. Blood poisoning.

traceable.

tradable.

trademark, trade name. A trademark is a name, symbol, or other depiction that formally identifies a product. A trade name is the name of the maker, not of the product. Cadillac is a trademark, General Motors a trade name.

Tralee, Ireland.

tranquillity, but **tranquilize, tranquilizer.**

transatlantic. Most dictionaries and style books (but by no means all) prefer *transatlantic* to *trans-Atlantic.* Similarly, *transalpine, transarctic, transpacific.*

Transdniestra. Breakaway part of Moldova.

trans fats. (Two words.)

transgressor. Not *-er.*

transship, transshipment.

transitive verb. In grammar, a verb that requires a direct object.

translucent is sometimes wrongly treated as a synonym for *transparent*. A translucent material is one through which light passes but through which images cannot be clearly seen, as with frosted glass. Note also the spelling; it is not -*scent*.

transsexual.

Trappist monk.

trattoria. Italian restaurant; pl. *trattorie*.

Traviata, La. Opera by Giuseppe Verdi (1853).

treiskaidekaphobia. Fear of the number 13.

trek, trekked.

Trentino-Alto Adige. Region of Italy.

TriBeCa. Short for Triangle Below Canal Street, New York City.

Triborough Bridge, New York City.

Trinidad and Tobago. Caribbean republic; capital Port-of-Spain. Natives are Trinidadians or Tobagonians, depending on which part of the republic they come from.

Trintignant, Jean-Louis. (1930–) French actor.

triptych. Painting on three panels hinged together.

trireme. Ancient Greek ship with three banks of oars.

Tristan da Cunha. British island colony in the south Atlantic Ocean.

Tristram Shandy, Gentleman, The Life and Opinions of. Novel by Laurence Sterne (1760–1767).

trivia is, strictly speaking, a plural, and a few dictionaries recognize it only as such. "All this daily trivia is getting on my nerves" should be "All these daily trivia are getting on my nerves." There is no singular form (the Latin *trivium* now has only historical applications), but there are the singular words *trifle* and *triviality*. The other option, if the plural form seems ungainly, is to convert *trivia* into an adjective: "All these trivial daily matters are getting on my nerves."

troglodyte. Cave dweller.

troika. A group of three.

Troilus and Cressida. Play by Shakespeare (c. 1601). The poem by Geoffrey Chaucer is "Troylus and Criseyde." In Boccaccio's *Il Filostrato* the spelling is *Criseida.*

Trollope, Anthony. (1815–1852) English novelist, son of **Frances Trollope** (1780–1863), novelist and travel writer.

trompe-l'oeil. (Fr.) Painting designed to deceive the viewer into thinking that the object depicted is not painted but real; pronounced *tromp loy.*

Trooping the Color. The annual event celebrating the British queen's official birthday in June (as opposed to her actual birthday in April) is not the Trooping of the Color, as it is often written, even in Britain, but just Trooping the Color.

troubadour.

trousseau, pl. *trousseaus/trousseaux.*

Trovatore, Il. Opera by Giuseppe Verdi (1853).

Trudeau, Garry. (1948–) American cartoonist, creator of Doonesbury.

Trudeau, Pierre (Elliott). (1919–2000) Prime minister of Canada (1968–1979, 1980–1984).

true facts is always either redundant or wrong. All facts are true. Things that are not true are not facts.

Truman, Harry S. (1884–1972) Democratic politician, president (1945–53). The *S* stands for nothing as Truman had no middle name, and for that reason some authorities spell it without a period.

try and, as in constructions such as "We'll try and come back next week," is regarded as colloquial by many authorities and thus is better avoided in serious writing. Use "try to" instead.

tse-tse fly.

tsunami.

Tsvangirai, Morgan. (1952–) Opposition leader in Zimbabwe, president of Movement for Democratic Change.

Tuckahoe, New York.

Tucson, Arizona.

Tuileries, Paris.

Tumucumaque, Serra de. Mountain range in northern Brazil.

tumult, turmoil. Both describe confusion and agitation. The difference is that *tumult* applies only to people, but *turmoil* applies to both people and things. *Tumultuous*, however, can also describe things as well as people ("tumultuous applause," "tumultuous seas").

turbid, turgid. The first means muddy or impenetrable; the second means inflated, grandiloquent, bombastic.

Turkmenistan. Former republic of the Soviet Union, now an independent state; capital Ashgabat (or Ashkhabad).

turpitude does not signify rectitude or integrity, as is sometimes thought, but rather baseness or depravity. "He is a man of great moral turpitude" is not a compliment.

turquoise.

Tuskegee, Alabama, home of **Tuskegee University** (formerly Tuskegee Institute).

Tussaud's, Madame. London waxworks museum.

Tutankhamun (or **Tutankhamen**). (c. 1359–c. 1340 BC) Egyptian pharaoh.

tutti-frutti.

TWA. Trans World Airlines (no hyphens), former airline.

Twain, Mark. Pen name of Samuel Langhorne Clemens (1835–1910), American author.

Tylers' and Bricklayers' Company. London livery company. Not *Tilers'*.

Tymoshenko, Yulia. (1960–) Prime minister of Ukraine (2005).

Tynedale (or **Tindale**), **William.** (c. 1484–1536) English biblical scholar.

tyrannosaur. Any dinosaur of the genus *Tyrannosaurus*. The largest tyrannosaur was *Tyrannosaurus rex*.

tyrannous.

tyro. A novice; pl. *tyros.*

Tyrol. Region of Austria and Italy; not *the Tyrol.* In German Tirol; in Italian, Tirolo.

Tyrrhenian Sea. Stretch of the Mediterranean between Italy, Corsica, Sardinia, and Sicily.

Tyus, Wyomia. (1945–) American sprinter.

Uu

U. A Burmese honorific, roughly equivalent to *Mr.*

UAE. United Arab Emirates.

UAL. United Airlines.

UAR. United Arab Republic, title used by Egypt and Syria together from 1958 to 1961, and by Egypt alone from 1961 to 1971.

Übermensch. (Ger.) Superman.

ubiquitous, ubiquity.

U-boat. Short for *Unterseeboot*, German term for submarine.

UBS PaineWebber Inc. Investment company.

Uccellina National Park, Tuscany, Italy.

Uccello, Paolo. (1397–1475) Italian painter; born Paolo di Dono.

UCLA. University of California at Los Angeles.

UDI. Unilateral declaration of independence.

Udmurtiya. Russian republic.

Ueberroth, Peter. (1937–) American businessman, former commissioner of Major League Baseball.

UEFA. Union of European Football Associations.

Ueno Park. Station and district, Tokyo.

Uffizi Gallery, Florence; in Italian, Galleria degli Uffizi.

UHF. Ultra-high frequency.

UHT. Ultra-heat tested (not *ultra-high temperature*), process for long-life milk products.

uisge beatha. Gaelic for *whiskey*.

ukase. An edict.

Ukraine. Former republic of Soviet Union, now an independent state; capital Kiev.

ukulele. Not *uke-*. Stringed instrument.

Ulaanbaatar (or **Ulan Bator**). Capital of Mongolia.

Ullmann, Liv. (1939–) Norwegian actress.

Ullswater. One of the Lake District lakes, Cumbria, England.

ulna. The larger bone in the forearm; pl. *ulnas/ulnae.*

Ulster. Province of Ireland, *not* coextensive with Northern Ireland; three counties are in the Republic of Ireland.

ultimatums.

ululate. To howl or hoot.

Uluru is the formal, and generally preferred, name for Ayers Rock in Australia; pronounced *oo-luh-roo*. It is part of Uluru-Kata Tjuta National Park. The resort alongside it is Yulara.

Ulysses/Odysseus. Two names for the same person: the leader of the Greeks in the Trojan war. The first is Latin, the second Greek.

Umayyad Dynasty. Muslim empire (661–750).

umbilicus. The umbilical cord.

unadulterated.

un-American, un-French, etc.

unanimous, unanimity.

una voce. (Lat.) With one voice, unanimously.

unbiased.

unbribable.

unchristian, but **non-Christian.**

UNCTAD. United Nations Conference on (*not* for) Trade and Development, agency set up in 1964 with the purpose of smoothing trade differences between nations and promoting economic development.

unctuous. Oily.

underdog. (One word.)

Underground. (Cap.) London subway system.

Under Milk Wood. (Three words.) Dylan Thomas play (1954)

under way (Two words.)

un-English, un-British, etc.

UNESCO. United Nations Educational, Scientific and Cultural Organization.

unexceptionable, unexceptional. Something that is *unexceptional* is ordinary, not outstanding ("an unexceptional wine"). Something that is *unexceptionable* is not open to objections ("In Britain, *grey* is the preferred spelling, but *gray* is unexceptionable").

Ungaretti, Giuseppe. (1888–1970) Italian poet.

unget-at-able. Note *unget* is one word.

unguent. Soothing cream or lotion.

UNHCR. Office of the United Nations High Commissioner for Refugees.

unicameral legislature. A legislature having just one chamber.

UNICEF. United Nations Children's Fund (formerly, United Nations International Children's Emergency Fund).

UNIDO. United Nations Industrial Development Organization.

unilateral, bilateral, multilateral are slightly numbing words and are often unneeded anyway, as in "Bilateral trade talks are to take place next week between Britain and Japan." Trade talks between Britain and Japan could hardly be other than two-sided. More often than not the context makes clear how much laterality is involved.

uninterested, disinterested. The first means not caring; the second means neutral.

Union of Soviet Socialist Republics. (Abbr. USSR.) In Russian, Soyuz Sovyetskikh Sotsialisticheskikh Respublik; ceased to exist in 1991. See also SOVIET UNION.

unique means the only one of its kind. A thing cannot be "more unique" or "one of the most unique," etc.

unison. All together.

Unisys. U.S. computer company.

United Airlines. (Abbr. UAL.) Not Air Lines.

United Arab Emirates. Formerly the Trucial States; composed of Abu Dhabi, Ajman, Dubai, Fujaira, Ras al Khaima, Sharja, and Umm al Qaiwain.

United Arab Republic. (Abbr. UAR.) Title used by Egypt and Syria together (1958–61) and by Egypt alone (1961–1971).

UnitedHealth Group. Health services company. Note UnitedHealth is one word.

United Kingdom. Formally, the United Kingdom of Great Britain and Northern Ireland; comprises England, Scotland, Wales, and Northern Ireland.

University College London. (No comma.)

unknown is often used imprecisely, as here: "A hitherto unknown company called Ashdown Oil has emerged as a bidder for the Wytch Farm oil interests." A company must be known to someone, if only its directors. It would be better to call it a little-known company.

unlabeled.

unless and until. One or the other, please.

unlicensed.

unmanageable.

unmistakable.

unmovable.

unnamable.

unnatural. Note *-nn-*.

unnecessary. Note *-nn-*.

unnerved. Note *-nn-*.

unnumbered. Note *-nn-*.

unparalleled.

unpractical/impractical. The words are synonyms.

unraveled.

unridable.

UNRRA. United Nations Relief and Rehabilitation Administration.

unselfconscious.

unshakable.

until, till, 'til, 'till. The first two are legitimate and interchangeable. The second two are wrong and, indeed, illiterate.

untimely death is often somewhat fatuous; few deaths are timely.

ununbiium, ununhexium, ununnilium, ununquadium, unununium. Chemical elements all discovered or first produced between 1994 and 2000.

unwieldy.

up-and-coming. (Hyphens.)

Upanishads. Ancient Hindu metaphysical treatises.

UPI. United Press International.

Upper Volta. Former name of Burkina Faso.

Uppsala, Sweden.

upsilon. Not -*ll*-. Twentieth letter of the Greek alphabet.

upsy-daisy.

Urdang, Laurence. (1927–) American lexicographer.

uremia. Toxic blood condition associated with kidney failure.

urethra. Urinary duct; pl. *urethrae* or *urethras*.

Uriah Heep. Character in Dickens's *David Copperfield*.

Uribe, Álvaro. (1952–) President of Colombia (2002–).

URL. Abbreviation of *uniform resource locator,* technospeak for a Web address on the Internet.

Urquhart. Scottish family name; pronounced *erk'-ert.*

Ursa Major, Ursa Minor. Constellations meaning respectively Big Bear and Little Bear.

ursine. Like or of a bear.

Ursuline. Order of nuns.

Uruguay. South American republic; capital Montevideo.

USAF. United States Air Force.

usage, use. The words are largely interchangeable. In general, *usage* appears in contexts involving languages ("modern English usage") and *use* in most other cases.

US Airways. Formerly USAir.

USB. Short for Universal Serial Bus.

US Bancorp. American banking group.

US Cellular Field. Home of the Chicago White Sox baseball team.

use, usage. *Usage* normally appears only in the context of formal practices, particularly in regard to linguistics ("modern English usage"), and *use* does duty for all other senses, but most dictionaries recognize the words as interchangeable in nearly all contexts. See also UTILIZE, USE.

USSR. See UNION OF SOVIET SOCIALIST REPUBLICS.

usufruct. The right to use another's property so long as no damage is done, as with walking on a path across farmland.

usury. The practice of lending money at a grossly inflated rate of interest; the adjectival form is *usurious*.

Uther Pendragon. Legendary father of King Arthur.

utilize, use. *Utilize* is the preferred term for making use of something that wasn't intended for the purpose ("He utilized a coat hanger to repair the car") or for extracting maximum value ("The farmers utilized every square inch of the hillside"). In other senses *use* is generally better.

Utrillo, Maurice. (1883–1955) French artist.

Utsunomiya, Honshu, Japan.

Uttar Pradesh. Indian state; capital Lucknow.

utterance.

Utzon, Jørn. (1918–) Danish architect, best known for designing Sydney Opera House.

uvula. The piece of flesh hanging at the back of the mouth above the throat.

uxoricide. The murder of a wife by her husband, and the man who commits such a crime.

Uzbekistan. Former Soviet republic, now an independent country; capital Tashkent.

Vv

vacillate.

vade-mecum. A handbook carried on the person for constant use.

vagary, pl. *vagaries.*

vagrant, vagrancy.

Vaishnava. Hindu devotee of Vishnu.

Vajpayee, Atal Bihari. (1924–) Prime minister of India (1996, 1998–2004).

valance, valence. The first is a short drapery; the second is a term from chemistry to describe molecular bonding.

Val-d'Isère. Ski resort in French Alps.

valediction. A farewell speech; adj. *valedictory.*

Valenciennes lace.

Valera, Éamon de. (1882–1975) U.S.-born prime minister of Ireland (1919–1921, 1932–1948, 1957–1959) and president (1959–1973).

valetudinarian. A person, particularly an invalid, obsessed with his or her health.

Valhalla. In Norse mythology, a great hall of slain warriors.

valiant.

Valium. (Cap.) Brand of tranquilizer.

Valkyrie. In Norse mythology, one of the twelve handmaidens of Odin.

Valladolid. Province and city in Castile, Spain.

Valle d'Aosta. Region of Italy.

Valletta. Capital of Malta.

vamoose. To flee or leave hurriedly.

Van Alen, William. (1883–1954) American architect who designed Chrysler Building, New York. Note unusual spelling of Alen.

Vanbrugh, Sir John. (1664–1726) English architect and playwright.

Van Buren, Martin. (1782–1862) U.S. president (1837–1841).

Van de Graaff, Robert J(emison). (1901–1967) American physicist and inventor of the Van de Graaff generator.

van der Post, Sir Laurens. (1906–1996) South African writer and explorer.

Vandross, Luther. (1951–2005) American entertainer.

Vandyke (or Van Dyck), Sir Anthony. (1599–1641) Born Anton Van Dijck, but that spelling is almost never encountered outside his native Belgium. In America his name is usually rendered as Sir Anthony Vandyke, though Van Dyck (the spelling favored in Britain) is also sometimes found. In both countries, objects associated with him are spelled *Vandyke*—e.g., "a Vandyke beard," "a Vandyke collar."

Vänern. Largest lake in Sweden.

van Eyck, Jan. (c. 1380–1440) Flemish painter.

van Gogh, Vincent. (1853–1890) Dutch painter.

Vanuatu. Island republic in the South Pacific, formerly the New Hebrides; capital Port-Vila (or Port Vila, without hyphen).

vaquero. Spanish for "cowboy."

Vargas, Getúlio Dornelles. (1883–1954) President of Brazil (1930–1945, 1951–1954).

varicella. Medical name for chickenpox.

varicose veins.

variegated.

various different is inescapably repetitive.

VDU. Visual display unit, a computer screen.

Veblen, Thorstein. (1857–1929) American economist.

Vecchio, Palazzo, Florence, Italy. The famous bridge across the Arno is the **Ponte Vecchio.**

VE Day (or **V-E Day**). May 8, 1945, the date of the Allied victory in Europe in World War II.

veins, but **venous.**

Velázquez (or **Velásquez**), **Diego Rodríguez de Silva y.** (1599–1660) Spanish painter.

veld (pref.)/**veldt** (alt.). Grassland.

vellum. The finest type of parchment.

venal, venial. *Venial,* from the Latin *venialis* ("forgivable"), means excusable; a venial sin is a minor one. *Venal* means corruptible. It comes from the Latin *venalis* ("for sale") and describes someone who is capable of being bought.

vendetta.

vendible.

veneer.

venerable.

venerate, worship. Although in figurative senses the words are interchangeable, in religious contexts *worship* should apply only to God. Roman Catholics, for instance, worship God but venerate saints.

Venezuela. South American republic; capital Caracas.

vengeance.

Veni, vidi, vici. (Lat.) "I came, I saw, I conquered."

venomous.

venous. Pertaining to veins.

ventilator.

ventre à terre. (Fr.) Full out, at top speed.

ventricles for the heart valves. Not *ventricals.*

Venus' fly-trap. (Note apos.)

veranda is the preferred spelling, but **verandah** is acceptable.

verbal agreement, because it can mean either a written or spoken agreement, can be ambiguous. Where the manner of agreeing is important, it is generally better to describe it as an oral or a written agreement.

verbatim means in exactly the same words.

verboten. (Ger.) Forbidden.

verdant. Green.

Verdi, Giuseppe. (1813–1901) Italian opera composer.

verdigris. Green rust on copper or brass.

verisimilitude. Air of truth, the quality of being realistic.

Vermeer, Jan. (1632–1696) Dutch painter.

vermicelli. Type of pasta.

vermilion (one *l*) for the color, but Vermillion (two *l*'s) for the towns in Kansas and South Dakota.

vermouth.

vernal. Pertaining to the spring, as in *vernal equinox*.

Veronese, Paolo. (1528–1588) Italian painter; born Paolo Cagliari.

Verrazano-Narrows Bridge, New York City.

Verrocchio, Andrea del. (1436–1488) Italian painter and sculptor.

Versailles. Palace near Paris.

vertebra, pl. *vertebrae.*

Verwoerd, Hendrik. (1901–1966) Dutch-born South African prime minister (1958–1966).

very should be made to pay its way in sentences. Too often it is used where it adds nothing to sense ("It was a very tragic death") or is inserted in a futile effort to prop up a weak word that would be better replaced by something with more punch ("The play was very good").

Vespucci, Amerigo. (1454–1512) Italian navigator and explorer after whom America was named.

vestibule. Entrance room or hall.

Veterans Administration. (No apos.) Former name of the U.S. Department of Veterans Affairs.

vetoes.

Veuve Clicquot. Champagne.

vexatious.

VHF. Very high frequency.

via, meaning "by way of," indicates the direction of a journey and not the means by which the journey is achieved. It is correct to say "We flew from London to Sydney via Singapore," but not "We traveled to the islands via seaplane."

viable does not mean feasible or promising, senses in which it is frequently used. It means capable of independent existence. A fetus is viable if it can live outside the womb.

Via Dolorosa. Jerusalem; "Way of sadness"; route taken by Jesus to the Crucifixion.

Vianchang. Capital of Laos; formerly called Vientiane.

vicereine. Female viceroy; the wife of a viceroy.

vichyssoise. Soup. Note *-ss-*.

vicious.

vicissitude. A change of circumstance. Although there is no compelling reason for it, the word is almost always used in the plural.

victualer. A provider of food and drink; pronouned *vittler*.

vie, vying.

Vientiane. Capital of Laos, now called **Vianchang.**

Vietcong, Vietminh. (Each one word.)

Vietnam. (One word.) Southeast Asian nation; capital Hanoi.

Vieux Carré. French quarter of New Orleans.

vigilance, vigilant, vigilante.

vignette. A decoration or sketch; an image with no definite border; a literary sketch.

vilify. Not *-ll-*. Defame.

Villa-Lobos, Heitor. (1887–1959) Not Hector. Brazilian composer.

Villaraigosa, Antonio. (1953–) Mayor of Los Angeles (2005–).

Ville Lumière. (Fr.) "City of light," nickname of Paris.

Villette. Novel by Charlotte Brontë (1853).

vinaigrette. A kind of salad dressing.

vin ordinaire. (Fr.) Inexpensive wine.

Virgil. Anglicized name of Publius Vergilius Maro (70–19 BC), Roman poet.

Virgin Atlantic Airways.

Virgin Islands comprise the British Virgin Islands (capital Road Town) and the U.S. Virgin Islands (capital Charlotte Amalie).

virtuoso, pl. *virtuosi* or *virtuosos.*

vis-à-vis. (Fr.) "Face-to-face"; with regard to.

Visconti, Count Luchino. (1907–1976) Italian stage and film director.

viscous. Sticky.

Vishnu. A Hindu god.

visitable.

vis major. (Lat.) "Greater force"; pl. *vires majores.*

visor. Sun shield.

VISTA, Volunteers in Service to America, is now AmeriCorps VISTA.

vita brevis, ars longa. (Lat.) "Life is short, art is long."

vitiate. Contaminate, ruin.

Viti Levu. Main island of Fiji, site of Suva, the capital.

vitreous, vitriform. The first describes something made of or having the quality of glass. The second means to have the appearance of glass.

vituperate, vituperative.

vivacious, vivacity.

Vivat regina! (Lat.) "Long live the queen."

Vivat rex! (Lat.) "Long live the king."

viva voce. An oral examination.

vivify. To bring to life.

viz., the abbreviation of *videlicet* (Lat.), means "namely" or "that is to say."

Vizcaíno, Sebastián. (c. 1550–1615) Spanish explorer.

V-J Day. August 15, 1945, the date of Japan's surrender in World War II.

Vlaanderen. Flemish for Flanders.

Vladivostok, Russia.

Vlaminck, Maurice de. (1876–1958) French artist and writer.

Vlissingen, the Netherlands.

vocal cords. Not *chords*. Vocal cords are so called because of their shape and structure, not because of their tonal qualities.

vociferous. Outspoken.

Vodafone. A telecommunications company.

voilà.

Volapük. Artificial language that once rivaled Esperanto in popularity.

volatile.

vol-au-vent. Puff pastry filled with savory foodstuffs and sauce.

volcano, pl. *volcanoes.*

volcanology, vulcanology. Both are the terms for the science of volcanoes. The first is the preferred American spelling, the second the preferred British one.

Volcker, Paul. (1927–) American banking executive and government official, chairman of the Federal Reserve (1979–1987).

Volgograd. Russian city; formerly Stalingrad and before that Tsaritsyn.

Volkswagen. German car company; formally Volkswagenwerk AG.

Volstead Act. Act passed in 1919 to enforce Prohibition.

Völsunga Saga. Scandinavian epic.

Voltaire. (1694–1778) Pen name of François-Marie Arouet, French writer; **Voltairean** is the somewhat awkward adjectival form of the name.

volte-face. (Hyphen.) A complete change or reversal, especially an unexpected one.

voluptuous.

von Braun, Wernher. (1912–1977) German-born American rocket scientist.

von Karajan, Herbert. (1908–1989) Austrian conductor.

Vonnegut, Kurt. (1922–2007) American novelist.

von Sternberg, Josef. (1894–1969) Austrian-born American film director.

von Stroheim, Erich. (1885–1957) German-born Hollywood actor and director.

Von Willebrand's disease. Genetic disorder that affects blood clotting.

voodoo.

voortrekker. Afrikaans for "pioneer."

Vorderasiatisches Museum, Berlin, Germany.

vortexes/vortices. For the plural of *vortex*, either is correct.

vox populi. (Lat.) "Voice of the people."

Voyageurs National Park, Minnesota.

voyeur. One who enjoys watching others engage in sexual acts.

Vuillard, Édouard. (1868–1940) French artist.

vulpine. Having the nature of a fox.

vying.

Ww

wacky.

Waikiki. Beach and district in Honolulu, Hawaii.

wainscot, wainscoting. Type of paneling.

Waitemata Harbor, Auckland, New Zealand.

waiver, waver. The first is a relinquishment of a claim; the second means to hesitate.

Wajda, Andrzej. (1926–) Polish film director; pronounced *vie'-da.*

Walden Pond. Small lake in Massachusetts associated with Henry David Thoreau.

Waldenses. Puritanical Christian sect originating in the twelfth century.

Waldheim, Kurt. (1918–2007) Austrian politician, secretary-general of the United Nations (1972–1982), and president of Austria (1986–1992).

Walesa, Lech. (1943–) President of Poland (1990–1995); awarded Nobel Peace Prize (1983).

walkie-talkie.

wallaby. Species of small kangaroo.

Wallace, Alfred Russel. (Not -*ll.*) (1823–1913) British naturalist.

Wallenberg, Raoul. (1912–1947?) Swedish diplomat who helped to save thousands of Hungarian Jews from being sent to concentration camps in World War II.

Wallis and Futuna Islands. South Pacific island cluster, formerly a French overseas territory, now formally a French overseas collectivity; capital Mata-Utu.

Walloon. A French-speaking Belgian, but **Wallonia** for the region.

Wal-Mart. Discount stores group. The company's full name is Wal-Mart Stores Inc.

Walpurgis Night (or **Walpurgisnacht**). The night of April 30, when witches were once thought to gather.

Walton, Izaak. (Not *Isaac.*) (1593–1683) English biographer and naturalist.

Wampanoag. Native American group, part of the Algonquin people.

Warszawa. The Polish spelling of Warsaw.

Wassermann test. Blood test for syphilis, named after German bacteriologist August von Wassermann (1866–1925).

wasteland is one word, but the poem by T. S. Eliot is **"The Waste Land."**

wastrel. Good-for-nothing person.

"Water, water, everywhere,/"Nor any drop to drink" are the lines from the Samuel Taylor Coleridge poem "The Rime of the Ancient Mariner."

Waterston, Sam. (Not *-son.*) (1940–) American actor.

Watteau, Jean-Antoine. (1684–1721) French painter.

Watusi. African people.

Waukegan, Illinois.

Waugh, Evelyn. (1903–1966) English novelist.

waver, waiver. The first means to hesitate; the second is the relinquishment of a claim.

Waverley Station, Edinburgh, Scotland.

wavy. Not *-ey.*

way, shape, or form. Choose one.

WCTU. Women's Christian Temperance Union.

Wealth of Nations, The, by Adam Smith; formally it is entitled *Inquiry into the Nature and Causes of the Wealth of Nations* (1776).

weasel.

weather conditions is redundant, as in "Freezing weather conditions will continue for the rest of the week." Delete *conditions*. Similarly tiresome is the weather forecasters' fondness for "activity," as in "thunderstorm activity over the plains states."

Weddell Sea, Antarctica.

Wedgwood china. Not *Wedge-*.

weevil. Type of beetle.

Wehrmacht. German armed forces (1935–1945).

Weidenfeld and Nicolson for the British publisher. Not *-field*, not *Nich-*.

Weil, Simone. (1909–1943) French philosopher; pronounced *vay*.

Weill, Kurt. (1900–1950) German-born American composer.

Weimar Republic. German republic (1919–1933).

Weimaraner. (Cap.) Breed of dog.

Weinmeister, Arnie. (1923–2000) American football player.

Weir, Peter. (1944–) Australian film director.

weird.

Weisz, Rachel. (1971–) British actress.

Weizmann, Chaim. (1874–1952) Russian-born Israeli scientist and statesman, president of Israel (1948–1952).

Welch Regiment, Royal Welch Fusiliers, but the **Welsh Guards** for British military units.

Welles, Orson. (1915–1985) American film actor and director.

Wellesley College, Wellesley, Massachusetts.

wellington boots. (No cap.)

weltschmerz. German for sadness over the state of the world.

werewolf, pl. *werewolves.*

West, Mae. (1892–1980) American actress.

West, Nathanael. Pen name of Nathan Wallenstein Weinstein (1903–1940), American novelist.

Westchester, New York, but **West Chester,** Delaware and Pennsylvania.

Western Australia for the Australian state, but the *West Australian* for its largest newspaper.

Westmeath. Irish county.

Westmoreland, William C. (1914–2000) American general.

Westmorland, not -*more*-, for the former English county, now part of Cumbria.

Westpac Banking Corporation. Australian bank.

West Point-Pepperell. U.S. textiles company, now **WestPoint Home.**

wether. A castrated sheep.

Weyerhaeuser Company. Forestry products company.

whacky (alt.)**/wacky** (pref.).

whammy. A curse.

wharf, pl. *wharves/wharfs.*

wheedle. Coax.

wheeze.

whelk. Edible mollusc.

whence. Although there is ample precedent for writing "from whence"—the King James Bible has the sentence "I will lift up my eyes unto the hills from whence cometh my help"—it is nonetheless tautological. *Whence* means "from where." It is enough to say "the hills whence cometh my help."

whereabouts is plural.

whether or not. The second two words should be dropped when *whether* is equivalent to *if,* as in "It is not yet known whether or not persons who become reinfected can spread the virus to others." *Or not* is necessary, however, when what is being stressed is an alternative: "I intend to go whether or not you like it."

whet one's appetite. Not *wet.* The word has nothing to do with heightened salivary flow or anything of the like. It comes from an old English word, *hwettan,* meaning "sharpen." Hence also *whetstone* for a stone used to sharpen knives.

which. The belief that *which* may refer only to the preceding word and not to the whole of a preceding statement is without foundation except where there is a chance of ambiguity. The impossibility of enforcing the rule consistently is illustrated by an anecdote cited by Gowers. A class in Philadelphia had written to a local paper's resident usage expert, asking him what was wrong with the sentence "He wrecked the car, which was due to his carelessness." Notice how the authority hoists himself with the last three words of his reply: "The fault lies in using *which* to refer to the statement 'He wrecked the car.' When *which* follows a noun, it refers to that noun as its antecedent. Therefore in the foregoing sentence it is stated that the car was due to his carelessness, which is nonsense." See also THAT, WHICH.

whim, whimsy.

whinny. The sound a horse makes.

whippet. Breed of dog.

whippoorwill. North American bird, so named because of its call.

whirligig for the fairground ride and beetle, but **whirlybird** is the slang term for a helicopter.

whiskey.

Whistler, James Abbott McNeill. (1834–1903) American painter.

White Friars. Carmelites.

whitish. Not *white-*.

Whit Sunday. The seventh Sunday after Easter.

Whittier, John Greenleaf. (1807–1892) American poet.

whittle. To pare wood; to reduce gradually.

whiz, whizzed, whizzing.

whiz kid, not *whizz-*, is generally the preferred spelling, though most dictionaries recognize both. The same applies for *whiz-bang*, but with the addition of a hyphen.

who, whom. *Whom* is used when it is the object of a preposition ("To whom it may concern") or verb ("The man whom we saw last night") or the subject of a complementary infinitive ("The person whom we took to be your father"). *Who* is used on all other occasions.

whodunit is the usual spelling for a mystery story. Note the single *n*.

whortleberry.

Who's Who. Biographical reference work.

Whyte & Mackay. Scotch whiskey.

widget. A gadget or other small undefined item.

wield.

Wien. German for Vienna.

Wiener, Norbert. (1894–1964) American mathematician, developed the science of cybernetics.

Wiener schnitzel. Fried breaded veal cutlet.

Wiesbaden, Germany. Not *Weis-*.

Wiesenthal, Simon. (1919–2005) Celebrated hunter of Nazi war criminals.

Wiest, Dianne. (1948–) American actress.

Wi-Fi. (Generally cap.) Short for *wireless fidelity.*

Wilde, Oscar (Fingall O'Flahertie Wills). (1854–1900) Irish poet and playwright.

wildebeest, pl. *wildebeeste/wildebeests.*

wildflower (adj.), **wild flower** (noun). A wildflower garden is filled with wild flowers.

Wilkes-Barre, Pennsylvania.

Wilkes Land, Antarctica. (Two words, no apos.)

willful.

Willkie, Wendell L(ewis). (1892–1944) American businessman chosen by Republican Party as its presidential candidate in 1940.

will-o'-the-wisp.

Wills, Garry. (1934–) U.S. historian.

willy-nilly.

Wilshire Boulevard, Los Angeles. Not *Wilt-*.

Wimbledon. Tennis club; officially, the All-England Lawn Tennis and Croquet Club.

Windhoek. Capital of Namibia.

Winger, Debra. (1952–) American film actress.

Winnemucca, Nevada.

Winnibigoshish, Lake, Minnesota.

Winnipeg. Capital of Manitoba, Canada.

Winnipesaukee, Lake, New Hampshire.

wisteria, not -*staria*, for the flowering shrub, though the American scientist for whom it was named was **Caspar Wistar.**

withal. Not -*all*. In addition, moreover.

withhold, withheld. Note -*hh*-.

Wittgenstein, Ludwig. (1889–1951) Austrian-born British philosopher.

Witwatersrand. South African region in which Johannesburg is located. The university commonly known as **Wits University** is formally **University of the Witwatersrand** (note *the*).

wizened. Shriveled.

Wobegon, Lake. Fictional town in stories by Garrison Keillor. The word itself is spelled **woebegone.**

Wodehouse, P. G. (1881–1975) Prolific comic novelist; formally Sir Pelham Grenville Wodehouse.

Wojciechowicz, Alex. (1915–1992) American professional football player.

Wolfe, Thomas. (1900–1938) American novelist.

Wollongong, New South Wales, Australia.

Wollstonecraft, Mary. (1759–1797) English author, mother of Mary Wollstonecraft Shelley.

wondrous. Not -*erous*.

Woods Hole Oceanographic Institution, Woods Hole, Massachusetts.

woofer. Type of loudspeaker.

woolen, but **woolly.**

Woolf, Virginia. (1882–1941) English novelist.

Woollcott, Alexander. (1887–1943) American journalist and critic.

Woolley, Monty. (1888–1963) American actor.

Woolloomooloo for the euphonious district of Sydney, Australia. Note the single *l* in the last syllable.

Woonsocket, Rhode Island.

Woosnam, Ian. (1958–) British golfer.

Worcestershire. English county famous for its sauce.

workaholic.

World Bank. Officially the International Bank for Reconstruction and Development, but that title is rarely used, even on first reference.

World Court. Officially the **International Court of Justice,** and that title should generally be used on first reference or soon thereafter.

Worrall Thompson, Antony. (1951–) British chef.

worshiped, worshiper.

worsted fabric. Not -*stead.*

would like. "I would have liked to have seen it" is a common construction and may be excused in conversation, but in writing it should be "I would like to have seen it" or "I would have liked to see it."

wound, scar. The two are not as interchangeable as writers sometimes casually make them. A scar is what remains after a wound heals. Thus it is always wrong, or at least stretching matters, to talk about a scar healing, including in figurative senses.

Wozniak, Steve. (1950–) Computer engineer, co-founder of Apple Computer with Steve Jobs.

wrack, rack. *Wrack* means to wreck; *rack* to strain. The expressions are *wrack and ruin, nerve-racking,* and *rack one's brain.*

Wrangell Mountains, Cape Wrangell, Wrangell–St. Elias National Park, Alaska.

wreak havoc.

Wroclaw, Poland; formerly Breslaw.

wunderkind, not *wonder-*, for a prodigy.

WWW. (Cap.) World Wide Web.

Wycherley, William. (1640–1716) English playwright.

Wyclif (or **Wycliffe**), **John.** (c. 1320–1384) English religious reformer.

Wylie, Elinor. (1885–1928) American poet and novelist.

Wynette, Tammy. (1942–1998) American country singer; born Virginia Wynette Pugh.

Xavier, St. Francis. (1506–1552) Spanish missionary, one of the founders of the Jesuit order.

XDR TB. Extensive drug-resistant tuberculosis.

Xenophon. (c. 430–c. 350 BC) Greek historian-soldier.

xerography. (No cap.) Photocopying process.

Xerox. (Cap.) Brand of photocopier and the copies it produces.

Xerxes. (519–465 BC) Persian king, defeated by Greeks at Salamis.

Xianggang. Pinyin name for Hong Kong, but use **Hong Kong.**

Xinhua. Chinese news agency; pronounced *shin-hwa'*.

Xizang. Pinyin name for Tibet, but use **Tibet.**

X-ray.

xylophone.

Yy

Yablonovy Range, Russia.

Yahoo! Computer search engine company. Note exclamation mark.

yakuza. (Not cap.) Japanese organized crime groups.

Yamaguchi, Kristy. (1971–) American figure skater.

Yamoussoukro. Capital of Côte d'Ivoire.

Yangon. Formerly Rangoon, capital of Burma.

Yangtze. China's greatest river, now increasingly known by its Pinyin name, Chang Jiang. Until the relationship between the two names is more generally known, however, Yangtze should also be used on first reference.

Yaoundé. Capital of Cameroon.

Yar'Adua, Umaru. (1951–) President of Nigeria (2007–).

yarmulke. Skullcap worn by Jews.

yashmak. Veil worn by Muslim women.

Yastrzemski, Carl. (1939–) American baseball star.

Yerevan. Capital of Armenia.

Yesilköy Airport, Istanbul, Turkey.

Yevtushenko, Yevgeny. (1933–) Russian poet.

yoicks. Fox hunter's call.

Yoknapatawpha County. Fictional county in William Faulkner novels.

Yokohama, Japan.

Yokosuka, Japan.

Yom Kippur. Jewish holy day, also called Day of Atonement.

Yourcenar, Marguerite. Pen name of Marguerite de Crayencour (1903–1987), Belgian-born French-American writer.

Yushchenko, Viktor. (1954–) President of Ukraine (2004); not to be confused with **Viktor Yanukovych** (1950–) whom he narrowly beat in a runoff election.

Yzerman, Steve. (1965–) Canadian ice hockey player; pronounced *eye-zer-man.*

Zz

Zaandam, Zaanstad, Netherlands.

zabaglione. Italian dessert.

Zacatecas. City and state in central Mexico.

Zaharias, Babe Didrikson. (1913–1956) American golfer and athlete; real first name Mildred.

Zaire. Central African republic; former name of the Democratic Republic of Congo. Capital Kinshasa.

Zákinthos. Greek island. Also variously known as Zacynthos, Zakyntos, and Zante.

Zambezi. African river.

Zambia. African republic; formerly Northern Rhodesia. Capital Lusaka.

Zanuck, Darryl F(rancis). (1902–1979) American film producer and studio executive, father of **Richard Darryl Zanuck** (1934–), film producer.

Zapatero, José Luis Rodríguez. (1960–) Prime minister of Spain (2004–).

Zappeion Gardens, Athens, Greece.

Zarathustra (Persian)/**Zoroaster** (Greek). (fl. sixth c. BC) Persian prophet, founder of Zoroastrianism.

Zarqawi, Abu Musab al-. (1966–2006) Jordanian insurgent associated with Al Qaeda.

Zatlers, Valdis. (1955–) President of Latvia (2007–).

Zátopek, Emil. (1922–2000) Czech long-distance runner.

Zeebrugge. Belgian port.

Zeffirelli, Franco. (1923–) Italian film, theater, and opera director.

Zeil, Mount, Northern Territory, Australia.

zeitgeist. Spirit of the age.

Zell am See. (No hyphens.) Austrian resort.

Zellweger, Renée. (1969–) American actress.

Zeppelin. Germany military airship in World War I.

Zermatt, Switzerland.

zeros.

Zeus. Preeminent Greek god.

Zhao Ziyang. (1910–2005) Prime minister of China (1980–87), general secretary of Chinese Communist Party (1987–89).

Zhonghua Remnin Gongheguo. Mandarin for the People's Republic of China.

Zhou Enlai (Pinyin)**/Chou En-lai.** (1898–1976) Prime minister of China (1949–1976).

Zia (ul-Haq), Muhammad. (1924–1988) President of Pakistan (1977–1988).

Zidane, Zinedine. (1972–) French soccer player.

Ziegfeld, Florenz. (1867–1932) American musical theater producer.

ziggurat.

Zimbabwe. African republic, formerly Rhodesia; capital Harare.

Zinnemann, Fred. (1907–1997) Austrian-born American film director.

Zions BanCorp. Utah-based banking company.

zip code. U.S. postal code.

zloty. Poland's basic unit of currency; pl. *zlotys.*

Zoellick, Robert. (1953–) American civil servant, made president of the World Bank in 2007 in succession to Paul Wolfowitz.

zoetrope. Nineteenth-century optical toy.

Zoroaster (Greek)**/Zarathustra** (Persian). (fl. sixth c. BC) Persian prophet, founder of **Zoroastrianism.**

Zorrilla y Moral, José. (1817–1893) Spanish poet.

Zsigmond, Vilmos. (1930–) Hungarian-born American cinematographer.

Zubaie, Salam al-. Iraq deputy prime minister, injured in bomb attack in 2007.

zucchini. American name for courgette.

Zukor, Adolph. (1873–1976) Hungarian-born American film producer and studio executive.

zum Beispiel. (Ger.) (Abbr. *z.B.*) For example.

Zurbriggen, Purmin. (1963–) Swiss skier.

zut alors! (Fr.) Cry of astonishment.

Zvonareva, Vera. (1984–) Russian tennis player.

Zwelithini, Goodwill. (1948–) King, Zulu Nation in South Africa (1968–).

zwieback. A kind of rusk.

Zwingli, Ulrich (or **Huldreich**). (1484–1531) Swiss religious zealot.

Zworykin, Vladimir. (1889–1982) Russian-born American scientist, one of the inventors of television.

Punctuation

The uses of punctuation marks are so numerous and the abuses so varied that the following is offered only as a very general guide to the most common errors. For those who wish to dig more deeply, I recommend the excellent *Mind the Stop*, by G. V. Carey.

apostrophe. The principal functions of the apostrophe are to indicate omitted letters (*don't, can't, wouldn't*) and to show the possessive (strictly, the genitive) case (*John's book, the bank's money, the people's choice*).

Two types of error occur with some frequency and are worth noting. They involve the following:

1. *Multiple possessives.* This problem can be seen here: "This is a sequel to Jeremy Paul's and Alan Gibson's play" (*Times*). The question is whether both of the apostrophes are necessary, and the answer in this instance is no. Because the reference is to a single play written jointly, only the second-named man needs to be in the possessive. Thus, it should be "Jeremy Paul and Alan Gibson's play." If the reference were to two or more plays written separately, both names would have to carry apostrophes. The rule is that when possession is held in common, only the nearer antecedent should be possessive; when possession is separate, each antecedent must be in the possessive.

2. *Plural units of measure.* Many writers who would never think of omitting the apostrophes in "a fair day's pay for a fair day's work" often do exactly that when the unit of measure is in-

creased. Consider "Laker gets further thirty days credit" (*Times* headline); "Mr. Taranto, who had nineteen years service with the company . . ." (*New York Times*). The words should appear as *days'* and *years'*. Alternatively, we could insert an *of* after the time elements ("thirty days of credit," "nineteen years of service"). One or the other is necessary.

The problem is often aggravated by the inclusion of unnecessary words, as in each of these examples: "The scheme could well be appropriate in twenty-five years time, he said" (*Times*); "Many diplomats are anxious to settle the job by the end of the session in two weeks time" (*Observer*); "The government is prepared to part with several hundred acres worth of property" (*Time* magazine). Each requires an apostrophe. But that need could be obviated by excluding the superfluous wordage. What is "in twenty-five years' time" if not "in twenty-five years"? What does "several hundred acres' worth" say that "several hundred acres" does not?

colon. The colon marks a formal introduction or indicates the start of a series. A colon should not separate a verb from its object in simple enumerations. Thus, it would be wrong to say, "The four states bordering Texas are: New Mexico, Arkansas, Oklahoma, and Louisiana." The colon should be removed. But it would be correct to say, "Texas is bordered by four states: New Mexico, Arkansas, Oklahoma, and Louisiana."

comma. The trend these days is to use the comma as sparingly as form and clarity allow. But there are certain instances in which it should appear but all too often does not. Equally, it has a tendency to crop up with alarming regularity in places where it has no business. It is, in short, the most abused of punctuation marks and one of the worst offenders of any kind in the English language. Essentially the comma's use is compulsory in three situations and recommended in a fourth.

1. *When the information provided is clearly parenthetical.* Consider these two sentences, both of which are correctly punctuated: "Mr. Lawson, the energy secretary, was unavailable for comment"; "The ambassador, who arrived in Britain two days ago, yesterday met with the prime minister." In both sentences, the information between the commas is incidental to the main thought. You could remove it and the sentence would still make sense. In the following examples, the writer has failed to set off the parenthetical information. I have provided slashes (the proper name, incidentally, is *virgules*) to show where the commas should have gone: "British cars/says a survey/are more reliable than their foreign counterparts" (editorial in the *Evening Standard*); "Operating mainly from the presidential palace at Baabda/southeast of Beirut, Habib negotiated over a sixty-five-day period" (*Time* magazine); "Mary Chatillon, director of the Massachusetts General Hospital's Reading Language Disorder Unit/maintains: 'It would simply appear to be . . .' " (*Time* magazine). It should perhaps be noted that failure to put in a comma is particularly common after a parenthesis, as here: "Mr. James Grant, executive director of the United Nations Children's Fund (UNICEF)/says . . ." (*Times*).

Occasionally the writer recognizes that the sentence contains a parenthetical thought but fails to discern just how much of the information is incidental, as here: "At nine she won a scholarship to Millfield, the private school, for bright children of the rich" (*Evening Standard*). If we removed what has been presented as parenthetical, the sentence would say: "At nine she won a scholarship to Millfield for bright children." There should be no comma after *school*, because the whole of the last statement is parenthetical.

A rarer error is seen here: "But its big worry is the growing evidence that such ostentatious cars, the cheapest costs £55,240, are becoming socially unacceptable" (*Times*). When the incidental information could stand alone as a sentence, it needs to be set off with stronger punctuation—either dashes or parentheses.

2. *When the information is nonrestrictive.* The problem here—which is really much the same as that discussed in the previous three paragraphs—is illustrated by this incorrectly punctuated sentence from the *Daily Mail:* "Cable TV would be socially divisive, the chairman of the BBC George Howard claimed last night." The writer has failed to understand the distinction between (1) "BBC chairman George Howard claimed last night" and (2) "The chairman of the BBC, George Howard, claimed last night." In (1), the name George Howard is essential to the sense of the sentence; it defines it. If we removed it, the sentence would say, "BBC chairman claimed last night." In (2), however, the name is nonrestrictive. In effect it is parenthetical. We could remove it without altering the sense of the sentence: "The chairman of the BBC claimed last night." When a name or title can be removed, it should be set off with commas. When it cannot be removed, the use of commas is wrong.

Two hypothetical examples may help to clarify the distinction. Both are correctly punctuated. "John Fowles's novel *The Collector* was a bestseller"; "John Fowles's first novel, *The Collector*, was a bestseller." In the first example the name of the novel is restrictive because *The Collector* is only one of several novels by Fowles. In the second example it is nonrestrictive because only one novel can be the author's first one. We could delete *The Collector* from the second example without spoiling the sense of the sentence, but not from the first.

When something is the only one of its kind, it should be set off with commas; when it is only one of several, the use of commas is wrong. Thus these two sentences, both from *The Times*, are incorrect: "When the well-known British firm, Imperial Metal Industries, developed two new types of superconducting wires . . ."; "The writer in the American magazine, *Horizon*, was aware of this pretentiousness . . ." The first example would be correct only if Imperial Metal Industries were the only well-known British firm, and the second would be correct only if *Horizon* were America's only magazine. The same error in reverse occurs here: "Julie Christie knows that in the week her new film *The Return of the Soldier* has opened . . ." (*Sunday Times*). Since *The Return of the Soldier* was Julie Christie's only new film of the week, it should have been set off with commas.

The error frequently occurs when a marriage partner is named: "Mrs. Thatcher and her husband Denis left London yesterday" (*Observer*). Since Mrs. Thatcher has only one husband, it should be "and her husband, Denis, left London yesterday."

3. *With forms of address.* When addressing people, you must use commas around the names or titles of those addressed. "Hit him Jim, hit him" (*Sunday Times*) should be "Hit him, Jim, hit him." The television program *Good Morning America* should really be *Good Morning, America*. The film *I'm All Right Jack* should have been *I'm All Right, Jack*. The lack of a comma or commas is always sloppy and occasionally ambiguous. In 1981, for instance, the *Sunday Express* illustrated a novel serialization with the heading "I'm choking Mr. Herriot" when what it meant was "I'm choking, Mr. Herriot"—quite another matter.

4. *With interpolated words or phrases.* Words such as *moreover, meanwhile*, and *nevertheless* and phrases such as *for instance* and *for example* traditionally have taken commas, but the practice has become increasingly discretionary over the years. In Britain they have been more freely abandoned than in America; Fowler, for instance, seldom uses them. I would recommend using them

when they suggest a pause or when ambiguity might result. This is especially true of *however*. Consider these two sentences: "However hard he tried, he failed"; "However, he tried hard, but failed." To keep from confusing the reader, if only momentarily, it is a good idea to set off *however* with commas when it is used as an interpolation. Much the same could be said of *say*: "She should choose a British government stock with [,] say [,] five years to run" (*Daily Mail*).

dash. Dashes should be used in pairs to enclose parenthetical matter or singly to indicate a sharp break in a sentence ("I can't see a damn thing in here—ouch!") or to place emphasis on a point ("There are only two things we can count on—death and taxes"). Dashes are most effective when used sparingly, and there should never be more than one pair in a single sentence.

There are two common errors with dashes:

1. Failing to mark the end of a parenthetical comment with a second dash: "The group—it is the largest in its sector, with subsidiaries or associates in eleven countries, says trading has improved in the current year" (*Times*). Make it "countries—says."

2. Allowing a word or phrase from the main part of the sentence to become locked within the parenthetical area, as here: "There is another institution which appears to have an even more— shall we say, relaxed—attitude to security" (*Times*). Removing the words between the dashes would give us an institution with "an even more attitude." *Relaxed* belongs to the sentence proper and needs to be put outside the dashes: "There is another institution which appears to have an even more—shall we say?—relaxed attitude to security." See also PARENTHESES.

ellipsis. An ellipsis (sometimes called an ellipse) is used to indicate that material has been omitted. It consists of three evenly spaced periods.(. . .) and not, as some writers think, a random scattering of them. When an ellipsis occurs at the end of a sentence, a fourth period is often added.

exclamation marks are used to show strong emotion ("Get out!") or urgency ("Help me!"). They should almost never be used for giving emphasis to a simple statement of fact: "It was bound to happen sometime! A bull got into a china shop here" (cited by Bernstein).

hyphen. Almost nothing can be said with finality about the hyphen. As Fowler says, "Its infinite variety defies description." Even the word for using a hyphen is contentious: some authorities hyphenate words, but others hyphen them. The principal function of the hyphen is to reduce the chances of ambiguity. Consider, for instance, the distinction between "the twenty-odd members of his cabinet" and "the twenty odd members of his cabinet." It is sometimes used to indicate pronunciation (*de-ice*), but not always (*coalesce, reissue*). Composite adjectives used before a noun are usually given hyphens ("a six-foot-high wall," "a four-inch rainfall"), but again, not always. Fowler cites "a balance-of-payments deficit" and Gowers "a first-class ticket," but in expressions such as these, where the words are frequently linked, the hyphens are no more necessary than they would be in "a real estate transaction" or "a post office strike." When the phrases are used adverbially, the use of hyphens is wrong, as here: "Mr. Conran, who will be fifty-years-old next month . . ." (*Sunday Times*). Mr. Conran will be fifty years old next month; he will then be a fifty-year-old man.

In general, hyphens should be dispensed with when they are not necessary. One place where they are not required by sense but frequently occur anyway is with *-ly* adverbs, as in *newly-elected* and *widely-held*. Almost every authority suggests that they should be deleted in such constructions.

parentheses. Parenthetical matter can be thought of as any information so incidental to the main thought that it needs to be separated from the sentence that contains it. It can be set off with dashes, brackets (usually reserved for explanatory insertions in quotations), commas, or, of course, parentheses. It is, in short, an insertion and has no grammatical effect on the sentence in which it appears. It is rather as if the sentence does not even know it is there. Thus this statement from *The Times* is incorrect: "But that is not how Mrs. Graham (and her father before her) have made a success of the *Washington Post.*" The verb should be *has.*

While the parenthetical expression has no grammatical effect on the sentence in which it appears, the sentence does influence the parentheses. Consider this extract from the *Los Angeles Times* (which, although it uses dashes, could equally have employed parentheses): "One reason for the dearth of Japanese-American politicians is that no Japanese immigrants were allowed to become citizens—and thus could not vote—until 1952." As written the sentence is telling us that "no Japanese citizens could not vote." Delete *could not.*

When a parenthetical comment is part of a larger sentence, the period should appear after the second parenthesis (as here). (But when the entire sentence is parenthetical, as here, the period should appear inside the final parenthesis.)

period (British, full stop). Two common errors are associated with the period, both of which arise from its absence. The first is the run-on sentence—that is, the linking of two complete thoughts by a comma. It is never possible to say whether a run-on sentence is attributable to ignorance on the part of the writer or to whimsy on the part of the typesetter, but the error occurs frequently enough that ignorance must play a part. In each of the following I have indicated with a slash where one sentence should end and the next should begin: "Although GEC handled the initial contract, much of the equipment is American,/the computers and laser printers come from Hewlett Packard" (*Guardian*); "Confidence is growing that OPEC will resolve its crisis,/however the Treasury is drawing up contingency plans" (*Times*); "Funds received in this way go towards the cost of electricity and water supply,/industries, shops and communes pay higher rates" (*Times*).

The second lapse arises when a writer tries to say too much in a single sentence, as here: "The measures would include plans to boost investment for self-financing in industry, coupled with schemes to promote investment and saving, alleviate youth unemployment, fight inflation, and lower budget deficits, as well as a new look at the controversial issue of reducing working hours" (*Times*). If the writer has not lost his readers, he has certainly lost himself. The last lumbering flourish ("as well as a new look . . .") is grammatically unconnected to what has gone before; it just hangs there. The sentence is crying out for a period—almost anywhere would do—to give the reader a chance to absorb the wealth of information being provided.

Here is another in which the writer tells us everything but his phone number: "But after they had rejected once more the umpires' proposals of $5,000 a man for the playoffs and $10,000 for the World Series on a three-year contract and the umpires had turned down a proposal of $3,000 for the playoffs and $7,000 for the World Series on a one-year contract, baseball leaders said the playoffs would begin today and they had umpires to man the games" (*New York Times*).

There is no quota on periods. When an idea is complicated, break it up and present it in digestible chunks. One idea to a sentence is still the best advice that anyone has ever given on writing.

question mark. The question mark comes at the end of a question. That sounds simple enough, doesn't it? But it's astonishing how frequently writers fail to include it. Two random examples: " 'Why travel all the way there when you could watch the whole thing at home,' he asked" (*Times*); "The inspector got up to go and stood on Mr. Ellis's cat, killing it. 'What else do you expect from these people,' said the artist" (*Standard*).

Occasionally question marks are included when they are not called for, as in this sentence by Trollope, cited by Fowler: "But let me ask of her enemies whether it is not as good a method as any other known to be extant?" The problem here is a failure to distinguish between a direct question and an indirect one. Direct questions always take question marks: "Who is going with you?" Indirect questions never do: "I would like to know who is going with you."

When direct questions take on the tone of a command, the use of a question mark becomes more discretionary. "Will everyone please assemble in my office at four o'clock?" is strictly correct, but not all authorities insist on the question mark there.

A less frequent problem arises when a direct question appears outside a direct quotation. Fieldhouse, in *Everyman's Good English Guide*, suggests that the following punctuation is correct: "Why does this happen to us, we wonder?" The Fowler brothers, however, call this an amusing blunder; certainly it is extremely irregular. The more usual course is to attach the question mark directly to the question. Thus: "Why does this happen to us? we wonder." But such constructions are clumsy and are almost always improved by being turned into indirect questions: "We wonder why this happens to us."

quotation marks (inverted commas). An issue that arises frequently in Britain but almost never in America is whether to put periods and other punctuation inside or outside quotation marks when they appear together. The practice that prevails in America and is increasingly common in Britain is to put the punctuation inside the quotes. Thus, "He said, 'I will not go.' " But some publishers prefer the punctuation to fall outside except when it is part of the quotation. Thus the example above would be "He said, 'I will not go'."

When quotation marks are used to set off a complete statement, the first word of the quotation should be capitalized ("He said, 'Victory is ours' ") except when the quotation is preceded by *that* ("He said that 'victory is ours' "). Fowler believed that no punctuation was necessary to set off attributive quotations; he would, for instance, delete the commas from the following: " 'Tomorrow,' he said, 'is a new day.' " His argument was that commas are not needed to mark the interruption or introduction of a quotation because the quotation marks already do that. Logically he is correct. But with equal logic we could argue that question marks should be dispensed with on the grounds that the context almost always makes it clear that a question is being asked. The commas are required not by logic but by convention.

semicolon. The semicolon is heavier than the comma but lighter than the period. Its principal function is to divide contact clauses— that is, two ideas that are linked by sense but that lack a conjunction. For instance, "You take the high road; I'll take the low road." Equally that could be made into two complete sentences or, by introducing a conjunction, into one ("You take the high road and I'll take the low road"). The semicolon is also sometimes used to separate long coordinate clauses. In this role it was formerly used much more extensively than it is today.

Words Ending in *-able* and *-ible*

-able	*-ible*

abominable	accessible
amenable	admissible
appreciable	collapsible
available	collectible (U.S., alt. UK)
collectable (UK, alt. U.S.)	compatible
conformable	comprehensible
confusable	contemptible
culpable	credible
delectable	deductible
dependable	defensible
describable	digestible
dispensable	forcible
estimable	discernible
execrable	divertible
expandable	exhaustible
impassable	impassible
impressionable	incorrigible
innumerable	irresistible
inscrutable	perceptible
inseparable	perfectible
knowledgeable	reprehensible
manageable	resistible
marriageable	revertible
peaceable	suppressible
perishable	
recognizable	
refusable	
reputable	

salable (U.S., alt. UK)
saleable (UK, alt. U.S.)
separable
sizable (U.S., alt. UK)
sizeable (UK, alt. U.S.)
unconscionable

Major Airports

Abbr.	City	Airport Name
AMS	Amsterdam	Schiphol
ATH	Athens	Elefthérios Venizélos
ATL	Atlanta	Hartsfield-Jackson Atlanta International
BCN	Barcelona	Barcelona International or El Prat
SXF	Berlin	Schönefeld
THF		Tempelhof
TXL		Tegel
BOS	Boston	Logan International
EZE	Buenos Aires	Ministro Pistarini (informally Ezeiza)
ORD	Chicago	O'Hare International
CPH	Copenhagen	Copenhagen Airport (informally Kastrup)
HAM	Hamburg	Hamburg-Fuhlsbüttel
HEL	Helsinki	Helsinki-Vantaa
LHR	London	Heathrow
LGW		Gatwick
LAX	Los Angeles	Los Angeles International
VNY		Van Nuys (pronounced *Van Nize*)
MAD	Madrid	Barajas
YUL	Montreal	Montreal–Pierre Elliott Trudeau International
YMX		Mirabel

Abbr.	City	Airport Name
SVO	Moscow	Sheremetyevo
VKO		Vnukovo
DME		Domodedovo
MUC	Munich	Franz Josef Strauss International
EWR	Newark	Newark Liberty International
JFK	New York	John F. Kennedy International
LGA		La Guardia
GMN	Oslo	Gardermoen
ORY	Paris	Orly
CDG		Charles de Gaulle
FCO	Rome	Leonardo da Vinci (Fiumicino)
CIA		Ciampino
GRU	São Paulo	Guarulhos International
VCP		Viracopos
CGH		Congonhas–São Paulo International
GMP	Seoul	Kimpo International
ICN		Incheon International
SIN	Singapore	Changi
ARN	Stockholm	Arlanda
BMA		Bromma
SYD	Sydney	Kingsford Smith
TPE	Taipei	Taiwan Taoyuan International
TLV	Tel Aviv	Ben Gurion
HND	Tokyo	Tokyo International or Haneda
NRT		Narita
YYZ	Toronto	Lester B. Pearson International
IAD	Washington, D.C.	Dulles International
WAS		Ronald Reagan–Washington National

Temperature Conversion Table

Celsius* ← F/C → Fahrenheit*			Celsius* ←F/C→ Fahrenheit*		
-18	0	32	0	32	90
-15	5	41	2	35	96
-12	10	50	4	40	104
-9	15	59	7	45	113
-7	20	68	10	50	122
-4	25	77	38	100	212
-1	30	86			

* Figures are rounded off to the nearest whole number.

Distance Conversion Table

km →miles/km← miles			km →miles/km← miles		
1.6	1	0.6	48.3	30	18.6
3.2	2	1.2	64.4	40	24.9
4.8	3	1.9	80.5	50	31.1
6.4	4	2.5	96.6	60	37.3
8.0	5	3.1	112.7	70	43.5
9.7	6	3.7	128.7	80	49.7
11.3	7	4.3	144.8	90	55.9
12.9	8	5.0	160.9	100	62.1
14.5	9	5.6	402.3	250	155.3
16.1	10	6.2	804.7	500	310.7
32.2	20	12.4			

* Figures are rounded off to one decimal place.

Metric Prefixes

Prefix	Meaning	Prefix	Meaning
deci-	one-tenth	deka-	10
centi-	one-hundredth	hecto-	100
milli-	one-thousandth	kilo-	1000
micro-	one-millionth	mega-	1 million
nano-	one-billionth	giga-	1 billion
pico-	one-trillionth	tera-	1 trillion

Main Units of Currency

Country	Currency	Country	Currency
Afghanistan	afghani	Colombia	peso
Albania	lek	Congo,	
Algeria	dinar	Democratic	
Argentina	peso	Republic of the	franc congolais
Australia	dollar	Costa Rica	colon
Austria	euro	Croatia	kuna
Belgium	euro	Czech	
Bolivia	boliviano	Republic	koruna
Bosnia-		Denmark	krone
Herzogovina	marka	Egypt	pound
Brazil	cruzeiro	El Salvador	U.S. dollar
Bulgaria	lev	Ethiopia	birr
Canada	dollar	Finland	euro
Chile	peso	France	euro
China	renminbi	Germany	euro
	yuan	Ghana	cedi

Country	Currency	Country	Currency
Greece	euro	New Zealand	dollar
Guatemala	quetzal	Nicaragua	córdoba
Haiti	gourde	Nigeria	naira
Honduras	lempira	Norway	krone
Hong Kong	dollar	Panama	U.S. dollar
Hungary	forint	Paraguay	guaraní
Iceland	krona	Peru	nuevo sol
India	rupee	Philippines	piso or peso
Indonesia	rupiah	Poland	zloty
Iran	rial	Portugal	euro
Iraq	dinar	Puerto Rico	U.S. dollar
Ireland	euro	Romania	leu
Israel	shekel	Russia	ruble
Italy	euro	Saudi Arabia	riyal
Jamaica	dollar	Singapore	dollar
Japan	yen	Slovakia	koruna
Kenya	shilling	South Africa	rand
Korea, North	won	Spain	euro
Korea, South	won	Sweden	krona
Kuwait	dinar	Switzerland	franc
Laos	kip	Syria	pound
Lebanon	pound	Taiwan	dollar
Libya	dinar	Thailand	baht
Luxembourg	euro	Tunisia	dinar
Malawi	kwacha	Turkey	lira
Malaysia	ringgit	Uganda	shilling
Malta	euro	United Kingdom	pound
Mexico	peso	United States	dollar
Morocco	dirham	Uruguay	peso
Netherlands	euro	Venezuela	bolívar

Country	Currency
Vietnam	dong
Zambia	kwacha
Zimbabwe	dollar

Numerals

Arabic	Roman	Arabic	Roman
1	I	50	L
2	II	60	LX
3	III	90	XC
4	IV	100	C
5	V	500	D
6	VI	1,000	M
7	VII	5,000	$\bar{V}$
8	VIII	10,000	$\bar{X}$
9	IX	100,000	$\bar{C}$
10	X		

Bibliography and Suggested Reading ←

Throughout the text I have in general referred to the following books by the surname of the author, ignoring the contributions of those who revised the originals. Thus although Sir Ernest Gowers substantially revised *A Dictionary of Modern English Usage* in 1965, that book is referred to throughout the text as "Fowler." References to "Gowers" are meant to suggest Gowers's own book, *The Complete Plain Words*.

Aitchison, Jean. *Language Change: Progress or Decay?* London: Fontana, 1981.

American Heritage Dictionary of the English Language. Boston: Houghton Mifflin, 2000.

Austin, Tim, compiler. *The Times Guide to English Style and Usage.* London: Times Books, 1999.

Bernstein, Theodore M. *The Careful Writer.* New York: Free Press, 1995.

———. *Dos, Don'ts and Maybes of English Usage.* New York: Free Press, 1995.

Burchfield, R. W., ed. *The New Fowler's Modern Usage*, third edition. Oxford: Clarendon Press, 1996.

Concise Oxford Dictionary of Current English. New York: Oxford University Press, 1995.

Encarta World English Dictionary. New York: St. Martin's Press, 1999.

Evans, Bergen and Cornelia Evans. *A Dictionary of Contemporary American Usage.* New York: Random House, 1957.

Fieldhouse, Harry. *Everyman's Good English Guide*. London: J. M. Dent & Sons, 1982.

Fowler, E. G., and H. W. Fowler *The King's English*, third edition. London: Oxford University Press, 1970.

Fowler, H. W. *A Dictionary of Modern English Usage*, second edition. Revised by Sir Ernest Gowers. New York: Oxford University Press, 1983.

Gowers, Sir Ernest. *The Complete Plain Words*, second edition. Revised by Sir Bruce Fraser. Harmondsworth, England; Penguin, 1980.

Grimond, John. *The Economist Pocket Style Book*. London: Economist Publications, 1987.

————. *New Words for Old*. London: Unwin, 1980.

Howard, Philip. *Weasel Words*. London: Hamish Hamilton, 1978.

————. *Words Fail Me*. New York: Oxford University Press, 1981.

————. *A Word in Your Ear*. Harmondsworth, England: Penguin, 1985.

————. *The State of the Language*. Harmondsworth, England: Penguin, 1986.

Hudson, Kenneth. *The Dictionary of Diseased English*. London: Papermac, 1980.

Jordan, Lewis, ed. *The New York Times Manual of Style and Usage*. New York: Times Books, 1976.

Manser, Martin H., ed. *Good Word Guide*. London: Bloomsbury, 2000.

Michaels, Leonard, and Christopher Ricks, eds. *The State of the Language*. Berkeley: University of California Press, 1990.

Morris, William and Mary Morris. *Harper Dictionary of Contemporary Usage*. New York: Harper & Row, 1975.

Newman, Edwin. *Strictly Speaking*. New York: Warner Books, 1975.

————. *A Civil Tongue*. New York: Warner Books, 1976.

Onions, C. T. *Modern English Syntax*, seventh edition. Prepared by B. D. H. Miller. New York: St. Martin's Press, 1971.

Oxford Dictionary for Writers and Editors. Oxford: Oxford University Press, 2000.

Oxford Dictionary of English Etymology. Oxford: Oxford University Press, 1982.

Oxford English Dictionary, compact edition. Oxford: Oxford University Press, 1971.

Palmer, Frank. *Grammar*. New York: Viking Penguin, 1989.

Partridge, Eric. *Usage and Abusage*. New York: W.W. Norton, 1997.

Phythian, B. A. *A Concise Dictionary of Correct English*. Lanham, Md.: Rowman & Littlefield, 1979.

Potter, Simeon. *Our Language*. Harmondsworth, England: Penguin, 1982.

Quirk, Randolph. *The Use of English*. London: Longmans, 1969.

Safire, William. *On Language*. New York: Avon, 1980.

———*What's the Good Word?* New York: Avon, 1983.

Shaw, Harry. *Dictionary of Problem Words and Expressions*. New York: Pocket Books, 1985.

Shipley, Joseph T. *In Praise of English: The Growth and Use of Language*. New York: Times Books, 1977.

Shorter Oxford English Dictionary. London: Book Club Associates, 1983.

Siegal, Allan M., and William G. Connolly. *The New York Times Manual of Style and Usage*, second edition. New York: Times Books/Random House, 1999.

Simon, John. *Paradigms Lost: Reflections on Literacy and Its Decline*. New York: Clarkson N. Potter, 1980.

Strunk, William, Jr., and E.B. White. *The Elements of Style*, third edition. New York: Macmillan, 1979.

Wallraff, Barbara. *Word Court*. New York: Harcourt, 2000.

Wood, Frederick T. *Current English Usage*, second edition. Revised by R. H. and L. M. Flavell. London: Papermac, 1981.

Grammatical terms are, to quote Frank Palmer, "largely notional and often extremely vague." In "I went swimming," for instance, *swimming* is a present participle; but in "Swimming is good for you," it is a gerund. Because such distinctions are for many of us a source of continuing perplexity, I have tried to use most such terms sparingly throughout the book. Inevitably, however, they do sometimes appear, and the following is offered as a simple guide for those who are confused or need refreshing. For a fuller discussion, I recommend *A Dictionary of Contemporary American Usage* by Bergen and Cornelia Evans and *A Concise Dictionary of Correct English* by B. A. Phythian.

adjective. A word that qualifies a noun or pronoun: "a *brick* house," "a *small* boy," "a *blue* dress." Most adjectives have three forms: the positive (*big*), the comparative (*bigger*), and the superlative (*biggest*). Although adjectives are usually easy to recognize when they stand before a noun, they are not always so easily discerned when they appear elsewhere in a sentence, as here: "He was *deaf*"; "I'm glad to be *alive*"; "She's *awake* now." Adjectives sometimes function as nouns (the *old*, the *poor*, the *sick*, the *insane*) and sometimes as adverbs (a *bitter* cold night, a *quick*-witted man). The distinction between an adjective and an adverb is often very fine. In "a great book," *great* is an adjective, but in "a great many books," it is an adverb.

adverb. A word that qualifies (or describes) any word other than a noun. That may seem a loose definition, but, as Palmer says, the classification is "quite clearly a 'ragbag' or 'dustbin,' the category into which words that do not seem to belong elsewhere are placed." In general, adverbs qualify verbs (*badly* played), adjectives (*too* loud), or other adverbs (*very* quickly). As with adjectives, they have the three forms of positive, comparative, and superlative (seen respectively in *long, longer, longest*). A common misconception is the belief that words that end in *-ly* are always adverbs. *Kindly, sickly, masterly*, and *deadly*, for example, are usually adjectives.

case. The term describes relationships or syntactic functions between parts of speech. A pronoun is in the nominative case (sometimes called the subjective) when it is the subject of a verb ("*He* is here") and in the accusative (sometimes called the objective) when it is the object of a verb or preposition ("Give it to *him*"). Except for six pairs of pronouns (*I/me, he/him, she/her, they/them, we/us*, and *who/whom*) and the genitive (which see), English has shed all its case forms.

clause. A group of words that contains a true verb (i.e., a verb functioning as such) and subject. The sentence "The house, which was built in 1920, was white" contains two clauses: "The house was white" and "which was built in 1920." The first, which would stand on its own, is called a main or principal or independent clause. The second, which would not stand on its own, is called a dependent or subordinate clause.

Sometimes the subject is suppressed in main clauses, as here: "He got up and went downstairs." Although "and went downstairs" would not stand on its own, it is a main clause because the subject has been suppressed. In effect the sentence is saying, "He got up and he went downstairs." See also PHRASE.

complement. A word or group of words that completes a predicate construction—that is, that provides full sense to the meaning of the verb. In "He is a rascal," *rascal* is the complement of the verb *is*.

conjunction. A word that links grammatical equivalents, as in "The president and prime minister conferred for two hours" (the conjunction *and* links two nouns) and "She came yesterday, but she didn't stay long" (the conjunction *but* links two clauses).

genitive. A noun or pronoun is in the genitive case when it expresses possession (*my* house, *his* car, *Sally's* job). Although some authorities make very small distinctions between genitives and possessives, many others do not. In this book, I have used the term *possessives* throughout.

gerund. A verb made to function as a noun, as with the italicized words here. "*Seeing* is *believing*"; "*Cooking* is an art"; "*Walking* is good exercise." Gerunds always end in -*ing*.

infinitive. The term describes verbs that are in the infinite mood (i.e., that do not have a subject). Put another way, it is a verb form that indicates the action of the verb without inflection to indicate person, number, or tense. There are two forms of infinitive: the full (*to go, to see*) and bare (*go, see*), often called simply "an infinitive without *to*."

mood. Verbs have four moods:
1. The indicative, which is used to state facts or ask questions (I *am* going; What time *is* it?).
2. The imperative, which indicates commands (*Come* here; *Leave* me alone).
3. The infinite, which makes general statements and has no subject (*To know* her is *to love* her).
4. The subjunctive, which is principally used to indicate hypothe-

ses or suppositions (If I *were* you . . .). The uses of the subjunctive are discussed more fully in the body of the book.

noun is usually defined as a word that describes a person, place, thing, or quality. Such a definition, as many authorities have noted, is technically inadequate. Most of us would not think of *hope, despair*, and *exultation* as things, yet they are nouns. And most of the words that describe qualities—*good, bad, happy*, and the like—are not nouns but adjectives. Palmer notes that there is no difference whatever in sense between "He suffered terribly" and "His suffering was terrible," yet *suffered* is a verb and *suffering* a noun. There is, in short, no definition for *noun* that isn't circular, though, happily, for most of us it is one part of speech that is almost always instantly recognizable.

object. Whereas the subject of a sentence tells you who or what is performing an action, the object tells you on whom or on what the action is being performed. In "I like you," *you* is the object of the verb *like*. In "They have now built most of the house," *most of the house* is the object of the verb *built*. Sometimes sentences have direct and indirect objects, as here: "Please send me four tickets"; "I'll give the dog a bath" (cited by Phythian). The direct objects are *four tickets* and *a bath*. The indirect objects are *me* and *the dog*. Prepositions also have objects. In the sentence "Give it to him," *him* is the object of the preposition *to*.

participle. The participle is a verbal adjective. There are two kinds: present participles, which end in *-ing* (*walking, looking*), and past participles, which end in *-d* (*heard*), *-ed* (*learned*), *-n* (*broken*), or *-t* (*bent*). The terms *present participle* and *past participle* can be misleading because present participles are often used in past-tense senses ("They were looking for the money") and past participles are often used when the sense is the present or future ("She has broken it"; "Things have never looked better"). When present-tense participles are used as nouns, they are called gerunds.

phrase. A group of words that does not have a subject and verb. "I will come sometime soon" consists of a clause (*I will come*) and a phrase (*sometime soon*). Phrases always express incomplete thoughts.

predicate. Everything in a sentence that is not part of the subject (i.e., the verb, its qualifiers and complements) is called the predicate. In "The man went to town after work," *The man* is the subject and the rest of the sentence is the predicate. The verb alone is sometimes called the simple predicate.

preposition. A word that connects and specifies the relationship between a noun or noun equivalent and a verb, adjective, or other noun or noun equivalent. In "We climbed over the fence," the preposition *over* connects the verb *climbed* with the noun *fence*. Whether a word is a preposition or a conjunction is often a matter of function. In "The army attacked before the enemy was awake," *before* is a conjunction. But in "The army attacked before dawn," *before* is a preposition. The distinction is that in the first sentence *before* is followed by a verb, whereas in the second it is not.

pronoun. A word used in place of a noun or nouns. In "I like walking and reading; such are my pleasures," *such* is a pronoun standing for *reading* and *walking*. Pronouns have been variously grouped by different authorities. Among the more common groupings are personal pronouns (*I, me, his,* etc.), relative pronouns (*who, whom, that, which*), demonstrative pronouns (*this, that, these, those*), and indefinite pronouns (*some, several, either, neither,* etc.).

subject. The word or phrase in a sentence or clause that indicates who or what is performing the action. In "I see you," the subject is *I*. In "Climbing steep hills tires me," *Climbing steep hills* is the subject.

substantive. A word or group of words that performs the function of a noun. In "Swimming is good for you," *Swimming* is a substantive as well as a gerund.

verb. Verbs can be defined generally (if a bit loosely) as words that have tense and that denote what someone or something is or does. Verbs that have an object are called transitive verbs—that is, the verb transmits the action from subject to an object, as in "He put the book on the table." Verbs that do not have an object are called intransitive verbs, as in "She slept all night"; in these the action is confined to the subject.

When it is necessary to indicate more than simple past or present tense, two or more verbs are combined, as in "I *have thought* about this all week." Although there is no widely agreed term for such a combination of verbs, I have for convenience followed Fowler in this book and referred to them as compound verbs. The additional or "helping" verb in such constructions (e.g., *have* in the example above) is called an auxiliary.

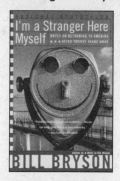
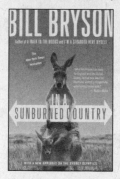